MW00763797

ONE HUNDRED GOOD SCHOOLS

Jack Frymier
Catherine Cornbleth
Robert Donmoyer
Bruce M. Gansneder
Jan T. Jeter
M. Frances Klein
Marian Schwab
William M. Alexander

Library of Congress Cataloging in Publication Data
Main entry under title:

One hundred good schools.

    Bibliography: p.
    1. Schools--United States--Evaluation--Methodology.
2. Educational surveys--United States. I. Frymier,
Jack Rimmel, 1925-   . II. Kappa Delta Pi.
LA210.065 1984   371'.00973   84-819
ISBN 0-912 099-02-X

Published by Kappa Delta Pi
An Honor Society in Education
P.O. Box A
West Lafayette, Indiana 47906

Table of Contents

Appendix

A Message from the President

Kappa Delta Pi has as its theme for the 1982–1984 biennium "Education for Freedom, Strength, and Peace." Much of the programming for Kappa Delta Pi for these two years has been related to this theme in one way or another.

The theme for the biennium was drawn from George Orwell's famous novel *Nineteen Eighty-Four*—in particular, the slogans that appear on the face of the Ministry of Truth: "War is Peace"; "Freedom is Slavery"; and "Ignorance is Strength." These contradictory phrases summarize, to a large extent, the essence of the dismal society that Orwell projected.

When Orwell wrote his novel in the late 1940s, he spoke of many aspects of society as he projected what it might become. Interestingly, he said next to nothing about formal education and schooling, but the thoughtful reader can easily project, from Orwell's views on related subjects, what he probably would have said about schools and the educational process, had he spoken directly to that subject.

Had Orwell described the schools and educational processes that would be consistent with the remainder of the society of *Nineteen Eighty-Four,* he probably would have described two (or possibly three) types of structures. For the children of the "proles," there would have been rudimentary schooling, such as to provide the students with a certain level of literacy necessary to understand the instruction of the government. This schooling would probably have been laced with heavy doses of political indoctrination in order to further the interests of the party. Such subjects as science, history, and the arts would have been given little or no consideration.

Inasmuch as the resources of Oceania went heavily into the permanent war effort, Orwell probably would have described schools as being held in antiquated, crowded, ill-heated buildings. Teachers (or at least the principals) probably would have been party hacks. Large classes and few and old instructional materials would have been the norm, except for the ever-present telescreen.

For the children of members of the Outer Party, schools might have been a bit better. Considering the importance of military technology, there would have been places that taught mathematics, physical science, and engineering to trusted persons. Political indoctrination would probably have been even stronger in the schools for party members' children than in the schools for the "proles." Levels of literacy would have been higher in order to have trained bureaucrats and technicians. There would even have been training in the popular art forms to provide television programs, cinema, and popular music for the masses. Children (or grandchildren) of members of the Inner Party might have had even additional advantages in their schooling, as would have befitted the status of their parents.

Throughout the schooling that Orwell might have depicted for 1984, there is a common and ominous thread—central control of thought, brought about by complete central control of structure. Not only would Big Brother be watching each student and teacher, but he would be dictating the curriculum, placing the teachers, providing the facilities and instructional materials, and molding the minds of youth toward his own ends. In short, like every other aspect of the society that Orwell projected, the schools of that time and place would be uniform for each social class, tightly controlled by the central government, and justified as a means to accomplish the evil goals of Big Brother.

How does *One Hundred Good Schools* relate to the implementation of the theme of Kappa Delta Pi for this biennium? In the Preface, which follows, Jack Frymier gives a brief history of Kappa Delta Pi's Good Schools Project. This history mentions that the concern which led to the formation of the Good Schools Project was that of the nature and quantity of the centralization of control of schools and schooling in the United States. However, as it evolved, the activity that became the Good Schools Project focused on much more than the control of schools.

In fact, as it developed, the Good Schools Project did not address directly the matter of control of schools at all. It did not need to. Some degree of control of education in North America exists at many levels—the learners, the teacher, the principal, the central office staff, the school board, the state or provincial education agency, the legislature, the national government, just to name a few. We might also include the writers and publishers of textbooks and instructional materials, the standardized test publishers, the colleges and universities, and the accrediting associations.

No school just happens to become good. A school becomes good because some person or some group of persons or some structure causes it to become good. Excellence can come about in a number of ways. We could have good schools throughout the country by action of the federal government, if such were high enough on the priorities of the public. Similarly, we could have good schools throughout any state or province if decision makers were of a mind to have it so. Principals or teachers, if of one mind on the matter and willing to pay the price, could bring about excellence in every classroom. If enough parents—or even students—wanted high quality education to abound and wanted it badly enough, it would come about. The control of education in North America is diverse enough and balanced enough that if any one structure wishes to promote excellence strongly enough for its constituency, it is likely to come about.

In this respect, education in the United States and Canada differs from that in much of the rest of the world. In many respects, our educational systems are highly decentralized in comparison with the educational systems of most of the other countries.

The issue of centralized control versus decentralized control is an unresolved one and is, in some respects, an irrelevant one. Under our structures, excellence can come about at any of several levels.

One Hundred Good Schools shows that excellence is unrelated to public or private control; that excellence is independent of the age or grade level of the students; that excellence does not depend on wealth or geographical location; and that the socioeconomic make-up of the student body of a school is not necessarily a determiner of excellence. The data in *One Hundred Good Schools* show that concerned principals and teachers and parents and students can take matters as they are and transform them into high-quality educational programs. Big Brother has neither been watching them nor directing their efforts.

Perhaps our schools, more than any other segment of our society, have kept us from the worst of the social evils projected by Orwell. Perhaps our schools *have* kept us free. Perhaps the better our schools, the longer our freedoms will last. May *One Hundred Good Schools* blossom into tens of thousands of good schools.

Jerry Robbins
Atlanta, Georgia
December 1983

Preface

One Hundred Good Schools is the story of an organization at work. Organizations, however, do not work. People do. In fact, people often join an organization because it represents an idea or a set of ideals with which they want to become involved. Kappa Delta Pi is such an organization.

Kappa Delta Pi is an honor society in education. Dedicated to excellence and scholarship in education, Kappa Delta Pi has about fifty thousand members who belong to more than four hundred chapters throughout the United States and in Canada.

Traditionally, people join Kappa Delta Pi while they are graduate or advanced undergraduate students enrolled in teacher education programs. After their initial contact with the organization, many continue their membership and maintain communication with Kappa Delta Pi by reading *The Educational Forum* and the *Record.* They consider it an honor to belong, but they do not participate in any other way.

The Good Schools Project changed some of that. *One Hundred Good Schools* is the story of how some members of Kappa Delta Pi tried to *understand* and *promote* excellence and scholarship in education by studying good schools across America. Hundreds of committed people rolled up their sleeves and went to work to learn about good schools.

How did it all begin? The idea of a study was first suggested to the executive council of Kappa Delta Pi in early 1980. The emphasis of the project, which originally focused on centralization and control, shifted in 1981 to improvement of the schools.

During September 1981, the president of Kappa Delta Pi appointed a seven-member research committee to accomplish this project: Catherine Cornbleth at the University of Pittsburgh; Robert Donmoyer at The Ohio State University; Bruce Gansneder at the University of Virginia; Jan Jeter at St. Mary's Dominican

College in New Orleans; Frances Klein at the University of Southern California; Marian Schwab at the Athenaeum of Ohio; and Jack Frymier at The Ohio State University. Jack Frymier was asked to serve as chairman. William Alexander at the University of Florida and laureate counselor of Kappa Delta Pi was asked to serve as liaison between the executive council and the research committee. Although the title was not formally adopted until several months later, the Good Schools Project was officially underway.

In December 1981, the newly appointed research committee met for several days in Columbus, Ohio. Five scholars agreed to meet with the committee to conceptualize the project: Roald Campbell at the University of Utah; John Goodlad at the University of California, Los Angeles; Maxine Greene at Teachers College, Columbia University; Harold Hodgkinson at the National Training Laboratories; and Harold Shane at Indiana University. The general plan was for the scholars to interact with the project committee over a three-day period. On the basis of those interactions, each scholar was to prepare a conceptual paper for the project committee. (Maxine Greene and John Goodlad were unable to attend the meeting, but they agreed to prepare a paper for the committee.)

Following the meeting with the scholars, the project committee met for two additional days in an attempt to think through, on the basis of the discussions with the scholars, the theoretical dimensions of the study.

In March 1982, the project committee met in New Orleans for four days to discuss the papers prepared by the scholars. Discussions proceeded at both a general and specific level, with attention to various kinds of considerations: theoretical, empirical, practical, and organizational.

During those discussions, the project committee reached agreement on several important considerations. First, we wanted our research effort to focus on the positive. Second, we were concerned that whatever activities we planned would be of such a nature that they would strengthen chapters of Kappa Delta Pi and produce good data. Third, we intended to use quantitative and qualitative approaches in data collection. Fourth, we agreed to focus on individual schools rather than teachers or school districts. Fifth, we decided to accomplish all data collection activities during the course of one academic year. Finally, we agreed that all communications would be through Kappa Delta Pi chapter counselors rather than through individual members of Kappa Delta Pi or school principals.

The research committee left New Orleans in March 1982 with these "agreements" about *what* we were going to do and *how* we were going to do it. One month later the committee met in San Antonio, prior to the biennial convocation of Kappa Delta Pi, to firm up our plans. We presented our suggestions for a revised title of the endeavor—Good Schools Project—to the executive council of Kappa Delta Pi for approval, then we conducted a highly structured two hour meeting with representatives of the chapters who were in attendance at the San Antonio meeting. This meeting proved beneficial to the committee in that participants highlighted many of the problems we would probably encounter. These participants also suggested procedures for dealing with the problems that might arise. Further, in a pilot study of sorts, participants indicated the kinds of criteria they thought might be employed by people in their own communities if those people identified schools that were known to be "good" for further study.

The research committee left San Antonio with a clear sense of direction and a good "feel" for some of the practical problems we thought we might encounter in studying good schools. This monograph describes exactly what was accomplished in the Good Schools Project and how it was accomplished.

This report was written by members of the Good Schools Project research committee, but represents the efforts of hundreds of members of the society who worked together in their own communities to help all of us learn about good schools. This project has been a major effort for Kappa Delta Pi.

One Hundred Good Schools is intended for people who want to improve the quality of life in schools today. Kappa Delta Pi members are concerned about excellence and scholarship in education, and we believe that they will find this information provocative and useful. However, we are convinced that many people—educators and parents, policy makers and others—will find the information helpful, too.

For too long, Americans have been obsessed with the negative aspects of schools and schooling. This report presents information from more than 28,000 students and 3,200 teachers who live and work in 106 good schools across America.

Chapter One describes the focus of this project—good schools—and was written by Jack Frymier. Chapter Two describes the logic and rationale employed for identifying the schools and was prepared by Robert Donmoyer and Bruce Gansneder. Chapter Three, written by Frances Klein, reports the criteria that were used to identify the schools and the significance of those criteria. Chapter Four, which details how we collected data in each of the schools in the study, was prepared by Jack Frymier.

In the fifth chapter, Bruce Gansneder reports information regarding the characteristics of the participating schools. Chapter Six, prepared by Catherine Cornbleth, describes the basic beliefs of teachers about curriculum in the schools which were identified as good. In Chapter Seven, the extent to which both teachers and students feel that the schools attain their goals is reported by Frances Klein, who also prepared Chapter Eight, which includes information about classroom practices. Chapter Nine, written by Marian Schwab, portrays the interpersonal relationships that exist within the schools.

Chapter Ten was written by Robert Donmoyer and deals with the nature and extent of commitment in the schools. Jan Jeter reports on safety and discipline in the schools identified as good in Chapter Eleven and on support services and facilities in Chapter Twelve. Chapter Thirteen, which is devoted to decision making within the schools, was prepared by Bruce Gansneder. Catherine Cornbleth provides some historical perspective about these schools in Chapter Fourteen, and Robert Donmoyer devotes Chapter Fifteen to a description of educators as inquirers—how people in the local chapters of Kappa Delta Pi participated in the project. Chapter Sixteen, prepared by Jack Frymier, is a general summary of what we learned from the study. In the final chapter, William Alexander asks, "What now?" What are the implications of the Good Schools Project for members of Kappa Delta Pi, for the profession at large, and for persons interested in making schools better?

Many people have made it possible for this research to be accomplished. The Delegate Assembly of Kappa Delta Pi authorized a study in April 1980. Representatives at the San Antonio biennial convocation in April 1982 "worked through" a list of questions that proved extremely helpful to the committee. The members of the executive council supported the project by making funds available and by encouraging the research committee in various ways. Jay Hostetler and the national office staff have been helpful with special mailings, special materials, and assistance of various kinds. Mary Lou Evans and James Ferrell assisted with logistics, and Nancy Swearengin accomplished all of the communications, plus her usual editorial responsibilities. Donald Anderson and the staff in the dean's office in the College of Education at The Ohio State University expedited materials production and data processing. Special thanks to Bruce Gansneder and the staff at the Bureau of Educational Research at the University of Virginia for their work with the statistical analysis of the data.

Those who have done the most, however, have been those members of Kappa Delta Pi in local chapters who chose to participate in this project "all the way." They identified the schools. They administered the survey instruments. They conducted the intensive interviews. They collected all the materials and sent those materials back to the research committee in time for analysis. To those loyal and hardworking members of Kappa Delta Pi who worked to make this study possible, we say: "Thank you. This project never would have been accomplished without your help. We hope the effort has been worthwhile for you."

Jack Frymier
Columbus, Ohio
November 1983

1

The Focus: Good Schools

Introduction

These are fascinating but frustrating times for people who are concerned about the schools. "American schools are in trouble," one thoughtful researcher claims.[1] "Our nation is at risk," the National Commission on Excellence in Education asserts.[2] "Where do we go now?," almost everyone is asking.

It was Einstein, supposedly, who once stated that our age was characterized by "obfuscation of ends and clarification of means." Even those who seem to be clear in their own minds about the ends schools ought to be pursuing are often at variance with others who are equally concerned.

The history of the Good Schools Project reflects some of the shifting sentiments and varying enthusiasms which have imbued the American public about its schools in recent years. When the project was initially conceptualized, it was to be a study of centralization and control of the schools. Later, the emphasis of the project was changed to continuation and improvement. Finally, the project came to be a study of "good schools."

The Good Schools Project research committee thought that the focus on good schools would be appropriate and useful. We were convinced that looking carefully at good schools would generate information different from much of the information researchers have been producing in recent years. We were also convinced that a focus on good schools would be helpful to persons who want to "get a handle" on their efforts to help the schools become better institutions.

Much of the history of human endeavor reflects a preoccupation with the negative aspects of human existence. It is true, of course, that this preoccupation with the negative is usually seen as a prelude to "making things better," but there is no doubt that many persons come to focus on the negative almost exclusively.

Terman, for instance, reviewed the history of the attention given the gifted child, and he reported that a hundred or more years ago precociousness was talked about in terms of "early ripe, early rot."[3] Almost universally, researchers in medicine have been concerned with illness rather than wellness; with the pathological rather than the healthful aspects of human life.

Much of the research in psychology has been devoted to a study of "personality disorders," "learning disabilities," "mental deficiencies," and things of that kind. Further, factories and schools have traditionally looked for "mistakes" or "errors"—in production and in learning—as the key to improved quality. Attention has been directed to the negative.

Today the tide is turning some. There is concern about "correcting errors," but the emphasis is changing. Researchers are directing more and more attention to the "healthful," the "effective," the "best." Policy makers are interested in learning from the successful institutions and individuals: "good" departments; "outstanding" corporations; the "very best" salespersons, managers, teachers, or whatever.

Fromm epitomizes the shift in psychological thought that has developed during the past forty years.

> There is no more fundamental distinction between men, psychologically and morally, than the one between those who love death and those who love life, between the *necrophilous* and the *biophilous*.[4]

Maslow's study of self-actualizing people,[5] Allport's discussion of "becoming,"[6] and Combs and Snygg's description of the adequate personality[7] illustrate the shift in focus among psychologists from disintegration to integration of personality; from unhealthy to healthy behavior.

In the corporate world, Peters and Waterman's study of America's best run companies illustrates the same negative to positive trend.[8] Ouchi's description of Theory Z companies[9] and Flory's characterization of "managers for tomorrow"[10] follows the same logic. The basic question reflected in each of these studies seems to be: "What can we learn from the best?"

The shift from negative to positive considerations is evident also in some researchers' focus on the schools. The "effective schools" approach, for example, illustrates that trend.[11]

Berman's conception of curriculum is predicated on the same devotion to the positive that undergirds the illustrations that have been cited here.[12] Sanders and Schwab's study of Annehurst, "the natural history of a good school," is yet another illustration of the tendency to emphasize the positive.[13]

The point is, there has been a shift—modest to be sure—from the problematic and pathological to the fully-functioning individual and institution in our society. Increasingly, researchers are interested in and attentive to the best in human experience.

The Problem

It may be true, as Whorf maintained, that "language shapes behavior."[14] If that is so, the language of research itself may be debilitating. Researchers usually start out by trying to "define the *problem*," for example. But problems are reminders of difficulty or failure. Perhaps researchers should learn to ask their questions in terms of possibilities or potentialities. Our research committee members were less concerned about different approaches to research than we were about what we could learn from a careful study of certain schools identified as good. We decided to focus the study on good schools.

There were four basic purposes of the Good Schools Project. First, we intended to identify the good schools in America today, wherever they might be: elementary, middle, or secondary level schools; public, private, or parochial schools; and urban, rural, or suburban schools. Second, we planned to study carefully those good schools to see what they were like. Third, we intended to look at the schools in depth and over time to learn how those good schools came to be; what made it possible for the people there to create the policies, practices, and programs that were recognized as superb. Finally, from what we learned about good schools, we planned to make inferences that would be useful and sound for those who want to make their own schools better.[15]

The Frame of Reference

Once the purposes were clarified, the Good Schools Project research committee did five things. First, we established a number of agreements regarding the practical aspects of the project. Second, we prepared a working paper on what seemed to be appropriate conceptual dimensions for the study. Third, we proceeded to develop survey and interview questions that might be used in a study of good schools. Fourth, those questions were then related to the conceptual dimensions that had been articulated. Fifth, we revised our conception of the dimensions as a result of the learning that took place when we tried to relate the survey and interview questions to the dimensions that had been proposed.

In the sections that follow, steps one and five are described in detail. The intervening, process steps have not been so described. Those were important events in the evolution of the framework for members of the Good Schools Project research committee, but they are probably less important to a reader of our report.

Procedural Agreements

Every research effort has practical limitations. Some are imposed by financial constraints. Others are the result of temporal considerations. Still others are inherent in the capabilities of the researchers and the nature of the phenomena under investigation.

Once the decision was made to focus the study on good schools, the committee began to sort out a number of agreements that would guide our work. Six factors were identified. First, we clarified why we were going to focus on the positive aspects of schooling. Second, we decided to work in ways that would strengthen local chapters of Kappa Delta Pi and also produce good data. Third, we committed ourselves to try to employ quantitative and qualitative approaches to data collection. Fourth, we agreed to aim our research efforts at individual schools rather than classrooms or school districts. Fifth, we decided to collect all data during the course of one academic year. Sixth, we agreed that all formal communications about the project would be through chapter counselors rather than through individual members of Kappa Delta Pi or other persons, such as building principals. Each of these six agreements is described more fully in the sections that follow.

Focus on the Positive: The decision to study good schools was a decision to emphasize the positive. More than that was involved, however. Most of the attention schools tend to receive seems to emphasize the negative aspects of schooling: declining test scores; lack of discipline; vandalism; sagging morale; incompetent staff; lack of public support; and the like. Anyone who knows anything about the reality of schools knows that that is a serious distortion of what actually exists.

Schools have their share of problems, but there are also many positive aspects of schooling that go unheralded. For example, even though it is correct that the Gallup poll has consistently identified discipline as the number one problem of schools, it is also true that only once in the last fifteen years have more than 25 percent of the respondents actually indicated that discipline was a problem. In other words, 75 percent or more of the people have *never* felt that discipline was a problem in the schools.[16]

Even in those efforts aimed at "looking at the bright side" of schools, a very narrow definition of what makes a school good seems to be emerging. For instance, many people who talk or write about "effective" schools seem to be preoccupied with standardized achievement test scores as the only important factor for school people to be concerned about. Almost everybody would say: "Obviously it is important to be concerned about things other than achievement scores." However, many of those same people then turn around and focus all energies on raising achievement scores. One recent publication states it this way:

> . . . there is reason to believe that planning to cover skills and objectives that are to be tested will increase the overlap between content taught and content tested.[17]
>
> One way districts or individual schools might help is by developing a curriculum guide that at least represents the majority of the content to be tested. This will likely require some adjustments in the present guide (if one has already been developed), since finding a test that overlaps with the content and skills in the curriculum guide is difficult, if not impossible.[18]

What is being advocated here, of course, is "teaching for the test." The implication is clear: achievement tests ought to be the central concern of people who want to create "effective schools and classrooms." To those of us on the Good Schools Project research committee, that seemed to be an extremely narrow and limiting conception of effective or good schools. We wanted to focus on the positive, but we wanted to look at schooling in a more wholistic, realistic way.

We also felt that experienced, competent professionals in the field could clarify for themselves what they think is "good" about schools without an *a priori* set of criteria or a stipulative definition from us. That is, while we felt that achievement scores were too limiting and too narrow as a criterion for defining or identifying good schools, we were reluctant also to impose our own preconceived definition or set of criteria without a broad base of professional input.

Researchers often specify criteria unilaterally when they set about to study anything, and we could have done that, too. However, it was our considered judgment that, if we solicited the intelligence and experience of competent professionals in the field on this matter, we would probably generate a broader and more reality-based set of criteria regarding what made schools "good" than if we imposed our own conception of criteria on all of the schools we hoped to study.

We agreed, therefore, that we would lean on the skill and judgments of able, experienced professionals in the field to identify schools they thought to be good. Further, we also agreed to study carefully their criteria for determining a good school and to compare that list with the criteria that conventional researchers employ. We hoped at least to learn something about the way other people think about schools they consider good. On the other hand, we might produce important information for helping people re-think what is really important about schools.

Strengthen Chapters and Collect Good Data: Given the fact that this project was being conceptualized within the framework of Kappa Delta Pi as an organization, was being funded by the society, and was to be accomplished by members of the society, two considerations emerged. We wanted to strengthen Kappa Delta Pi as an organization, and we wanted to collect data that would be valid and useful for the profession at large.

Because we intended to accomplish the study in conjunction with local chapters of Kappa Delta Pi, we agreed to approach the chapters in ways that would allow them to become better and stronger if they became involved. We were conscious that we would be making demands that would create tensions and difficulties on people at the local level, but we were also conscious of the opportunities that such an involvement might create for people to acquire new understandings and new skills.

Whatever processes we might create for chapters to use in collecting data could be helpful to those chapters and to us. However, as a committee we were committed to the idea of doing a good study of good schools. Validity and reliability of data were absolutely essential. It was imperative that the data we planned to collect be trustworthy.

Employ Different Approaches for Collecting Data: The original proposal that was submitted to the executive council of Kappa Delta Pi had outlined the possibility of collecting "survey-type data" along with "case study-type data." Those concepts had not been described carefully, but members of the research committee had been recruited with those two basic orientations in mind.

Our plan initially was to procure survey data from a fairly large number of individuals and then to use in-depth interview techniques and other procedures. This two-pronged approach to data collection persisted in our thinking during the conceptualization process and eventually was incorporated into the research design.

Study Individual Schools: From the evidence made available to us by the scholars, and from our own understandings of schools and schooling, the individual school building (rather than the classroom or school district) seemed to be the most appropriate level on which to focus our observational efforts. The building principal and his or her staff constitute a working group with assigned responsibilities for teaching a given set of young people in a defined geographical region. The school—as a functioning entity—promised to be a meaningful unit of analysis in which to try to comprehend the complexities and nuances of teaching and learning.

Collect Data During One Academic Year: Schools and school people organize their efforts and activities around the concept of an "academic year." In most cases, staff members are hired and assigned on the basis of an academic year. Student activities, formal evaluations, program changes, and other aspects of schooling generally fall conveniently into the academic year time frame. September through June becomes a useful and practical time slot through which to study a school.

Local Kappa Delta Pi chapters, whose members' energies we

hoped to enlist, also organize their activities around the academic year schedule. Elections of officers are held annually, programs are developed "for the year," and counselors assume their own responsibilities within that time frame, too.

Therefore, the research committee agreed that, whatever data collection processes were to be devised, everything that involved local chapters would have to take place between early September of one year and the end of May the next year. We concluded such a time frame would be constraining, but it was the only realistic approach.

Work Through Chapter Counselors: Kappa Delta Pi is a large organization with thousands of members and hundreds of chapters across the United States and in Canada. Further, it has a functioning governance structure of various committees and working groups. There were many ways in which the research committee might have decided to relate to Kappa Delta Pi. For various reasons, some of which have already been implied, we decided to conduct all communications and data collection efforts through the chapter counselors.

The committee knew from the beginning that a decision to channel everything through the local chapter counselors could be problematic. Counselors differ in their abilities and enthusiasms for Kappa Delta Pi activities. One of the purposes of this whole project, however, was to strengthen chapter efforts and program activities. We hoped that counselors would see this research project as an opportunity and a way to vitalize or revitalize their local chapters of Kappa Delta Pi.

We agreed, therefore, that all communications, all requests for participation, and all instructions regarding data collection would be directed to local chapters of Kappa Delta Pi through the chapter counselors. If many counselors elected to participate, the number of schools that we would study might be very large. If only a few counselors decided to become involved, the number of schools in our sample would be smaller, but the data would be meaningful and useful, just the same.

Conceptual Dimensions

From the beginning, the Good Schools Project research committee explored the conceptual aspects of the study with the intention of allowing the concepts to evolve. We explored Sarason's ideas regarding the "culture of the school"[19] and

Bronfenbrenner's notions of the ecological environment as a set of nested structures.[20] We looked carefully at Rutter and his colleagues' study of students over time in twelve English secondary schools.[21] We examined the data regarding successful urban schools,[22] and we studied the "meaning of school success" as Garbarino and Asp defined that term.[23]

Over time and through discussion, our understanding of what should and could be studied was modified as we made decisions, selected survey items, shaped interview procedures, and the like. What follows is a description of the finally agreed-upon dimensions that served as a conceptual framework for our study of more than one hundred good schools. By definition, these dimensions became restrictive when we began to use them as a basis for the study. Our hope was that we had broadened and defined the conceptual framework to the point where we could make observations of the reality of schooling in a reasonably comprehensive but accurate way.

Demographics: The demographics dimension includes such factors as community environment, school environment, characteristics of students, teachers, and principals, along with special programs in the school and co-curricular and extracurricular activities. Information regarding teacher experience, teacher turnover, class size, incidents of theft and vandalism, percentage of students who receive free lunch, age of building, percentage of students who failed the previous year, number of students suspended, expelled, and the like are also included.

Curriculum Perspectives: This dimension refers to beliefs about the nature of knowledge and learning that influence the curriculum opportunities provided to students. These beliefs are assumed to influence and be influenced by classroom practices and other aspects of the school milieu and, less directly, the institutional–community context in which the school is located. The subdimensions include expectations for students, including teachers' expectations for student learning, students' self-expectations for learning, and achievement emphasis; and teachers' conceptions of knowledge and learning, including teachers' perceptions of the nature, selection, and use of knowledge in curriculum, and the organization and distribution of knowledge in curriculum, including provision for variety and student choice.

Goal Attainment: The goal attainment dimension refers to the ends of education that schools strive to achieve. Goals give direction to the educational enterprise, and the importance of particular goals and the extent to which they are achieved are significant considerations. The subdimensions include such factors as reading skills, factual knowledge, study skills, attitudes towards people of different races, religions, or cultures, sense of self-worth, respect for the rights of others, independence and self-reliance, ability to evaluate information, and effective expression of opinions.

Classroom Practices: The classroom practices dimension refers to actual practices that take place which indicate how students attain the goals of education that are deemed to be important. Subdimensions include such factors as opportunities for critical thinking, student choice options, use of classroom time, homework, evaluation of student learning, availability of instructional materials and supplies, use of textbooks, extent to which cooperation in learning is encouraged or allowed, the nature and degree of individualized instruction, and instructional practices.

Interpersonal Relations: This dimension refers to the ways people in the school perceive, understand, evaluate, and react to one another. Subdimensions addressed are task support, personal support, inclusion, and respect.

Commitment: Commitment refers to attitudes and beliefs which result in dedication to the school and its goals, and behavior which is motivated by this dedication rather than the likelihood of extrinsic reward or punishment. The subdimensions of commitment include staff commitment, student commitment, parent commitment, factors that cause high levels of commitment, teacher pride and morale, teacher openness, and teacher acceptance of responsibility.

Discipline and Safety: This dimension relates to the perceived reasonableness of school rules and their enforcement procedures, compliance with school rules and regulations, extent to which the school environment is safe and conducive to teaching and learning, and the use of drugs, alcohol, and tobacco. The subdimensions include school rules, rule enforcement, compliance, safety and security, drugs, alcohol, and tobacco, and student behavior.

Support Services and Facilities: This dimension refers to the perceived adequacy of school support services and to the condition and use of the school building. Subdimensions include library services, secretarial services, worthwhileness of inservice programs, pleasantness and cleanliness of the school, and use of the building.

Decision Making: The decision making dimension of the study refers to the institutional functioning of the school and the degree of staff satisfaction with these processes. How school-wide problems are identified and acted upon, and how responsibility is shared or denied are aspects of this dimension. The specific subdimensions include looking at decision making in terms of the people who are involved—administrators, teachers, students, and parents—and according to the procedures employed, the success achieved, and the extent to which cooperation is involved.

History: Schools change, and this dimension refers to the aspects of classroom practices, school milieu, and institutional–community context as they have developed to their present state. In other words, how have these schools come to be as they are now? Even a rich description of the characteristics and dynamics of good schools, including identification of patterns of beliefs and practices that distinguish them from other schools, is not sufficient to guide improvement efforts. Also needed is knowledge about how good schools came to be so that others might benefit from the experience.

Achievement Scores: Standardized achievement and ability test scores routinely administered in each school during the past three years were collected.

Summary

This chapter outlined what might be described as a cautious shift in research from the negative aspects of human existence (e.g., sickness, errors, problems) to the more positive aspects of the human experience (e.g., wellness, successes, possibilities). Following that, the purposes of the Good Schools Project were set forth: to identify good schools; to study those schools; to find out how those schools came to be; and then to make inferences that would be helpful to others. Finally, the procedural agreements and conceptual dimensions of the study were described. How we identified the schools to be included in the study is reported in the next chapter.

Notes

1. John I. Goodlad, *A Place Called School* (New York: McGraw Hill Book Co., 1984), p. 1.
2. David P. Gardner et al., *A Nation At Risk* (Washington, D.C.: U.S. Department of Education, 1983), p. 5.
3. Lewis M. Terman and Melita H. Oden, *The Gifted Child Grows Up* (Stanford: Stanford University Press, 1947), p. 1.
4. Erich Fromm, *The Heart of Man* (New York: Harper and Row, Publishers, 1964), p. 38.
5. Abraham H. Maslow, *Motivation and Personality* (New York: Harper and Row, Publishers, 1954).
6. Gordon W. Allport, *Becoming* (New Haven: Yale University Press, 1955), 106 pp.
7. Arthur W. Combs and Donald Snygg, *Individual Behavior*, rev. ed. (New York: Harper and Row, Publishers, 1957).
8. Thomas J. Peters and Robert H. Waterman, Jr., *In Search of Excellence* (New York: Harper and Row, Publishers, 1982).
9. William G. Ouchi, *Theory Z* (Reading, Ma.: Addison-Wesley Publishing Co., 1981).
10. Charles D. Flory, ed., *Managers for Tomorrow* (New York: New American Library, 1965), 288 pp.
11. Donald E. Mackenzie, "Research for School Improvement: An Appraisal of Some Recent Trends," *Educational Researcher* 12 (April 1983): 5-17.
12. Louise M. Berman, *New Priorities in the Curriculum* (Columbus, Oh.: Charles E. Merrill Publishing Co., 1968), 241 pp.
13. Donald P. Sanders and Marian Schwab, *Annehurst: The Natural History of a Good School* (West Lafayette, In.: Kappa Delta Pi, 1981), 82 pp.
14. Benjamin Lee Whorf, *Language, Thought, and Reality* (New York: John Wiley and Sons and the Technology Press of Massachusetts Institute of Technology, 1956), 278 pp.
15. Jack Frymier, "Good Schools Project: A Call to Action," *The Educational Forum* 46 (Summer 1982): 388-90.
16. Stanley M. Elam, ed., *A Decade of Gallup Polls of Attitudes Toward Education 1969-1978* (Bloomington, In.: Phi Delta Kappa, 1978), 377 pp.
17. David A. Squires, William G. Huitt, and John K. Segars, *Effective Schools and Classrooms* (Alexandria, Va.: Association for Supervision and Curriculum Development, 1983), p. 15.
18. Ibid., p. 17.
19. Seymour B. Sarason, *The Culture of the School and the Problem of Change* (Boston: Allyn and Bacon, Inc., 1971), 246 pp.
20. Urie Bronfenbrenner, *The Ecology of Human Development* (Cambridge, Ma.: Harvard University Press, 1979), 330 pp.
21. Michael Rutter et al., *Fifteen Thousand Hours* (Cambridge, Ma.: Harvard University Press, 1979), 285 pp.
22. Willard R. Duckett, ed., *Why Do Some Urban Schools Succeed?* (Bloomington, In.: Phi Delta Kappa, 1980), 225 pp.
23. James Garbarino and C. Elliot Asp, *Successful Schools and Competent Students* (Lexington, Ma.: D.C. Heath and Co., 1981), 170 pp.

2

Identifying the Good Schools

The procedure used to identify the sample of schools for the Good Schools Project was one of the more unique aspects of the project. Most studies of successful schools first articulate explicit criteria which are then used to select a sample for study. The effective schools literature, for example, normally employs student achievement as measured by standardized tests as selection criteria. The Good Schools Project research committee developed no *a priori* criteria for purposes of sample selection. Rather, the project's research committee delegated both the task of developing the criteria on which the selection of a good school would be made and the task of selecting a good school to the various local Kappa Delta Pi chapters participating in the study. The first part of this chapter briefly describes the criteria development procedure and sample selection procedure (see Appendix J for complete instructions). The second part of the chapter presents the research committee's rationale for employing this untraditional method of identifying good schools.

Procedures

In August 1982, the research committee invited all 400 Kappa Delta Pi chapter counselors to participate in the Good Schools Project. Each chapter participating in the study was to identify one or more exceptionally good schools in the local chapter's geographic area by following a six-step procedure.

Step one directed the local chapter counselor to form a selection committee, consisting of Kappa Delta Pi members only, to make the final decisions regarding which schools were to be identified as good. Counselors were encouraged to include only experienced professionals. This was designed to ensure the competence of selection committee members. The national research committee reasoned that, since Kappa Delta Pi was an honor society, limiting membership to Kappa Delta Pi members would help ensure that the local selection committees were staffed by highly competent and experienced individuals. A computerized mailing list of all current Kappa Delta Pi members residing in the immediate area of each local chapter was sent to chapter counselors to facilitate the identification of possible selection committee members.

Step two directed the newly-formed selection committee to solicit recommendations of good schools from every member of Kappa Delta Pi in its area. A mailing list and a form letter to be sent on the local counselor's stationery were provided to each selection committee to make the job easier. Included with each letter to be mailed to Kappa Delta Pi members was a special form for recommending a school as good. Descriptive data about each school was requested, and those who recommended schools to be included in the project were asked to describe in detail, and with as much specificity as possible, why they felt that the school they were recommending was an especially good school.

Step three directed the selection committee to have the local chapter members return their recommendations of schools they considered good to the selection committee by October 15, so those recommendations could be reviewed.

Step four directed the selection committee to analyze the recommendations and rationales which accompanied the recommendations and to use these analyzed data, along with the committee members' general experience and wisdom, to determine criteria that could be used to make the final identification of schools to be included in the Good Schools Project. After the criteria had been determined by the local selection committees, those groups were directed to "write the criteria down" and then to "develop a process for employing the criteria to identify good schools. . . ." Final decisions about schools identified as good were to be made by November 1, 1982.

Step five directed the selection committee to contact all of the schools identified as good, to verify the descriptive information made available by the person who had originally recommended the school, to describe the general purpose and nature of the Good Schools Project to the building principal, and to encourage that person to participate in the project. The nature of the demands on the participating schools and the general time line for collecting data in the schools were to be described to the building principal.

Step six directed the selection committee to send all factual information and recommendation forms for each school identified as good to the Good Schools Project research committee by November 15, 1982, along with statements of the criteria used, processes for employing the criteria, and the names and responsibilities of all local selection committee members.

Over 4,700 letters to individual members of Kappa Delta Pi were mailed by local selection committees. A total of 218 persons responded by recommending one or more schools as good. In all, 209 schools were recommended by Kappa Delta Pi members for inclusion in the project. By January 1, 1983, complete information on 132 schools identified as good was received from thirty-nine chapters of Kappa Delta Pi. Four schools refused to participate. Ultimately, data were collected in 106 schools.

Rationale

As noted at the outset of this chapter, the procedure for identifying a sample of good schools, which was just outlined, is hardly a conventional one, in large part because no common definition of school success was formulated to serve as a basis for sample selection. The research committee chose this unconventional procedure for three interrelated reasons: (1) problems the research committee perceived with previous studies of successful schools resulting from the too limited definitions of school success employed by these studies; (2) financial constraints; (3) the unique benefits the research committee believed would accrue from using the procedures outlined above. Each of these reasons is discussed briefly below.

Limitations of Previous Studies

The research committee members who designed the Good Schools Project study believed that most previous studies of successful schools, such as the effective schools research, were seriously flawed because of the criteria used to define the samples of good schools employed in the studies. The criteria were normally limited to student academic achievement as measured by standardized achievement test scores. The problem with these studies lies with the criteria in general and with the way the criteria are made operational.

At a general level, the problem is that the term "student academic achievement" in no way exhausts what most people expect from schools. Normally, schools are expected also to contribute to their students' social and emotional development, and it is unlikely that most people would consider a school successful or effective or good if that school attained academic achievement by seriously impairing either social or emotional development.

Even with respect to the criteria of academic achievement, however, there are problems with most prior studies because of the way academic achievement has been operationally defined. In most instances, achievement has been made operational by using students' scores on standardized achievement tests. Such scores in no way exhaust the common sense meaning of the term "academic achievement," just as academic achievement in no way exhausts most people's goals for schooling. Performance on standardized achievement tests, in fact, is not intrinsically worthwhile, but receives its meaning because it is assumed that such performance is an index of later success. Unfortunately, the predictive validity of such scores has not been established and, in fact, the evidence that does exist suggests that performance on most standardized tests given at the elementary and secondary levels is not a predictor of later success.[1] Thus, even if one wished to define school success solely in terms of student academic achievement it does not seem appropriate to define student academic achievement solely in terms of students' standardized achievement test scores.

Financial Considerations

Because of the problems discussed above, the research committee became committed to the principle of using multiple, divergent, and possibly even contradictory criteria for identifying its sample of good schools. One procedure would have been to carefully define a series of different sets of criteria, then to identify a sample of good schools which was composed of subsets of schools which met the different sets of criteria defined. Financial considerations precluded this option; the search for the right schools to meet multiple, predefined sets of criteria would have been too costly for the project's relatively meager resources. The research committee decided instead to identify the study's sample by following the procedures outlined in the first half of this chapter. The approach, as described previously, was an inductive rather than a deductive one: the Good Schools Project did not define good schools *a priori,* but made the definition a central question for empirical inquiry. Most of the remaining chapters in this book describe what the average school in the sample was like in terms of the criteria used to direct data collection.

Advantages of the Inductive Approach

Beyond the cost advantage, the research committee believed the inductive approach to defining good schools had two additional advantages. First, the criteria developed by the local selection committees (in the process of following the identification procedures outlined previously) constitute data which can be analyzed and used to articulate multiple definitions by which the goodness of a school can be judged. Chapter Three presents the outcomes of such an analysis. One unfortunate consequence of the effective schools literature has been the tendency to focus attention on questions of means and, in the process, to give the impression that questions of ends have been resolved and need no further discussion. By identifying and articulating the wide range of values employed by an array of educators in identifying good schools, the Good Schools Project is a reminder of the importance of value issues in education, and it serves as an antidote to the effective schools literature with its relatively narrow definition of educational goodness.

A second advantage of the sample identification procedures developed by the Good Schools Project research committee is that these procedures netted a more diverse sample of good schools than probably would have been produced if the committee had identified its sample on the basis of predefined criteria, even multiple sets of predefined criteria. This diversity is not especially important for this initial publication, which simply aggregates data from the entire sample and reports characteristics of the sample's average school. The research committee, however, plans further study of the data that have been collected. For example, the committee plans to identify outliers in the sample and, either through additional analysis of existing data or through in-depth case studies, to analyze the characteristics of these especially unique schools. Correlational studies also are planned to explore relationships among variables. For example, the relationship between academic achievement (as measured by standardized tests) and interpersonal relationships will be explored to determine whether these criteria for defining good schools are complementary, or whether hard choices have to be made with respect to these dimensions. Correlational studies also are planned to determine other possible relationships, such as the relationship among staff participation in decision making, staff commitment, and student achievement.

Summary

This chapter described the untraditional procedure used to identify good schools and the rationale for using these unconventional procedures. These procedures not only treat value questions in education as problematic, but they also provide a rich data source to explore empirically the educational consequences of various values.

Note

1. C. Jencks and M. Brown, "Effects of High Schools on Their Students," *The Harvard Educational Review* 45 (August 1975).

3

Criteria Used in Identifying the Good Schools

This is a time of great emphasis upon academic excellence, effective schools, quality education, and a general recognition of the importance of schooling. Governmental agencies at the federal and state level, national commissions, citizens' groups, prestigious educators, parents, business and industrial groups, legislators, community organizations, school administrators, and teachers echo the call for quality education and the need for good schools. People are in accord that the schools must improve so that all students will receive the best education possible.

There is not as much agreement, however, as to how the schools are to improve as there is with the general goal that something must be done. A variety of ways has been proposed as to how schooling should be improved. The recent report from the National Commission on Excellence in Education calls for increased graduation requirements for students, more homework, longer hours in school, and more rigorous and measurable standards in the academic areas.[1] Institutions of higher education throughout the United States are requiring of their entering students more English, science, mathematics, and foreign language courses. High schools are tightening up their requirements for graduation in response to university and general community pressures for higher standards. Some high schools are even anticipating future needs and are requiring, in addition to the traditional academic areas, computer literacy and keyboard skills as basic competencies for graduation. Higher achievement scores in reading and mathematics have become an expectation for all schools. Communities are encouraged to examine their schools and become involved with the faculties in order to assure that the communities are served by good schools—schools which meet at least some of the above standards.

Are these the standards by which schools ought to be judged? Do they adequately define good schools? These questions became one research focus for the Good Schools Project. The research committee wanted to investigate how a group of knowledgeable educators within the participating chapters of Kappa Delta Pi would identify good schools. What criteria would be used to define and nominate good schools by those persons who knew the schools in their area? This question became an important part of the research study. Thus, the research committee deliberately decided not to specify in advance what criteria should be used to identify the schools which were to be recommended for participation in this study; i.e., those schools which were considered good or even exemplary. Rather, the research committee was interested in finding out what criteria would be used in the process of identifying good schools.

Research on Effective Schools

Other approaches to studying good schools or effective schools have been taken. There is a body of research findings, for example, which describes effective schools. In these studies, the criteria have been decided upon in advance by the researchers. Effective schools were usually defined as those which have higher achievement test scores in reading and mathematics than might normally be expected of the students. As the results of these studies have become available to the education profession, the studies have generated considerable interest and effort. School faculties are admonished to see that their schools possess the characteristics identified through the research. College courses and staff development workshops, based on these research findings, are held for teachers. Thus, the results of these studies are having a considerable impact upon schools. For some educators, the results of these studies have become the standards by which effective schools are defined.

What are these standards as currently defined from the effective schools research studies? Several summaries of the research provide an overview of the findings. Mackenzie identified three clusters of characteristics from the literature on effective schools: leadership, efficacy, and efficiency dimensions.[2] Each of those three dimensions was then divided into core elements, or those most frequently found in the literature, and facilitating elements, or those less frequently found in the literature on effective schools. The facilitating elements were also specific conditions concerning implementation, according to Mackenzie.

Core elements in the leadership dimension were: a positive climate or atmosphere; activities focused on clear and reasonable objectives; teacher-directed classrooms; and staff development on effective teaching. Facilitating elements were: a shared consensus on values and goals; long-range planning and coordination; stability of key staff; and support for school improvement at the district level.

Core elements in the efficacy dimension were: high expectations with a press for excellence; rewards for academic growth and excellence; cooperation and group interaction within classrooms; complete involvement in improvement; freedom to implement adaptive practices; learning tasks of appropriate difficulty; and empathy, rapport, and interaction of the teacher with students. An emphasis on homework, accountability with acceptance of responsibility for learning, avoidance of nonpromotion, and interaction with successful peers with deemphasis on ability grouping were the facilitating elements or ways in which the core elements might be implemented.

The core elements in the efficiency dimension centered on effective use of instructional time; orderly and disciplined environments; diagnosis, prescription, and feedback in learning; instruction based upon content coverage; and an emphasis on basic and high level skills throughout the school. Two facilitating elements were named: opportunities to have individualized work and the number and variety of opportunities for learning.

Other reviews of the literature on effective schools are in basic agreement with the above synthesis. Purkey and Smith reviewed several different types of research conducted on effective schools and summarized the important characteristics identified by each type of study as well as the methodological weaknesses of each design.[3] Major characteristics of effective schools as synthesized from all the different types of studies were: order, control, and discipline; high staff morale and expectations for student achievement; emphasis on instructional leadership by the principal or other staff members; a clear set of goals and emphasis for the school; schoolwide staff development effort; a system for monitoring student progress; and considerable control by staff over training and instructional decisions within the school.

Ralph and Fennessey cited five characteristics typically mentioned in the literature: strong administrative leadership, safe and orderly climate of the school, emphasis on basic academic skills, high teacher expectations of all students, and a system for assessing and monitoring student performance.[4] Edmunds also cited the same criteria as Ralph and Fennessey.[5] Squires, Huitt, and Segars identified three major characteristics from the literature on effective schools: positive school climate with an academic emphasis, an orderly environment, and expectations for success.[6] The leadership processes of modeling, consensus building, and feedback contributed to the maintenance of the three preceding characteristics.

From the above summaries of the research, then, several characteristics can be identified as being persistent qualities or practices of effective schools. These characteristics cluster around four dimensions: administrative leadership, staff development and involvement, school qualities, and classroom qualities or practices.

The first dimension of strong administrative leadership has been found consistently in effective schools. Sometimes more specific forms of leadership were named, such as an emphasis upon instruction or use of the processes of modeling, consensus building, and feedback.

The second dimension emphasized staff development and involvement. The characteristics for this dimension were: the existence of staff development activities; considerable staff control over instructional and development decisions; complete staff involvement in improvement; and staff morale.

The third dimension related to general school qualities. The characteristics for this dimension were: an emphasis on basic academic skills and high level thinking skills; rewards for academic growth and excellence; clear, high expectations for success; agreed upon goals; positive school climate with an academic emphasis; and a safe, orderly, disciplined environment.

The fourth dimension identified classroom qualities or practices. The characteristics for this dimension were: cooperation and group interaction in classrooms; empathy, rapport, and interaction of the teacher with students; freedom to implement adaptive practices; teacher-directed classrooms; activities focused on clear and reasonable objectives; learning tasks of appropriate difficulty; effective use of instructional time; instruction based on content coverage; diagnosis, prescription, and feedback in learning; and a system for assessing and monitoring student progress.

Characteristics included in the literature, but less frequently found in the research, according to Mackenzie were: long-range planning and coordination; stability of key staff; support for school improvement at the district level; an emphasis on homework; accountability with an acceptance of responsibility for learning; avoidance of nonpromotion; interaction with successful peers with a deemphasis on ability grouping; opportunities for individualized work; and the number and variety of opportunities for learning.[7]

These characteristics have been summarized from several types of research studies and appear in the literature as findings from the major studies on effective schools. As these findings are reported, however, there are some important limitations identified regarding this body of research.

Limitations of the Effective Schools Literature

In spite of the eagerness and open reception with which many educators have received the findings of the effective schools research, some scholars have cautioned about generalizing too much from those studies. Rowan, Bossert, and Dwyer cited three major limitations of the research.[8] The first was the use of achievement test scores as the narrow definition of instructional effectiveness. This neglects the variety of other goals schools are expected to achieve. The second criticism was the use of only effective versus ineffective schools in research designs. These designs provide little help in understanding the causes of why the schools became effective or ineffective. An examination of only global factors in schools was the third criticism named. This ignores important variations within a single school. Rowan, Bossert, and Dwyer also cited a validity problem in selecting effective schools. In one study, the assessment of a panel of district personnel asked to identify effective schools was used. This was different from the usual quantitative methods used to assess instructional effectiveness. The results of these two selection processes proved to be negatively correlated. Rowan, Bossert, and Dwyer further cautioned that some of the measures used for determining school effectiveness are not stable over long periods of time.

Cuban noted the narrowness of the definition of effective,

and he called attention to the broad array of outcomes which any school has.[9] Additionally, Cuban cited these problems: the language used to describe the schools is fuzzy, no study provides blueprints or prescriptions on how to create effective schools, and the research has been conducted primarily in elementary schools. Firestone and Herriott echoed the latter concern and cautioned that elementary and secondary schools are different organizations and, thus, findings applicable to elementary schools may not be applicable to secondary schools.[10]

Purkey and Smith noted the same caution as Firestone and Herriott: most of the research had been conducted on elementary schools with successful mathematics and reading programs.[11] In addition, Purkey and Smith cited the difficulty in generalizing from the studies.

Perhaps the most serious limitation of all the research is the acceptance of a very narrow definition of school effectiveness—reading and mathematics achievement scores on standardized tests. Test results repeatedly have been the criteria used to select the schools initially and, thus, have determined, in part, what has been found in the effective schools studied. Such a narrow definition of effectiveness is extremely limited and unnecessarily restricted. It may well be possible that a school effective in fostering achievement in reading and mathematics is not a good school based upon the other important characteristics of a place where teachers and students live and learn effectively.

Few would delete achievement in the basic skills as an important outcome of schooling, but many would challenge it as the only desired outcome of schooling. Recent research from the "Study of Schooling," for example, reported that students, teachers, and parents within that sample of schools expected their schools to meet a diversity of functions or outcomes. They wanted schools to attend not only to intellectual development, but also to personal, social, and vocational development.[12] If schools are expected to meet an array of goals, various practices will be necessary which nurture and encourage the development of all.

Practices which encourage one set of expectations, e.g., intellectual development, do not necessarily encourage the development of other expectations, e.g., social development. Further, the current research suggests that a teacher-directed classroom is related to the development of basic skills and higher thinking skills, but such a practice may not be related to the development of skills in social interaction, respect for diversity among people, decision-making skills, and creative endeavors. More peer interaction as well as more personal autonomy may be necessary to achieve these outcomes than would be present in a classroom where the teacher always directs learning. Encouraging practitioners to model their schools after the findings of the current research on effective schools and classrooms may well ignore or even impede other learning outcomes which are considered important. A narrow definition of school effectiveness used as the sole basis for determining classroom practices could be harmful to other equally important educational outcomes. A broader definition of school effectiveness is essential in future research and practice.

The Kappa Delta Pi Good Schools Project was undertaken in the belief that there are good schools within local communities, and these good schools can be identified by thoughtful, knowledgeable educators. Given the skepticism about and the frequent condemnations of the public schools, the decision was made to locate a sample of schools thought to be good and to study them in detail. It was expected that the schools might be good on several dimensions, not only in academic achievement. To restrict unnecessarily the definition of good schools would be to deny the variety of functions the schools serve and the array of outcomes to which schools contribute. The research committee wanted to allow "goodness" to be broadly defined and not to restrict the sample to the criterion of achievement only.

Analysis of the Criteria

A total of twenty-nine chapters of Kappa Delta Pi submitted criteria by which they identified the good schools that were included in this study. In the later stages of this study, these chapters also collected data which described the schools based on the various dimensions reported in other chapters in this monograph. Kappa Delta Pi chapters that did not participate in both of these phases of the study were eliminated from the sample for the analysis of criteria used to identify good schools. The total number of criteria named was 320. The range of criteria reported by the chapters was from two to thirty-two. The mode number of criteria for the chapters was ten, and the mean for all chapters was eleven.

A unit of analysis had to be established for the criteria sent by each participating chapter of Kappa Delta Pi. Some criteria were redundant, and sometimes a single statement had several different criteria within it. The following decisions were made as to how these problems were to be handled. When a single criterion was repeated in other statements, and if it clearly meant the same thing, the criterion was tallied only once. When a single statement referred to two or more criteria, each criterion was considered to be a separate one.

A preliminary analysis of the criteria made as the data came in from chapters suggested that several broad categories would account for many of the criteria. When the sample finally was identified as being twenty-nine chapters, the broad categories previously developed became the basis for organizing the criteria. Each criterion, then, was placed in an appropriate category. Eight broad categories were used in the final analysis: curriculum or programs; climate or atmosphere; school and community relations; facilities and resources; qualities of administrative leadership; characteristics of faculty or teachers; characteristics of staff; and characteristics of students. A ninth category of miscellaneous was used so that no criterion was placed into a particular category unless the focus of it clearly seemed to match the title of the category. Table 1 summarizes the number of criterion items in each category, and the percentage of

Table 1

Categories of Criteria Used to Identify Good Schools

Category	N	% of Responses
Curriculum or Programs	86	27
Climate or Atmosphere	52	16
School and Community Relations	41	13
Facilities and Resources	30	9
Qualities of Administrative Leadership	27	8
Characteristics of Faculty or Teachers	25	8
Characteristics of Staff	24	8
Characteristics of Students	13	4
Miscellaneous	22	7
TOTAL	320	100

each category based upon the total number of criteria.

It became apparent quickly that there would be sub-categories of similar criteria within each of the categories. This proved to be true for all categories, so each of the nine broad categories were refined further into subcategories of criteria. Again, there was no attempt to force a criterion into any existing subcategory; if the criterion did not match the focus of the others, a new subcategory was begun. Thus, some subcategories contained only a single criterion. Each single criterion clearly matched the broad category, however. Appendix S describes the breakdown by category and subcategory.

An independent rater, not involved with the project, was provided with operational definitions of the major categories and a sample of 285 criteria. For the 240 criteria in the six most frequent categories, the percentage of interrater agreement was 82.5 percent. The percentages of agreements for each of those six categories were as follows: curriculum or programs 80.6 percent; climate or atmosphere 79.6 percent; school and community relations 97.4 percent; facilities and resources 81.5 percent; administrative leadership 66.7 percent; and characteristics of teachers 86.5 percent.

Curriculum or Programs

The largest category of criteria used to identify the good schools in this study focused upon the qualities or characteristics of the curriculum or programs of the school. This category generally contained criteria which dealt with expectations and goals; means for achieving them; and outcomes of student learning. Also included were criteria citing extracurricular activities or aspects of the co-curriculum. This one category contained eighty-six criteria, or 27 percent of the total number. The major subcategories of this category are shown in Appendix S. Only those subcategories accounting for more than 10 percent of the category total are discussed here.

Within the category of curriculum or programs, the largest subcategory of criteria had to do with providing for students' needs. Typical criteria were: meets the needs of all students; has an individualized approach; and recognizes individual differences. Fourteen criteria were in this subcategory, or 16 percent of the total in the category. Two other subcategories had thirteen criteria each, or 15 percent of the total within the category. These centered on an orientation to achievement or named academic excellence as a quality. Typical responses were: a basic skills emphasis; achievement oriented; academic excellence emphasized; and academic accomplishments. The other subcategory was similar in orientation, but did not make clear what the thrust or orientation to learning was. It emphasized that clear expectations existed for the curriculum or noted only that a philosophy, goals, objectives, or a scope and sequence existed for the curriculum. Typical responses in this subcategory were: an emphasis on success; clear expectations; a planned philosophy; existence of set goals or objectives; and scope and sequence. A fourth subcategory had ten criteria, or 12 percent of the category total. These criteria mentioned a broad, flexible, or balanced curriculum. Typical responses in this subcategory were: develops the whole person; nurtures students; wide range of flexible programs; flexible curriculum; and contains both the academics and the arts. The remaining subcategories are shown in Appendix S.

The curriculum was featured prominently in the criteria listed and used by the chapters of Kappa Delta Pi in identifying good schools. Criteria from the research literature on effective schools clearly were used—academic achievement; clear expectations; academic excellence; and important classroom practices, such as diagnostic and prescriptive teaching and flexibility of methods—but there were other criteria considered very important which did not reflect so clearly that research literature. The largest subcategory of criteria was an emphasis on meeting the individual differences of students. Another large subcategory emphasized a broad, balanced, and flexible curriculum which nurtured all aspects of the students, not just the academic. Other subcategories emphasized factors not mentioned at all in the research literature: a changing curriculum; one emphasizing personal development; and one with provisions for extending learning beyond the classroom.

The criteria used in the Good Schools Project extended the characteristics considered important in the effective schools research literature. A wide array of attributes about the curriculum was seen as important for identifying good schools. The prominence of this category suggested that to identify effective schools based only on achievement data was indeed restricting.

The number of criteria in this largest category, eighty-six, reflected clearly the importance of the curriculum or school program in defining a good school. This category had, by far, the largest number of criteria of any of the categories. Curriculum is the substance of schooling and it was central to the criteria used by chapters of Kappa Delta Pi for identifying good schools.

Climate or Atmosphere

The second broad category of criteria had to do with the climate or atmosphere of the school. The criteria in this category emphasized interpersonal relationships; the learning atmosphere; respect for people; an orderly, efficient environment; and morale or spirit of the school. Within this category there were fifty-two different criteria which accounted for 16 percent of the total number of criteria.

Within the climate category, the largest subcategory centered on interrelationships: sharing; open communication; positive relationships; and rapport among the various groups within the school. In this subcategory there were eleven criteria, or 21 percent of the total number in the category. The next largest subcategory had nine criteria, or 17 percent of the category total This subcategory focused on general characteristics of climate, such as positive school climate; humanistic respect for others; a student-centered climate; and general positive attitudes or expectations. Eight criteria, or 15 percent of the category total, formed the next subcategory, and these criteria were concerned with orderliness and discipline. Typical responses in this subcategory were an emphasis on discipline; orderliness; self-discipline; respect for authority; and a code for conduct. The next largest subcategory had six criteria, which accounted for 12 percent of the category total. This subcategory focused on the climate for learning, but named slightly different aspects of it than the ones discussed above. For example, some of the responses were freedom to try and fail; commitment to learning as a lifelong process; inspired to excel; time for learning; sense of purpose; and a learning atmosphere.

The two preceding subcategories of criteria clearly reflected one of the characteristics of the effective schools research literature: a safe, orderly, purposeful climate for learning. There was, however, another subcategory, also containing six criteria, or

12 percent of the category total. This subcategory emphasized quite a different aspect of climate; the emotional climate of the school. The criteria in this subcategory named a warm, loving, caring, happy climate as being an essential characteristic of good schools. These criteria were not mentioned in the effective schools research, but were cited by a few chapters of Kappa Delta Pi as criteria for identifying good schools. All of the other subcategories accounted for less than 10 percent of the category total, and these are summarized in Appendix S.

The category of school climate reflected the effective schools research literature in that subcategories of criteria identified an orderly, disciplined environment and a sense of purpose for learning. However, a concern for a happy, warm, caring climate and an overall humanistic, broad concern for students were added. Such difficult concepts to define as school spirit and pride are part of the category. The past research efforts have not used these characteristics extensively. Future research should consider these important attributes of school climate in order to further understand good schools.

School and Community Relations

The third broad category of criteria dealt with school and community relations: support; involvement; and use of resources. A two-way relationship was apparent from some criteria: the community should be involved in the school and the school should be involved in the community. There were forty-one criteria in this category, which accounted for 13 percent of the total number. The largest subcategory of criteria had to do with parent and school relationships. This subcategory had twelve criteria, or 29 percent of the total, within the category. All of these criteria focused on parental involvement in the school or parent, teacher, and school communication. Another subcategory of eight criteria, or 20 percent of the category total, emphasized community involvement or community cooperation with the school. These subcategories were kept separate because of the broader focus upon community than the particular focus upon parents as in the former subcategory. A small subcategory of three criteria combined both community and parent support for involvement.

Two other distinctions were kept in the subcategories of

criteria. One subcategory emphasized only support or recognition, not necessarily involvement, with the school. There were seven criteria in this subcategory, or 17 percent of the category total. Examples of these criteria were positive perceptions from the community; means for community support; and understanding and awareness of the community. Another smaller subcategory named only general support from parents, again not necessarily involvement with the school.

A final subcategory suggested the other direction of school and community relationships—the school using or being concerned with the community. There were eight criteria in this subcategory, or 20 percent of the category total. Typical responses were: involvement in community activities; community use of school building for various activities; and the utilization of community resources. This subcategory indicated the belief that schools must be a part of their community, support it, and utilize those resources in the schools.

School and community relations was not a common characteristic in the effective schools research. Most educators, however, know the importance of being in touch with the surrounding community and, particularly, with parents. Neither effective schools nor good schools can ignore this relationship.

Facilities and Resources

A fourth broad category of criteria dealt with the facilities and resources of the school: buildings; grounds; materials; finances; and other types of support. In this category there was a total of thirty criteria named that accounted for 9 percent of the total number. The largest subcategory had eight criteria or 27 percent of the total in the category and referred to the adequacy, size, and design of the building. The criteria clearly did not focus on the newness of the buildings. Another subcategory related to the physical facilities, but reflected a far more affective judgment about them rather than an assessment of their adequacy. This subcategory had four criteria, or 14 percent of the category total. Responses in this subcategory named pride in the facilities and aesthetics, attractiveness, and safety of the facilities.

Another subcategory of criteria named facilities and materials or other resources. There were five criteria, or 17 percent of the category total. The criteria emphasized the adequacy

of the facilities and materials or other resources. A similar subcategory, which focused more on support, named specifically the
adequacy of learning resources or that materials were provided.
Five criteria were in this subcategory, accounting for 17 percent
of the category total. Another subcategory of three criteria, accounting for 10 percent of the category total, emphasized that
the facilities or resources enabled achievement; provided motivations; or were respected. The other subcategories, each containing only a single criterion, are shown in Appendix S.

The actual physical facilities and resources were not
featured in the summaries of the effective schools research, and
yet some aspect of this category was mentioned thirty different
times in the Good Schools Project. Perhaps it is possible to have
an effective school without an emphasis on the physical
resources, but they may be more important to a good school. To
be identified as good, it seemed necessary that the physical
facilities and resources of the school be acceptable.

Qualities of Administrative Leadership

A fifth broad category of criteria focused on qualities of administrative leadership in the school. There were twenty-seven
criteria within this category, which accounted for 8 percent of the
total. The largest subcategory had twelve criteria, or 44 percent
of the category total. These criteria named general qualities of
administrative leadership, such as effective, supportive, positive,
helpful, outstanding, and cooperative. There was one other subcategory of criteria which included three items, or 11 percent of
the category total. This subcategory specifically named the instructional leadership of the administration. Twelve other subcategories, each containing only a single criterion, are listed in
Appendix S.

Clearly, administrative leadership was considered by the
chapters of Kappa Delta Pi to be important to good schools.
When compared with the eighty-six criteria centered upon the
curriculum, however, strong administrative leadership was not
emphasized in the Good Schools Project as much as in the effective schools research. Strong administrative leadership was consistently mentioned in the effective schools research studies. For
this sample of schools, however, administrative leadership was

important, but not so prominent as in the effective schools research.

Characteristics of the Faculty or Teachers

A sixth broad category of criteria used in selecting the sample of schools for this study involved the characteristics of the faculty or teachers. This category was kept separate from characteristics of the staff, since the staff of a school can be composed of professionals such as teachers, administrators, counselors, librarians, and nurses; paraprofessionals such as aides; and nonprofessionals such as secretaries, receptionists, and custodians. Criteria for staff might be different from criteria for teachers or the faculty of professional educators. Characteristics of the faculty or teachers was not a large category of criteria, however. This category had a total of twenty-five criteria, or 8 percent of the total. These criteria were then grouped into different subcategories, each with five or less criteria. The largest subcategory included five criteria, or 20 percent of the category total, and named general or specific competencies; qualifications; and skills the teachers or faculty possessed such as being professionally competent or current in the profession. There were three subcategories, each with three criteria. Each subcategory accounted for 12 percent of the total in this category. One subcategory identified criteria such as professional pride; dedication; and enthusiasm. Another focused specifically on what teachers did to encourage learning: provides time for teaching and learning and views his or her role as establishing a learning community. The third subcategory emphasized being warm, caring, and responsive to students. All other subcategories are shown in Appendix S.

This category of criteria did not reflect the characteristic of teacher involvement in instructional decision making which was named in some of the effective schools research studies. This was suggested in the category of curriculum or programs and, yet, even there it did not have a great deal of prominence. The emphasis on a climate for learning from the effective schools literature was reflected here to some degree. It is difficult, of course, to separate teachers and curriculum as separate factors in practice. The skills, values, and preparation of teachers have a significant impact on what the planned curriculum actually becomes. Thus, some of the criteria named in these two categories overlapped. The categories were separated for analysis purposes in the preliminary stages, however, because the emphasis was clearly upon the curriculum or clearly upon the teacher. From both of the categories, it was obvious that teacher competence and skill in dealing with the curriculum accounted for a significant number of criteria.

Characteristics of Staff

A seventh broad category was staff characteristics. Since it was unclear whether these criteria were limited to the professional staff or included everyone on the payroll, those criteria focusing clearly upon the teacher or faculty were separated from criteria dealing with the staff. There were twenty-four criteria in this category, accounting for 8 percent of the total number of criteria. One subcategory of seven criteria, or 29 percent of the category total, had to do with staff development or professional growth opportunities. The other subcategory of six criteria, or 25 percent of the category total, included criteria dealing with the quality of staff relations; cooperation; and open channels of communication.

One subcategory of four criteria, or 18 percent of the category total, contained criteria about the competence and qualifications of the staff or that the staff was carefully selected. This particular subcategory could have been included with the category of teachers or faculty, but such a decision might not have been an accurate interpretation of what was meant. Secretaries, custodians, and cafeteria workers also need to be (and usually are) competent, qualified, and carefully selected. They, too, are part of the staff of a school. For this reason, a distinction was made in categorizing those criteria clearly focusing upon teachers or faculty and those which collectively focused on the staff. The remaining small subcategories are shown in Appendix S.

The staff development emphasis in this category clearly reflected the effective schools research. Opportunities for staff growth and involvement in staff development was an important characteristic of many of the effective schools studied. Once again, however, the affective qualities of the staff also seemed to be at least equally important to this sample of schools identified as good. Cooperation, open communication, morale, and collaborative leadership were considered to be important criteria of good schools.

Characteristics of Students

The eighth category was a small one of only thirteen criteria, accounting for 4 percent of the total. It dealt with characteristics of students. Each subcategory of criteria was less than five. The largest subcategory included four criteria, or 31 percent of the category total. This subcategory identified as criteria students who were alert; attentive; involved in their schooling; and well-disciplined. Another subcategory of three criteria, or 23 percent of the category total, emphasized attitudes toward learning: motivated; working purposefully toward learning; and responsible. A subcategory of two criteria, or 15 percent of the category total, emphasized the performance of students after leaving school. Another subcategory of two items identified happy students as an important characteristic of schools identified as good. Two subcategories, each containing only a single criterion, are shown in Appendix S.

This category, which included only a small number of criteria overall, did not figure explicitly in the research literature on effective schools. For students to have higher than expected achievement test scores, however, it appeared, from the Good Schools Project research, that students must be motivated, work purposefully, be alert, attentive, and well-disciplined. Several chapters of Kappa Delta Pi also emphasized pride, happiness, and responsible citizenship, all of which are not reflected in the effective schools literature.

Miscellaneous

A final category of miscellaneous was necessary for all those criteria which did not fit clearly into the preceding eight categories. There were twenty-two such criteria, but some of these did fit together in a subcategory. Five of them, or 23 percent of the category total, named accreditation by a state or regional association as being a criterion of a school identified as good. Four criteria, or 18 percent of the category total, centered on descriptions of demographics or sampling for this study: schools vary in size, location, population, or type; support by administrators for this project; professional judgments that the schools were indeed good schools; and knowledge of the schools in the area. Other smaller subcategories are shown in Appendix S. None of these criteria were mentioned in the effective schools research.

Conclusions

A Caution

The synthesis of criteria used for identifying good schools reported in this chapter is a preliminary analysis of the data. Other analyses yet to be made may allow a more direct comparison with the characteristics of the schools in the sample, with the dimensions included in the questionnaires, and with the data obtained from the interviews. These later analyses also may allow for a more direct comparison with the synthesis of characteristics of effective schools. A detailed comparison between the synthesis of criteria for schools identified as good and the synthesis of the characteristics of effective schools is clearly a task for the future. At the present stage of analysis, the criteria for schools identified as good and the characteristics of effective schools can only be examined at a broad level of generality, and this must be done with the full knowledge that these studies were arrived at through research efforts designed for very different purposes and by methodologies which are distinctly different. Given this caution, however, some interesting observations can be tentatively made from the existing summary of criteria used to identify good schools and the characteristics of effective schools.

Commonalities

The synthesis of criteria used to identify good schools for the Good Schools Project contains many, if not all, of the characteristics summarized in the effective schools research literature. Many of the criteria are worded exactly the same or unquestionably reflect the same idea. Criteria or characteristics, clearly included in both the Good Schools Project and the effective schools research literature, are: strong administrative leadership; an emphasis on academic skills; staff development activities; high expectations for success; a positive school climate; and a safe, orderly environment, for example. At the same time, however, there are some important differences which must be recognized.

Differences

Although the characteristics of effective schools identified from the research literature are clearly reflected in the synthesis of criteria used to select the good schools for this study, their importance does not seem as dominant. High expectations for success and an orderly, safe, disciplined climate, for example, are mentioned by about half of the chapters, but not consistently by all. The effective schools research has a much more frequent citing of the above characteristics.

There is also another important difference: some of the similar criteria are expanded in their meanings, as well as having new ones which are mentioned frequently. For example, criteria within the climate of the school category reflect the emphasis from the effective schools literature on the safe, orderly, disciplined climate for learning. About the same number of Kappa Delta Pi chapters also reflects the sense of purpose and learning atmosphere from the effective schools research. However, that is not all that is considered important in the synthesis of the good schools criteria. The good schools criteria extend the concept of climate in important ways. About a third of the chapters focus on a student-centered, humanistic climate, and positive human relationships. Thus, the climate of the school dimension includes more and different aspects for good schools than it does for effective schools.

Other new dimensions of criteria are added: facilities and resources, and school and community relations, for example. Criteria within these categories are not mentioned frequently enough, if at all, to be included in the summaries of the effective schools research. Yet for the good schools sample, they are important categories of responses.

Good Schools and Effective Schools

It is clear that the chapters of Kappa Delta Pi participating in the Good Schools Project believe that a wide range of criteria are important to use in identifying good schools. Schools identified as good by these criteria appear to be schools in which academic achievement occurs, but in which the curriculum also fosters a much broader array of outcomes. Good schools have an orderly, safe, disciplined climate, but also one which is happy, caring, warm, and humanistic. Good schools have teachers who are professionally competent and who provide time for learning, but who also have pride, dedication, enthusiasm, and are warm to and caring for students. Good schools have students who are purposeful and motivated in their learning, but who are also happy and responsible citizens. Good schools have adequate, not necessarily new or extensive, facilities and resources. Good schools have positive relationships with their communities and parents. Good schools are places where learning occurs and where students and teachers live and grow in many ways, supported and nurtured by the school climate, community facilities, and resources. They are places where administrators, teachers, and students accept, trust, and recognize each other.

Good schools with many of these characteristics do exist. More of them ought to exist. As the research efforts on good schools and effective schools grow and become more mature, there will be increased understanding as to how schools get to be that way and what must be done in order for them to stay that way. It is in these schools—good and effective schools which are continuing to improve—that students will receive the best possible education.

Future Research Agenda

The synthesis of criteria for identifying good schools as defined in this study is much broader than the characteristics of effective schools. Perhaps there is a difference between effective schools and good schools. Perhaps it is possible to have an effective school as currently defined which is not a good school and vice versa. Perhaps there is more overlap than is now apparent. That is an agenda for future research which must be planned and conducted carefully. Can what is meant by a humanistic, warm, caring, student-centered climate be made operational and studied by traditional research methods? Are new and different research methodologies needed? Why are school and community relationships considered important in this study, and yet they have not been shown to be a significant factor in the effective schools research? What types of community support are most important to good schools, and how are they developed and maintained? The answers to these questions are not known and become important areas to study for future research efforts.

It must be recognized that the assumptions and standards, used implicitly or explicitly in any research, determine in part what will be found. When schools with higher achievement scores than might normally be expected are selected to be studied, that decision directs attention more heavily to modes of teaching and support mechanisms thought to be related to achievement. Other important variables such as caring, trust, pride, and cooperative social interaction, which are difficult to make operational, are not frequently considered.

When knowledgeable people are asked to name criteria by which to identify good schools, the focus is broader than achievement and its related constructs. This process of identifying good schools encourages consideration of more affective, and perhaps even more lasting, attributes of schools. Thus, how the research problem is defined becomes a significant factor in the results obtained.

A significant research task for the future is to examine further the impact of how effective schools or good schools are selected, based upon what is found in the study. The need for effective and good schools is great, and much of the future rests upon all students having the opportunity to attend such schools. The future research agenda for effective and good schools must include a broad array of criteria which more closely matches the hopes and expectations held by most people for the schools. Fostering achievement is not enough. Schools must also be places where education is broadly defined and where learning occurs in a nurturing enviornment. This future research agenda is an extremely challenging one, but one which is imperative for students who will live most of their lives in the twenty-first century.

Notes

1. David P. Gardner et al., *A Nation At Risk* (Washington, D.C.: U.S. Department of Education, 1983).
2. Donald E. Mackenzie, "Research for School Improvement: An Appraisal of Some Recent Trends," *Educational Researcher* 12 (April 1983): 5-17.
3. Stewart C. Purkey and Marshall S. Smith, "Too Soon To Cheer?: Synthesis of Research on Effective Schools," *Educational Leadership* 40 (December 1982): 64-69.
4. John H. Ralph and James Fennessey, "Science or Reform: Some Questions About the Effective Schools Model," *Phi Delta Kappan* 64 (June 1983): 689-94.
5. Ronald R. Edmunds, "Programs of School Improvement: An Overview," *Educational Leadership* 40 (December 1982): 4-11.
6. David A. Squires, William G. Huitt, and John K. Segars, *Effective Schools and Classrooms: A Research-Based Perspective* (Alexandria, Va: Association for Supervision and Curriculum Development, 1983).
7. Mackenzie, "Research for School Improvement."
8. Brian Rowan, Steven T. Bossert, and David C. Dwyer, "Research on Schools: A Cautionary Note," *Educational Researcher* 12 (April 1983): 24-31.
9. Larry Cuban, "Effective Schools: A Friendly But Cautionary Note," *Phi Delta Kappan* 64 (June 1983): 695-96.
10. William A. Firestone and Robert E. Herriott, "Prescriptions for Effective Elementary Schools Don't Fit Secondary Schools," *Educational Leadership* 40 (December 1982): 51-53.
11. Purkey and Smith, "Too Soon To Cheer?"
12. John I. Goodlad, *A Place Called School: Prospects for the Future* (New York: McGraw Hill, 1984).

4

Collecting Data in the Good Schools

The basic purposes of the Good Schools Project were to identify good schools all over America, study those schools carefully, look at the schools in depth and over time, and then make inferences that would be useful to those persons who might want to make their own schools better.

By December 1982, the Good Schools Project research committee had received information from thirty-six chapter counselors in Kappa Delta Pi. Their chapters had identified 136 schools to be included in the study. Materials for the chapters to use in collecting data from each of the participating schools were shipped in early January 1983. By June 1983, reasonably completed sets of information from 106 schools had been returned. In the sections that follow, the number and characteristics of participating schools, data collection procedures, and data analysis procedures are described.

Information about Participating Schools

In all, data were received from chapter counselors for 106 schools that had been identified as good. Appendix R presents pertinent information about each of the 106 schools. Table 1, in this chapter, summarizes by grade level the number of schools that participated in the study.

Data were collected from 70 elementary level, 15 middle level, and 21 secondary level schools. In all, survey data were collected from approximately 28,000 students, 3,200 teachers, and 106 principals. Interview data were collected from approximately 500 persons. All data were aggregated by school, so the 106 schools described in Table 1 and in Appendix R comprise the sample for this study.

Table 1

Number of Schools Participating in the
Good Schools Project by Grade Level

Elementary		Middle		Secondary	
Grades	Number	Grades	Number	Grades	Number
K-2	1	4-7	1	6-12	1
K-3	7	5	1	7-12	1
K-4	3	5-6	1	8-12	1
K-5	23	6	1	9	1
K-6	26	6-8	6	9-12	10
K-7	7	7-8	3	10-12	6
K-8	3	7-9	2	11-12	1
	70		15		21

Collection of Data

Counselors in participating chapters were directed to do four things: (1) interview the principal in every school; (2) survey all of the teachers in every school; (3) have the regular teachers survey about half of the students in every school; and (4) interview a number of teachers, students, parents, and others in one specific school (see Appendix K). In addition, counselors were also directed to collect various materials from each school regarding standardized achievement and ability test scores.

Sixteen different kinds of printed materials (or sets of materials) were included in a box prepared for each school. All materials were color coded and labeled clearly to ensure appropriate use, but the box of materials was undoubtedly seen as a formidable task to be accomplished by the counselor who received it in early January. However, the instructions stated that all materials were to be returned to the Good Schools Project office by early May, so each chapter had at least three and a half months in which to collect the data. In fact, all materials received on or before June 15th were included in the study.

Interviewing the Principal

Complete interview data, using the interview schedule described in Appendix L, were obtained from ninety-nine of the building principals. Special instructions for all interviewers suggested that the interviews be conducted by teams of two persons and tape recorded (see Appendix M).

Four different sets of questions were posed to each principal interviewed: background questions; open ended questions; questions about specific aspects of school life; and questions about the school and its community. The open ended questions and the questions about specific aspects of school life were the same questions asked of parents, students, teachers, and others in one school in which multiple interviews were accomplished. Questions about the school and its community that were asked of every principal (see Part V, Appendix L) generated the detailed information about each school that is described in Chapter Five.

Surveying the Teachers

Instructions to counselors in local chapters of Kappa Delta Pi directed those persons to administer the Teacher Survey (see Appendix O) to all teachers in each of the schools identified as good. The Teacher Survey was a printed booklet of 216 questions which teachers were asked to respond to on an optical scan-type answer blank. Usable responses were received from 3,230 teachers in the 106 schools studied. According to the information provided by the principals interviewed regarding the number of teachers in the schools, this constituted about a 71 percent response. Information about how the teachers responded is reported in Chapters Six through Fourteen, according to the conceptual dimensions of the study that were described in Chapter One.

Surveying the Students

Counselors were directed to have the regular classroom teachers, in each of the schools identified as good, administer the Student Survey (see Appendix P) to approximately half of their students in grades four through twelve. The Student Survey was a printed booklet of 100 questions which students were asked to respond to on an optical scan-type answer blank. Students were told not to put their names or any other identifying marks on their answer blanks.

Students in grades two and three were asked to respond to a

one page, "Yes" or "No"-type survey instrument which was read aloud to them by their regular classroom teachers (see Appendix Q, *Young Children's Survey*). Students did not put their names or any other identifying marks on their answer blanks.

Detailed instructions were provided to local chapter counselors regarding how to select the 50 percent sample of students in each school in order to ensure representativeness (see Appendix N). In all, 22,088 students in grades four through twelve responded to the *Student Survey,* and 6,194 students in grades two and three responded to the *Young Children's Survey.* Information about how the students responded is described in Chapters Six through Fourteen, according to the conceptual dimensions of the study.

Extensive Interviewing in One School

Instructions to chapter counselors directed them to do several things in each of the schools that their chapters had identified as good: interview every principal, survey every teacher, and survey about half of the students. In one school, however, the counselors were instructed to conduct hour-long interviews with five students, five teachers, five parents, and five other persons in the school (e.g., guidance counselors or assistant principals). Special instructions were provided to those who actually conducted the interviews to assure comparability and quality of the interview data (see Appendix M, "Instructions for Conducting Interviews").

The questions posed to these respondents were the same questions as those asked of principals in parts three and four of the principal's interview schedule (see Appendix L). The logic of the questions went from very open ended questions (e.g., "If you were to sum up this school in a phrase, what would that phrase be?") to more specific aspects of school life (e.g., "Do students who go to this school learn different things than students who go to other schools? If so, what are those things?" or "What person or groups of persons make the decisions in this school? Please tell what kinds of decisions each person or group makes and provide an example of each type of decision.").

In all, interviews were conducted with more than 500 persons in thirty schools. These interviews have not been fully analyzed as of this writing, although excerpts and illustrative incidents have been incorporated into Chapters Six through Fourteen. The intention of the Good Schools Project research committee is to do careful analyses of these interview protocols in the months ahead.

Collecting Standardized Achievement Scores

Those who conducted the interviews with the school principals were directed to collect detailed information about students' ability and achievement scores, as measured by the standardized tests regularly used by the school being studied (see question 79, Appendix L).

Partial or complete information or actual copies of achievement data reports were obtained from 83 of the 106 schools. Because the data vary extensively (by test publisher and by grade level reported), careful analyses of these data have not yet been completed. The intention of the research committee is to accomplish such analysis in the near future.

Analysis of the Data

The basic purpose of the Good Schools Project was to identify and study good schools. The *school* was assumed to be the basic unit of analysis. Data were collected from more than 3,000 teachers and over 28,000 students, and interviews with more than 500 persons were conducted. All data were aggregated *by school,* however, so the size of the sample was actually 106 schools.

In this monograph, descriptive data only are reported, by grade level, for the 106 schools studied. Descriptive information (i.e., percentages) is reported about every item of the *Teacher Survey, Student Survey, Young Children's Survey,* and Part V of the "Principal's Interview Form."

Chapter Five describes the demographic characteristics of the 106 schools studied. Most of this information was obtained from the principal's interview, although certain items from the *Teacher Survey* are reported, too. Chapters Six through Fourteen describe the data in terms of the conceptual dimensions of the study that were described in Chapter One. Appendices A through I include complete information about responses to every item on the three survey instruments. Each of these appendices includes complete information from teachers and students, reported according to grade level and by conceptual dimension.

5

Demographic Characteristics

What are the schools that have been identified as good actually like? Where are they located? What kinds of communities do they serve? What are the characteristics of their staff and student populations?

Most of the data in this section were obtained through interviews with the principal of each school. Interviews were available from one hundred schools: sixty-eight elementary, twelve middle schools, and twenty secondary schools. However, the numbers reported here sometimes do not add up to one hundred, because some questions were not answered by all principals.

General Characteristics

Ninety-six of the schools identified as good were public, two were private, and two were parochial. One private school was elementary and the other middle; one parochial school was an elementary school and the other was a secondary school. Four schools in the study were special purpose schools: one elementary level special education school, one secondary level vocational school, and two secondary level alternative education schools for gifted students.

Forty-eight percent of the elementary schools were in a city, as were 27 percent of the middle schools and 28 percent of the secondary schools. Twenty-eight percent of the elementary schools, 64 percent of the middle schools, and 44 percent of the secondary schools were in county districts. Only one middle school was in a rural or suburban area, while 23 percent of elementary schools and 28 percent of the secondary schools were in rural or suburban areas.

The smallest school district had 350 students, while the largest had more than 100,000. The median size of the school districts was 5,638 students. Eighteen schools were in school districts with less than 3,000 students. Twenty-five schools were in districts with 3,000 to 7,100 students. Fourteen schools were in school districts with 7,100 to 16,000 students. Thirteen schools were in school districts with 16,000 to 42,000 students. Sixteen schools were in school districts with 50,000 to 100,000 or more students.

The smallest school had 106 students and the largest had 3,750 students, with a median of 514. Thirty-six of the schools had 400 or less students, fifty had 401 to 999 students, and fourteen had from 1,000 to 3,750 students. Although elementary schools tended to have less than 400 to 1,000 students and secondary schools tended to have 400 to 1,000 or more students, one elementary school had more than 1,000 students and two secondary schools had 400 or less students.

Community Environment

Type of Community

The communities in which these schools were located were characterized as rural for twenty schools, urban for eighteen schools, suburban for thirty-six schools, and some combination of these for twenty-three schools. Location did not vary substantially by school level. The educational level of the school community was characterized as above average for forty-one schools, average for thirty-six schools, and below average for sixteen schools. No secondary school communities were characterized as below average.

Socioeconomic Status

If we consider those schools in which 50 percent or more of the students came from home environments characterized as "affluent," "middle class," "working class," or "poor," there were two schools in affluent communities, twenty-six schools in middle class communities, twenty-seven schools in working class communities, and twelve schools in poor communities. The communities in the remaining thirty-three schools were more heterogeneous than these sixty-seven schools. A similar picture emerges if the home environments were characterized as executive, professional, skilled labor, and unskilled or unemployed. Three communities were executive, eleven were professional, thirty-eight were skilled, eighteen were unskilled or unemployed, and the remainder were mixed. While specific analyses have not been completed at this time, it does appear, as one would expect, that the secondary schools tended to have a more heterogeneous student body than the elementary schools.

In all but six schools, some students received free lunches. In twenty-one schools, 10 percent or less of the students were provided free lunches. Twenty-seven schools provided free lunches for 11 to 25 percent of the students. Over 25 percent of the students received free lunches in forty-two schools. In one school, all of the students received a free lunch. These percentages were higher at the elementary and middle school level than at the secondary level.

Fifty-seven schools had no textbook fees, and twenty-one schools had no children who could not afford the textbook fees that were required. In twelve schools, 1 to 10 percent of the students were relieved of textbook fees because they could not afford them. In four schools, this was the case for 11 to 29 percent of the students.

Stability

The stability of the community in terms of people moving in and out of the community was described as very stable for thirty-nine schools, moderately stable for fifty-four schools, and unstable for six schools. When asked how many parents do volunteer work in the school at least twice weekly, principals indicated none in 13 percent of the elementary schools, none in 25 percent of the middle schools, and none in 55 percent of the secondary schools. Ten or more parents did weekly volunteer work in 58 percent of the elementary schools, in 42 percent of the middle schools, and in 15 percent of the secondary schools.

Racial Composition

There were fifteen schools in which 50 percent or more of the students were black, seventy-nine schools in which 50 percent or more of the students were white, two schools in which 50 percent or more of the students were Hispanic, and one school in which 50 percent or more of the students were American Indian. Fifteen schools included no blacks, three schools included no whites, eighty-seven schools included no American Indians, sixty-four schools included no Hispanics, and fifty-one schools included no Orientals. In none of the schools was 50 percent of the student body Oriental. When principals were asked if any ethnic groups were predominant in their school community, twenty-five said blacks, thirty said whites, three said Hispanics, two said Orientals, and two said American Indians. When principals were asked if any religious groups were predominant in their school community, sixty-eight said Protestants, thirty-eight said Catholics, three said Buddhists, two said Muslim, and one said Jewish.

Busing

Students were bused to school at ninety-four of the 100 schools. The main reason children were bused was because of geographic location. Busing for the purpose of racial integration occurred at 25 percent of the elementary schools, at none of the middle schools, and at 15 percent of the secondary schools. Geographic location was the reason for busing in the other seventy-three schools. The median distance that children were bused one way was four miles. The range was from one to twenty-two miles. Middle and secondary students were bused further than elementary students. Two-thirds of the elementary school students had an average bus ride of one to five miles, while the students in 50 percent of the middle schools and 50 percent of the secondary schools had an average bus ride of one to five miles.

School Environment

School Building

The buildings of these 100 schools were not new. Only twenty-one were built in the last ten years. Eighteen school buildings were fifty or more years old. Three were over seventy-five years old, and one was one hundred years old. The median age of the buildings was twenty-five years. In seventeen schools no major additions or remodeling had been done. In one school, the last major addition or remodeling was done forty-two years ago. Forty-three of the schools had a major addition or remodeling in the last ten years.

Vandalism

Thirty-nine of the schools had no incidents of vandalism last year. This included thirty-three of the elementary schools, three of the middle schools, and three of the secondary schools. Fifteen schools had one incident, thirteen schools had two incidents, sixteen schools had three to five incidents, and eleven schools had more than five incidents.

The cost of vandalism was not reported by twelve schools. Of the remaining eighty-eight schools, forty-two had no cost due to vandalism. Thirteen schools had vandalism costs of less than $100. In twelve schools vandalism cost between $100 and $200. In fourteen schools vandalism cost between $200 and $900, and in seven schools vandalism cost $3000 or more. The cost of vandalism per student enrolled was zero in thirty-nine schools, five cents to fifty cents in twenty-five schools, fifty-one cents to one dollar in ten schools, one to two dollars in six schools, and more than two dollars in five schools.

When asked about the worst incident of vandalism, thirty-nine schools had none, forty-six had minor graffiti or a few broken windows, eight reported breaking and entering or minor theft, and three reported major damage. In sum, eighty-five of the ninety-six schools reported either no vandalism or only minor incidents.

Theft

Fifty-seven schools reported no incidents of theft against teachers last year. Twenty schools reported one incident, thirteen schools reported two to three incidents, and seven schools reported more than three incidents. Theft against teachers increased with school level. One or no incident was reported in fifty-nine of the elementary schools, eight of the middle schools, and ten of the secondary schools.

Thirty-two of the elementary schools reported no incidents of theft against students. Seventy-eight percent of the schools averaged one theft or less per month. Theft against students was more prevalent in middle and secondary schools. Of the middle and secondary schools which reported incidents of theft, all had one or more incidents against students. The range was from one to forty-five, with one school reporting 200 thefts. Twenty-four of the elementary schools, five of the middle schools, and seven of the secondary schools reported one to nine incidents last year. Only six of the elementary schools had ten or more incidents against students. Three of the middle schools and four of the secondary schools reported ten to eighteen incidents, and three of the middle schools and six of the secondary schools had twenty or more incidents.

Violence

Ninety-two of the schools reported no incidents of physical attacks against teachers. Two elementary and two secondary schools each reported two attacks. One school reported one attack against a staff member. Fifty-three schools reported that there were no incidents of physical attack (e.g., fighting) against students. This included forty-one of the elementary schools, six of the middle schools, and six of the secondary schools. Twelve of the schools reported one or two incidents, thirteen reported three to ten incidents, and fourteen reported eleven to sixty-six incidents against students. Eighteen of the elementary schools, three of the middle schools, and four of the secondary schools had one to ten incidents. The remaining schools reported from eleven to sixty-six incidents including five of the elementary schools, two of the middle schools, and seven of the secondary schools. Incidents occurred once a month or less in 92 percent of the elementary schools, 82 percent of the middle schools, and 59 percent of the secondary schools. Eighty-eight percent of the elementary schools, 82 percent of the middle schools, and 76 percent of the secondary schools had less than two incidents per year per hundred students.

Characteristics of Students

Attendance

Average daily attendance ranged from 84 percent to 100 percent. In eight schools it was 84 to 90 percent, in thirty-nine schools it was 91 to 95 percent, in thirty-one schools it was 96 to 97 percent, and in thirteen schools it was 98 to 100 percent. Percentage of attendance was 95 to 100 in thirty-six of the elementary schools, in four of the middle schools, and in four of the secondary schools.

Dropout Rate

The dropout rate was zero in sixty-nine schools; ranged from 1 to 7 percent in twenty-three schools; and was 20 percent in one school. Five percent or less of the students transferred out in thirty-eight schools, 6 to 10 percent transferred out in twenty-six schools, and more than 10 percent transferred out in thirty-four schools. Transferring out appeared to occur less in middle and secondary schools than in elementary schools. The number of schools from which 11 percent or more of the students transferred was twenty-six at the elementary level, two at the middle level, and six at the secondary level.

Transferring in occurred at about the same rate across school levels. The percentage of students transferring in was 5 percent or less in thirty-six schools, 6 to 10 percent in twenty-seven schools, and above 10 percent in thirty-four schools. More than 10 percent of the students transferred in at twenty-four of the elementary schools, three of the middle schools, and seven of the secondary schools.

Suspensions

There were no suspensions last year in forty-six of the schools and no expulsions in eighty-two of the schools. The number of each of these increased with school level. While two-thirds (forty-four) of the elementary schools had no suspensions, only one of the middle schools and one of the secondary schools had no suspensions. There were no expulsions in 97 percent of the elementary schools, 67 percent of the middle schools, and 53 percent of the secondary schools.

Graduation Rate

Eighteen of the twenty secondary schools reported graduation data. The percentage of students graduating ranged from 65 to 99 percent. Two schools had a 65 to 75 percent graduation rate. Six schools graduated 80 to 90 percent of the students. In ten schools 95 to 99 percent of the students graduated.

Student Failure Rate

Twenty-four schools did not report the percentage of students who failed one or more classes last year. In nine of the seventy-six schools that reported data, no students failed one or more courses. In thirty-six schools, 1 to 5 percent of the students failed one or more courses. In sixteen schools, 6 to 10 percent of the students failed one or more courses. In eight schools, 11 to 20 percent of the students failed one or more courses, and in seven schools more than 20 percent of the students failed one or more courses. Grade level retention occurred for no children in eight schools, for 1 percent of the students in thirty-two schools, for 2 to 3 percent of the students in twenty schools, for 4 to 5 percent of the students in twenty-one schools, and for more than 5 percent of the students in thirteen schools.

In fifty-eight of the schools, students were tracked or grouped by ability. Tracking increased with school level. Tracking existed in 54 percent of the elementary schools, 67 percent of the middle schools, and 80 percent of the secondary schools.

College Bound Students

The percentage of college bound students in these schools ranged from 1 percent to 100 percent. Fifty-one percent or more college bound students were reported by twenty-nine of the seventy-one schools responding to this question. This was true for 40 percent of the elementary schools, 27 percent of the middle schools, and 47 percent of the secondary schools. In 38 percent of the elementary schools, 55 percent of the middle schools, and 16 percent of the secondary schools, 25 percent or fewer of the students were reported to be college bound.

The principals at the secondary schools also reported the percentages of their graduates who go on to college or vocational schools. The percentage of students going to college ranged from 5 to 99 percent. At five schools, 5 to 25 percent of the students went to college. At six schools, 30 to 40 percent went to college. At six schools, 60 to 76 percent went to college, and at two schools, 90 to 99 percent went to college. Finally, an average of about 16 percent of the students in these schools went on to vocational schools, with a range of 0 to 45 percent.

Characteristics of Teachers

Demographics

The majority of the teachers were female, but sex of teachers varied with grade level. Ninety-one percent of the elementary teachers were female, as were 68 percent of the middle school teachers and 57 percent of the secondary school teachers.

Race of teachers varied with grade level. Eighty-six percent of the teachers at the secondary level were white, as were 82 percent at the elementary level and 79 percent at the middle school level.

While similar percentages of teachers at the elementary level (45 percent) and middle level (42 percent) had the master's degree or the doctorate, substantially more of the secondary level teachers (57 percent) had the master's degree or the doctorate.

About three-fourths of the teachers at each grade level were married.

Classrooms

The median class size was twenty-four. Average class size was smaller in the secondary than in the middle and elementary schools. Average class size was twenty-three or less in 46 percent of the elementary schools, 33 percent of the middle schools, and in 60 percent of the secondary schools.

More middle school teachers (20 percent) than secondary (11 percent) or elementary teachers (6 percent) indicated that they had average classes of thirty-one or more students. Middle school teachers were also less likely to have classes of sixteen to thirty students (64 percent) than were elementary (81 percent) or secondary teachers (73 percent).

While the majority of the teachers taught alone, 90 percent of the secondary teachers taught alone as compared to 70 percent of the middle school teachers and 43 percent of the elementary teachers. Elementary teachers (45 percent) were more likely to teach with an aide than were middle school (11 percent) or secondary teachers (5 percent). Middle school teachers (19 percent) were most likely to teach in a team. Twelve percent of the elementary teachers and 5 percent of the secondary teachers taught in a team.

Forty-one of the schools had no part-time teachers. Eighty-seven of the schools had at least one full-time support person, and seventy-nine schools had at least one part-time support person.

Teaching Experience

Teachers at the middle school level had less teaching experience in general than did elementary and secondary teachers. The percentage of middle school teachers who taught ten years or less was 54, compared to 47 percent at the elementary level and 42 percent at the secondary level. The proportion of middle school teachers who had taught at their present school for ten years or less was 79 percent, as compared to 76 percent at the elementary level and 70 percent at the secondary level.

Professional and Sick Leave

The percentage of teachers who took sick leave last year ranged from 0 to 100. The median was 80 percent. At 57 percent of the elementary schools, 33 percent of the middle schools, and 31 percent of the secondary schools, 81 to 100 percent of the teachers took sick leave. The average number of sick leave days taken was four. Again, the number of sick leave days taken varied by school level. In 33 percent of the elementary schools, teachers took more than four days for sick leave. This was true in 8 percent of the middle schools and 20 percent of the secondary schools.

The average percentage of teachers taking professional leave in these schools ranged from 0 to 100. The median was 25 percent. Professional leave was taken by more than a fourth of the teachers in 46 percent of the elementary schools, in 33 percent of the middle schools, and in 67 percent of the secondary schools. In general, teachers took from none to ten days of professional leave, with the median being one day. Elementary and secondary school teachers also tended to take more days of professional leave than middle school teachers. An average of one and a half or more days of professional leave was taken by teachers in 41 percent of the elementary schools, 8 percent of the middle schools, and 53 percent of the secondary schools.

The average percentage of teachers in these schools taking personal leave ranged from 0 to 100, with a median of 50 percent. Personal leave was taken more often in middle schools than in elementary or secondary schools. Personal leave was taken by more than 60 percent of the teachers in twenty-two elementary schools, seven middle schools, and six secondary schools. The average number of personal leave days taken in these schools ranged from none to ten, with a median of one day. An average of one and a half or more personal leave days was taken by the teachers in 35 percent of the elementary schools, 50 percent of the middle schools, and 44 percent of the secondary schools.

Resignations

The percentage of teachers who voluntarily left these schools each year for another position ranged from 0 to 18. In forty-eight schools the percentage was 0, and in nineteen schools the percentage was 1. Two to 5 percent left at sixteen schools, and at twelve schools 6 to 18 percent left. Teacher resignations varied with school level. No teachers left at 62 percent of the elementary schools, 25 percent of the middle schools, and 22 percent of the secondary schools. There were twenty-nine schools at which the proportion of teachers leaving was 2 percent or higher. This included 18 percent of the elementary schools, 67 percent of the middle schools, and 50 percent of the secondary schools.

Characteristics of Principals

Demographics

Sixty of the schools had one principal, twenty-seven had two, and thirteen had more than two principals. Thirteen of the sixty-eight elementary schools had two principals. Nine of the middle schools had two principals, and one had more than two. Five of the secondary schools had two principals, and twelve had more than two.

The highest degree held by three principals was the baccalaureate. Eighty-nine principals held the master's degree, and five held the doctorate. All of those who held the doctorate had the degree in education. Eighty-one of the eighty-six principals who had the master's degree specified the area. Seventy-six of the eighty-one had the master's degree in education. Three had the master's degree in a social science. Sixty-eight of the principals indicated their undergraduate major. Forty-seven majored in education, eight in a social science, six in a physical science, two in English literature, and one each in business, engineering, and mathematics.

The number of years the principal had been at the school ranged from one to thirty-six years, with a median of six years. The length of tenure was longer for the elementary and secondary principals than middle school principals. At the elementary school level, 49 percent had been principal at the school for seven years or longer. This was true for 25 percent of the middle school principals and 42 percent of the secondary principals.

One-fourth of the principals came to their posts from within the school. Most of the principals came from within the district (86 percent). All of the middle school principals come from within the district, whereas only 74 percent of the secondary principals came from within the district.

The median age of the principals was forty-six years. While seven of the middle school principals were between forty-six and fifty, none were over fifty. The secondary schools had the largest number of principals over the age of fifty (35 percent) and had the largest number between the ages of forty and forty-five (40 percent).

All of the middle school principals, 90 percent of the secondary principals, and 65 percent of the elementary principals were male. Eighty-seven percent were white. All of the secondary principals, 83 percent of the middle school principals, and 84 percent of the elementary principals were white.

The median number of years the principals had been in education was twenty. The secondary principals had been in education longer. Fifty-eight percent of the secondary principals had been in education for more than twenty years. Forty-seven percent of the elementary principals had been in education over twenty years, as had 46 percent of the middle school principals.

Hiring

When asked the criteria the principal used for hiring teachers, sixty-two principals mentioned ability, twenty-nine mentioned experience, forty mentioned educational background, and fifteen mentioned that they got outside information on past performance (i.e., references). At thirty-eight schools the hiring decision was made jointly by the principal and central office staff (including supervisors). At twenty-one schools, teachers were hired through a joint decision by central office staff, the principal, and department heads. In eleven schools, the decision was made jointly by the principal and the teachers, and in eight schools the decision was made by all of these parties. In nine schools, the principal made the decision, and in nine other schools the central office made the decision. Teachers were not involved in hiring in any of the middle schools, but they were involved at 18 percent of the elementary schools and at 39 percent of the secondary schools.

Special Programs

Gifted and Talented

Twenty of the schools did not report a program for the gifted and talented. In the eighty schools which did report such a program, from 1 to 40 percent of the students were in the program. One to 3 percent were included in twenty schools, 4 to 5 percent were included in twenty-two schools, 6 to 10 percent in twenty-four schools, and more than 10 percent in fourteen schools.

Emotionally Disturbed and Learning Disabled

Thirty-four schools had a program for the emotionally disturbed. In seventeen of these schools the program served 1 percent of the students. In nine schools it served 2 to 3 percent of the students, and in eight schools it served 4 to 8 percent of the students.

Eighty-five schools had a program for learning disabled students. Of those which had such a program, nineteen schools served 1 to 2 percent of the students, thirty-three schools served 3 to 4 percent of the students, eighteen schools served 5 to 6 percent of the students, and fifteen schools served from 7 to 30 percent of the students.

Educable and Trainable Mentally Retarded

Forty-nine schools had a program for educable mentally retarded (EMR) students. Thirty-nine percent of the elementary schools, 75 percent of the middle schools, and 70 percent of the secondary schools had an EMR program. All of the secondary schools' EMR programs served from 1 to 5 percent of the students. Three of the elementary schools and two of the middle schools served 7 to 24 percent of their students with this program.

Eighteen schools had a program for the trainable mentally retarded which served 1 to 10 percent or less of their student populations. The existence of these programs was not related to school level.

Co-Curricular or Extracurricular Activities

Eighty-one of the schools had music activities. This included 75 percent of the elementary schools, 100 percent of the middle schools, and 90 percent of the secondary schools. Participation in music decreased as school level went up. In 74 percent of the elementary schools, in one middle school, and in two secondary schools, half or more of the students participated. In the majority of the middle schools, 21 to 50 percent of the students participated; in the majority of the secondary schools, 1 to 21 percent participated in music. Drama was available in forty-five schools (28 percent of the elementary schools, 83 percent of the middle schools, and 80 percent of the secondary schools).

Sports activities existed in sixty-seven schools (57 percent of the elementary schools, 83 percent of the middle schools, and 90 percent of the secondary schools).

Scholastic activities were available in forty-nine schools (34 percent of the elementary schools, 67 percent of the middle schools, and 90 percent of the secondary schools).

Summary

In summary, most of the schools identified as good in this study are public schools in stable middle class or working class communities. Racially, the schools are mixed, and the predominant religious groups in the community are Protestant and Catholic. Most of the teachers in the schools are female, have ten or more years experience, and are white. Generally, principals are experienced professionals, who have come up through the system.

The school buildings are generally old, and the student populations are of a manageable size. The schools are not for the elite or academically superior. Incidents of vandalism, theft, and violence are few.

6

Curriculum Perspectives

It is obvious that curriculum has been defined, designed, and experienced in various ways. What is less obvious is that all curriculum definitions, designs, and experiences respond in one way or another to these critical questions: What should be taught? How should it be taught? To whom should it be taught? Responses to questions of what, how, and to whom necessarily reflect our assumptions and values. Sometimes, these beliefs are directly stated. Often they remain unstated and unexamined.

Whether or not underlying curriculum perspectives (i.e., beliefs about the nature of knowledge, students, and learning) are made explicit, they have important implications and consequences. The implications are social and political, as well as philosophical. They are long range as well as immediate. They affect not only which students learn what, but also society at large, now and for the future. For example, how we teach something reflects assumptions and carries messages about the nature of knowledge. When the emphasis is on rote memorization of information, the assumptions and messages are likely to be that knowledge is fixed or certain, that it is determined by experts, and that it consists of accumulated bits of information. This view of the nature of knowledge does not accommodate discovery, invention, or personal meaning.

Similarly, to whom we teach or do not teach something reflects assumptions and carries messages about our perceptions of students' present competence and future prospects. When some students (e.g., boys) are provided opportunities to learn things that are not made available to other students (e.g., girls), the assumptions and messages are likely to be that some students are less capable and that they should limit their personal aspirations. This view of how knowledge should be distributed is not only discriminatory to individuals or groups, but also deprives society of the potential contributions of all its members.

In the Good Schools Project, two curriculum beliefs were examined: expectations for students, including teachers' expectations for student learning, students' self-expectations for learning, and achievement emphasis; and teachers' conceptions of knowledge and learning, including teachers' perceptions of the nature, selection, and use of knowledge in curriculum, and the organization and distribution of knowledge in curriculum, including provision for variety and student choice.

Directly or indirectly, teachers' expectations for students and teachers' conceptions of knowledge shape classroom practices, i.e., the teachers' responses to the questions of what should be taught, how, and to whom. In turn, teachers' classroom and other experiences, the school milieu, and the institutional–community context in which the school is located shape teachers' curriculum beliefs. The relationship among belief, decision, practice, and experience is interactive and dynamic, not linear or fixed. For example, teachers who have high expectations for their students are likely to provide students with more opportunities to learn (or, opportunities to learn more) than are teachers who have low expectations. Not surprisingly, the students of high expectation teachers are likely to learn more than the students of low expectation teachers. This occurrence confirms and perpetuates the teachers' initial expectations.[1]

Teachers' expectations have been shown to distinguish between more and less effective schools in several studies where effectiveness was determined largely or solely on the basis of standardized achievement test scores.[2] Teachers in these more effective schools consistently held high expectations for their students' learning. What are teachers' expectations for student learning in schools identified not merely as effective but as "good"? In the Good Schools Project, we also sought to determine teacher–school goals for student learning and the extent of teacher–school emphasis on achievement. In addition, we examined students' perceptions of their teachers' expectations for students, students' self-expectations, and students' perceptions of pressure for achievement.

In the school literature, teachers' conceptions of knowledge have received less attention than teachers' expectations. Until recently, most people tended to take knowledge for granted, as something to be transmitted from one person or generation to the next, like the passing of the baton in a relay race. This naive view of knowledge has been challenged by several developments, including the so-called knowledge explosion, increasingly sophisticated computer technology, new scientific theories that undermine previously established beliefs, and growing acceptance of social and intellectual pluralism. Diversity and change have become "facts" of contemporary life. It is now recognized as naive to view knowledge as revealed or discovered by disinterested experts, fixed or certain, or consisting of discrete bits or bodies of "objective facts" with instrumental utility. Increasingly, we are coming to recognize that knowledge is humanly created in social settings, tentative or problematic, consisting of interrelated process and substance whose utility is interpretive of experience and generative of further knowledge as well as instrumental in an everyday practical sense. This constructivist view of knowledge, however, seems not to be widely held by teachers or reflected in classroom practices.[3] What conceptions of knowledge and learning are held by teachers in good schools? To what extent are their conceptions naive or constructivist?

In the following sections, the teacher and student survey results and illustrative interview data regarding expectations for students' and teachers' conceptions of knowledge are presented and examined. (See Appendix B, Table 1 for survey items and teachers' responses by school level and Appendix B, Tables 2 and 3 for survey items and students' responses by school level.)

Expectations for Students

Teachers' Expectations

Three aspects of teachers' expectations for student learning tapped by the teacher survey were the extent to which the teachers believed that (1) teachers in their schools expected students to learn, (2) students would learn if teachers expected them to, and (3) all students were capable of higher-level learning. A large majority of teachers reported that the teachers in their schools "always" expected students to learn. They were less certain, however, that students would learn if their teachers expected them to learn. About half the teachers responded that all students "often" were capable of higher-level learning, while a sizeable minority responded that this "seldom" or "never" was the case. It may be that, while teachers expected students to learn, teachers' doubts about some students' capacities for higher-level learning limited the teachers' beliefs that positive expectations have the desired effect. Interestingly, on all three of these general expectation items, elementary teachers were more positive than middle school teachers, and middle school teachers were more positive than secondary teachers.

Parallel school level differences appeared in students' perceptions of their teachers' expectations for students. Overall, few students reported that their teachers "seldom" or "never" expected them to learn. However, younger students more often than older students reported that their teachers "always" believed students could learn and expected them to do so.

Ten teacher survey items referred to frequently expressed school goals or objectives for student learning. In order of perceived importance to elementary teachers, the goals were: reading skills, positive attitudes toward learning, a sense of self-worth, friendliness and respect toward people of different races and religions, independence and self-reliance, critical thinking and reasoning skills, factual knowledge and concepts in the subject area, effective expression of opinions, skills in evaluating information and arguments, and vocational skills. Middle and secondary teachers ranked the ten goals similarly. However, with the exception of vocational skills, elementary teachers perceived these school goals for student learning as "always" being important more often than did middle and secondary teachers.

The same pattern of school level differences was evident in teachers responded that academic learning "always" was a top elementary than middle and more middle than secondary teachers responded that academic learning was "always" a top priority at their schools and that teachers "always" felt responsible for the social development of students. Surprisingly, perhaps, 14 percent of the secondary teachers responded that academic learning "seldom" or "never" was a top priority at their schools, and 29 percent responded that teachers "seldom" or "never" felt responsible for the social development of students. There may be less consensus regarding school goals among secondary teachers. Alternatively, secondary teachers may be less likely to see some of these goals as the school's responsibility, or they may be less optimistic regarding what schools can accomplish.

Teachers at all levels tended to perceive generally stated goals as "always" important more often than specifically stated ones. For example, critical thinking and reasoning skills were perceived as "always" important more frequently than were effective expression of opinions and skills in evaluating information and arguments. Also, four of the five top ranked goals were not "academic" in the strict sense of that word, with the exception being reading. Recent attention to academic achievement as measured by standardized test scores seemed not to be reflected in the priorities of these good schools.

Students' Self-Expectations

Students' self-expectations showed that personal–social concerns were increasingly important across school levels. A majority of secondary students chose "To get along well with other people" or "To become a better person" as the most important goal for themselves. In contrast, elementary students were divided more evenly among that goal and "To get a good job" and "To learn a lot about the subjects in school." The latter goal ranked lowest among students at all grade levels. Consistent with these findings, how much students expected to learn in school during the year decreased by school level. Sixty-two percent of secondary students, compared to 85 percent of elementary students, responded that they expected to learn "a lot." While most students expected to learn a lot in school, less than one-third chose learning a lot about the subjects in school as their most important personal goal.

Regarding future expectations, more secondary than middle or elementary students expected to graduate from high school, perhaps because they were closer to doing so, but fewer were sure of going on to college. Generally, these school level differences in students' self-expectations were consistent with teachers' reports of academic emphasis in their schools. Academic goals seemed more important, or at least more salient, to elementary teachers and students than to secondary teachers and students.

Achievement Emphasis

Achievement emphasis, the third subset of the expectations dimension, referred to perceived pressure on students to score well on tests or to get good grades. It also included the recognition given to students' efforts compared to students' performances. Teachers perceived pressure on students to get good grades as moderate and coming from sources in addition to themselves. Perceived achievement pressure increased with school level, which seemed inconsistent with school level differences in reported academic emphasis. Perhaps achievement was seen as broader than academic performance. Particularly interesting were teachers' responses to the item "Achievement is more important than effort for getting good grades in this school." Twenty-eight percent of the secondary teachers responded "seldom" or "never" compared to 39 and 41 percent of the middle and elementary teachers respectively. Thus, a sizeable minority of teachers perceived achievement as less important than effort, with elementary and middle school teachers seeming more likely than secondary teachers to reward effort with good grades.

Generally, students more than teachers perceived more pressure on students to learn. Students agreed with teachers that effort counted for grades, and that effort counted more at the elementary than middle than secondary levels. Across school levels, most students reported that effort led to success in school, suggesting that they were defining success more broadly than getting good grades.

Together, teacher and student survey results regarding expectations for students suggested that what most people would consider positive expectations prevailed in these good schools. These survey results also suggested expectations broader than the "3 Rs" or "basic skills" or even academic performance. Teachers and students in good schools, it seemed, expected more.

Teachers' Conceptions of Knowledge and Learning

Nature, Selection, and Use

Teachers' conceptions of the nature, selection, and use of knowledge in curriculum shaped their responses to the critical curriculum questions of what should be taught and how. Teachers surveyed in the Good Schools Project recognized the tentativeness of knowledge, with a majority across school levels responding that what was considered to be true or important "often" changed as conditions changed. Textbooks seemed to be respected but not revered as sources of knowledge or the basis for selecting what to teach. Less than 25 percent of the teachers responded that it "always" was important for students to learn what was in the textbook, while approximately 70 percent responded that it "often" was important. A pragmatic or utilitarian view of the use of knowledge predominated, particularly among elementary teachers.

Although these teachers' beliefs suggested more constructivist conceptions of knowledge than found in other studies, the teachers' responses to two other survey items clouded this picture. Slightly more than one-third of the teachers—middle teachers more than either elementary or secondary teachers—responded that it "always" or "often" was more important that students learned what was right than to think for themselves. The teachers were divided as to whether open ended questions were confusing to students, with elementary teachers being more confident of students' abilities to deal with open ended questions than were middle and secondary teachers.

More teachers accepted that what was true or important changed than accepted that students could and should decide for themselves after careful reflection. These results suggested that the teachers saw themselves as the gatekeepers of school knowledge. A sizeable minority also seemed, at least implicitly, to endorse conservative socialization over prevailing school and societal norms. Yet, across school levels, teachers ranked critical thinking and reasoning skills higher than facts and concepts in subject areas as important school goals. Teachers appeared to hold diverse and possibly contradictory beliefs about the nature, selection, and use of knowledge in curriculum; beliefs that may well be reflected in classroom practices (see Chapter 8) that communicate mixed messages to students.

Diversity and apparent contradiction were also evident in the responses of the principals, teachers and other school personnel, students, and parents to interview questions relevant to curriculum perspectives.[4] Many respondents mentioned their schools' emphasis on "basics," presumably reading and arithmetic. The use of ditto handouts and worksheets was frequently mentioned, particularly by students. Generally, naive or fuzzy conceptions of knowledge and learning were indicated, combined with a strong work ethic and expression of concern and caring for students as individuals. This perspective was succinctly stated by one middle school teacher who noted that "we teach fifty-five minutes per hour. We work!"

Although respondents in several schools referred to student responsibility, skill development, and going beyond the basics, they usually did not provide specifics. One elementary school principal, for example, mentioned a "strong foundation of basic skills supplemented by opportunity to express their [students'] own creativity." Critical thinking or student questioning, reasoning, and decision-making were specifically cited in only a few schools, usually elementary schools, suggesting that these often-stated goals were not widely pursued in classroom practices.[5] The fact that there were schools in which knowledge was treated as tentative and subject to student interpretation and evaluation, however, indicated that constructivist conceptions were neither impractical nor incompatible with other demands of schooling.

Overall, the principals, teachers and other school personnel, students, and parents who were interviewed seemed not to have thought through their conceptions of knowledge and learning. The interview data suggested that they had difficulty expressing their ideas in this area, and they often resorted to popular slogans such as "educate the whole child." Few people, educators included, seemed to have had occasion to seriously examine their beliefs about knowledge and learning, tending instead to take them for granted.

Organization and Distribution

Teachers' beliefs regarding the organization and distribution of knowledge in curriculum, including provision for variety and student choice, shaped their responses to the critical curriculum questions of how to teach and what shall be taught to whom. A majority of teachers across school levels agreed that students "always" learned best when new subject matter was related to their previous experiences; very few believed that this "seldom" or "never" was the case. There was less agreement among teachers as to whether students learned best when they began with discrete skills and information rather than broad ideas. Approximately half believed that this "often" was the case, while the others were divided between "always" and "seldom" or "never." A majority also believed that content "often" was integrated across subject boundaries to promote learning. Not surprisingly, perhaps, given the organization of most schools, belief in content integration was stronger among elementary than middle than secondary teachers. These results suggested an inclination toward a constructivist conception of knowledge organization in curriculum, i.e., one that interrelates knowledge rather than focusing on discrete bits of information in isolation from each other and from student experience.

Regarding the distribution of knowledge in curriculum, in particular provision for variety and student choice, more teachers endorsed variety than student choice. Almost all teachers believed that students "always" or "often" learned best when a wide variety of activities was provided. However, a sizeable minority, especially among middle and secondary teachers, believed that students "seldom" or "never" learned best when they had some choice in the selection of materials and activities and that, given the opportunity, students "seldom" or "never" chose activities that were educationally worthwhile. Middle and secondary teachers seemed to have less confidence that students would choose wisely. Once again, the teachers seemed to be seeing themselves as gatekeepers of school knowledge, not only of what should be taught, but also of how and to whom.

The interview data were consistent with this picture. There was evidence of some ability grouping and opportunity for students to engage in independent study and projects of their own design. Mention was also made of some form of individualization, usually in vague terms of "matching learning style with teaching style," "individualized teaching," or encouraging students "to go further and reach their potential." However, whole class teacher-directed teaching and learning using varied materials seemed to be the norm, characterized by what one elementary teacher called "structured freedom."

Conclusions

Taken together, the findings regarding expectations for students and teachers' conceptions of knowledge and learning suggest that the curriculum perspectives of teachers in schools identified as good do differ, though not dramatically, from those of teachers in other schools and studies. Teachers surveyed in the Good Schools Project tend to have higher expectations for their students and more constructivist conceptions of knowledge and learning. The findings also suggest the complexity of teachers' curriculum perspectives. It is probably fruitless and misleading to attempt to categorize or label teachers on the basis of their beliefs about the nature of knowledge, students, and learning. More worthwhile, it seems, are efforts to increase self-awareness of our curriculum perspectives, their complexity, and possible contradictions. Then we can begin to consider the ways in which our beliefs shape and are shaped by classroom practices, how they affect our students, and what changes might be desirable.

Notes

1. See, for example, C. Braun, "Teacher Expectation: Socio-Psychological Dynamics," *Review of Educational Research* 46 (1976): 185-213; Jere E. Brophy and Carolyn M. Evertson, *Learning From Teaching* (Boston: Allyn and Bacon, 1976); Jere E. Brophy and Thomas L. Good, *Teacher–Student Relationships: Causes and Consequences* (New York: Holt, Rinehart and Winston, 1974).

2. See, for example, Donald E. Mackenzie, "Research for School Improvement: An Appraisal of Some Recent Trends," *Educational Researcher* 12 (April 1983):5-16; Stewart C. Purkey and Marshall S. Smith, "Effective Schools: A Review," *Elementary School Journal* (1983):427-52; Michael Rutter et al., *Fifteen Thousand Hours: Secondary Schools and Their Effects on Children* (Cambridge, Ma.: Harvard University Press, 1979).

3. On conceptions of knowledge and curricular implications, see Geoffrey M. Esland, "Teaching and Learning as the Organization of Knowledge," in *Knowledge and Control,* ed. Michael F. D. Young (London: Collier Macmillan, 1971); Thomas S. Popkewitz, "Whither/Wither the Curriculum Field?," *Contemporary Education Review* 1 (1982): 15-21. Studies of teachers' curriculum perspectives include: Anne M. Bussis, Edward A. Chittenden, and Marianne Amarel, *Beyond Surface Curriculum* (Boulder, Co.: Westview, 1976); Catherine Cornbleth and Willard Korth, "Teacher Perspectives and Curriculum Priorities" (Unpublished manuscript, University of Pittsburgh, 1982); B. Robert Tabachnick, Kenneth M. Zeichner, Kathleen Densmore, Susan Adler, and Kathleen Egan, "The Impact of the Student Teaching Experience on the Development of Teacher Perspectives" (Paper presented at the Annual Meeting of the American Educational Research Association, New York City, 1982); B. Robert Tabachnick, Kenneth M. Zeichner, Kathleen Densmore, and Glen Hudak, "The Development of Teacher Perspectives" (Paper presented at the Annual Meeting of the American Educational Research Association, Montreal, 1983).

4. I wish to thank Jane Holahan, University of Pittsburgh, for her invaluable assistance in reviewing the interview data.

5. This finding is consistent with those of other school studies. See, for example, Willard Korth and Catherine Cornbleth, "Classroom Activities as Settings for Cognitive Learning Opportunity and Instruction" (Paper presented at the Annual Meeting of the American Educational Research Association, New York City, 1982); Kenneth A. Sirotnik, *What You See Is What You Get: A Summary of Observations in Over 1000 Elementary & Secondary Classrooms* (Los Angeles: A Study of Schooling, Technical Report No. 29, Graduate School of Education, Laboratory in School and Community Education, University of California at Los Angeles, 1981).

7

Goal Attainment

Goal setting is not an idle activity. It is a fundamental curriculum decision affecting what students will learn. Goals are set with the expectation that teachers will use them as a basis for classroom practices; and classroom practices, in turn, determine what students will learn at school. Many schools share common goals for their students, e.g., basic abilities in communication, positive attitudes toward others, knowledge of the content areas, and a positive self-image. All students are expected to achieve these goals in most schools in the United States.

In a time of discontent about education, however, it is easy to forget that schools are expected to help students attain a variety of goals. It becomes a temptation to focus only on visible goals or those most easily attained and to neglect the others. When the basics are heavily emphasized, for example, positive attitudes toward others may be overlooked as the teacher devotes more and more time to reading, writing, and mathematics.

The research committee of the Good Schools Project was interested in examining the types of goals that good schools believed were important and whether these goals were being attained. Teachers and students were asked to respond to an array of commonly stated goals for schooling. Students responded to nine goal statements, indicating how important they were, and whether the school taught them. Teachers responded to ten goal statements, indicating how important each was, and how effective they perceived the school was in helping students attain each goal.

The preceding chapter reported that teachers and students in the 106 good schools had goals or expectations broader than just the basic skills or academic achievement. The teachers and students in these good schools also had expectations that students would develop, for example, a sense of self-worth and a friendliness and respect toward people of different races and religions. Although there were variations in the perceptions of how important teachers and students thought the different goals were, there was much importance attached to a broad array of goals by both teachers and students.

Whether the schools were actually helping students attain the goals thought to be important was the next question asked. This chapter reports the data on how effective the teachers believed their schools were in helping students attain the broad array of goals, and to what extent students believed they were being taught the same or similar goals. The goals were grouped into four categories: intellectual, social, personal, and vocational. Only the major trends are reported here. All the data pertaining to goal attainment are summarized in Appendix I.

Attainment Of Intellectual Goals

Intellectual goals include a fund of factual knowledge about the content areas, critical thinking and reasoning skills, and communication skills. Schools usually are thought to have unique opportunities to develop intellectual goals above any other category of goals. Other social institutions as well as schools contribute to the attainment of personal, social, and vocational goals, but the schools have been delegated primary responsibility for developing intellectual goals. The Good Schools Project asked teachers how effectively their schools helped students attain the intellectual goals of reading skills, writing skills, critical thinking and reasoning skills, and other intellectual goals such as gaining factual knowledge and concepts in the subject areas, skills in evaluating information and arguments, and effective expression of opinions. Students were asked to what extent they were taught, for example, reading skills, to read for understanding, to read for enjoyment, to write effectively, and thinking and reasoning skills.

Reading Skills

The development of reading skills was not neglected in the schools surveyed in the Good Schools Project. Over 70 percent of the teachers at the elementary level thought their schools "always" were effective at helping their students attain reading skills, and 79 percent of elementary students thought they "always" were taught reading skills. At the middle school level, 53 percent of the teachers thought their schools "always" were effective at helping their students attain reading skills, and 63 percent of the students thought their schools "always" taught them reading skills. At the secondary level, however, 57 percent of the teachers thought their schools "often" were effective in helping students attain reading skills. Secondary students were evenly divided among their beliefs that their schools "always," "often," or "seldom" or "never" (combined into one category) taught them reading skills with approximately 33 percent in each response category. There was a trend, then, for the percentages of teachers who responded that their schools "always" were effective at helping their students attain reading skills to decrease across school levels, while the percentages of teachers who responded "often" increased across school levels. A similar trend occurred for students at the elementary and middle school levels, but secondary students were evenly divided among the three response categories.

Most teachers at all levels believed that their schools were effective at helping students develop reading skills at least "often." The responses of the elementary and middle school students indicated that 90 percent or more of them believed they "always" or "often" were taught reading skills, but only 69 percent of the secondary students thought this. Clearly, then, reading skills remained an important emphasis in classroom practices in the elementary and middle schools in the Good Schools Project sample. Perhaps by the secondary level, teachers expected that students had these basic skills and teachers did not emphasize them as much in their classroom practices. Those students who had not achieved minimal competencies in reading were often segregated into special English classes at the secondary level.

Students were asked about additional goals related to reading. In addition to questions about reading skills, the students were asked if they were taught to read for understanding and to read for enjoyment. Reading for understanding "always" was taught, according to 63 percent of the elementary students, 49 percent of the middle students, but only 35 percent of the secondary students. As with reading skills, the percentages of students who responded "always" to reading for understanding decreased with the level of schooling, while the percentages responding "often" increased with the level of schooling. Thus,

46 percent of the secondary students responded that they "often" were taught to read for understanding. More of the elementary and middle school students responded "always." It is possible that the decreasing percentages of students responding "always" was due to an emphasis on reading for understanding at the earlier levels, with the expectation that most students would not need a continued emphasis. According to 81 percent of the secondary students, however, this goal was not neglected, and they were taught at least "often" to read for understanding.

Reading for enjoyment was a goal which fewer students at all levels thought they were taught. Most students thought they "often" were taught to read for enjoyment, about 40 percent at each level of schooling. The numbers of students who responded "always" decreased at each level, and those who responded "seldom" or "never" increased from 26 percent at the elementary level to 45 percent at the secondary level. Attention to the goal of reading for enjoyment did not receive as much emphasis at any level as did the other two goals in reading, according to the students.

In the Good Schools Project sample, students and teachers at all levels agreed that their schools were addressing reading goals. Most teachers at all levels believed their schools "always" or "often" were effective at helping students develop reading skills. Most students also thought their schools "often" or "always" taught reading skills, but a significant number, 31 percent at the secondary level, said they "seldom" or "never" were taught reading skills.

Most students also believed that their teachers taught students to read for understanding, even though the percentages decreased from the majority in the category of "always" for elementary and middle schools to higher percentages in the "often" category at the secondary level. While the secondary schools did not seem to help many students acquire reading skills, secondary schools did seem to help more students learn to read for understanding.

The smallest number of students reported that they were taught reading for enjoyment. Sizeable numbers of students at each level reported their schools "seldom" or "never" taught students to read for enjoyment. Even so, 55 to 74 percent of the students believed their schools were helping students attain this goal.

Writing Skills

Only students were asked to respond to what extent they believed their schools were helping students learn to write effectively. About 75 percent of the students at each level of schooling thought their schools taught students to "always" or "often" write effectively. The same trends in the data that existed for reading skills were apparent for developing writing skills. More elementary students (54 percent) than middle school students (33 percent) thought their schools "always" taught students to write effectively, and more middle school students thought their schools "always" taught students to write effectively than did secondary students (26 percent). At the same time, 42 percent of the middle school students and 46 percent of the secondary school students responded that their schools "often" helped students learn to write effectively.

The schools in the Good Schools Project did not neglect the basics of learning to read and write. The evidence was that students and teachers thought students were being taught to read and write. The goal of reading for enjoyment received less attention, according to students, however.

Thinking and Reasoning Skills

Another goal emphasized in American education is learning how to think and reason. Eisner has identified cognitive processing—thinking abilities—as a conception of curriculum held by many to be the primary or only emphasis for schools.[1] Many are exhorting the schools to give this goal top priority.

Teachers in the Good Schools Project were asked how effectively their schools helped students develop critical thinking and reasoning skills. An overwhelming majority of teachers at each level of schooling said their schools "always" or "often" were effective at this (94 percent at the elementary level, 84 percent at the middle level, and 80 percent at the secondary level).

More students than teachers thought students "always" were taught thinking and reasoning skills at each level of schooling. At the elementary level, 49 percent of the students said they "always" were taught thinking and reasoning skills and 38 percent responded "often" to this survey item. Among middle school students 36 percent responded "always" and 43 percent responded "often." Among secondary students 26 percent responded "always" and 48 percent responded "often."

It appeared that the elementary schools taught students thinking and reasoning skills more frequently than did middle or secondary schools. This finding was somewhat puzzling.

Other Intellectual Goals

Only teachers were asked about other intellectual goals: gaining factual knowledge and concepts in the subject areas, developing skills in evaluating information and arguments, and effective expression of opinions. Most teachers thought their schools "often" or "always" were effective at helping students gain factual knowledge.

Most teachers at all levels thought their schools "always" or "often" were effective at helping students develop skills in evaluating information and arguments (87 percent at the elementary level, 75 percent at the middle level, and 79 percent at the secondary level).

A similar pattern was true for the goal of effective expression of opinions (40 percent indicated "always" and 52 percent "often" at the elementary level; 24 percent indicated "always" and 58 percent "often" at the middle level; and 23 percent indicated "always" and 60 percent "often" at the secondary level).

The goals of developing factual or conceptual knowledge and the intellectual skills of evaluating information and arguments, along with effective expression of opinions, received considerable attention. For all these goals, however, there generally was a decreasing emphasis on "always" teaching them as the level of schooling increased, according to both teachers and students.

Attainment of Personal Goals

In addition to intellectual goals, teachers and students were asked to respond to several statements pertaining to personal goals. Personal goals were defined as goals not based upon the subject areas or basic skills, but those which assisted students to grow and develop as learners and people, such as to develop a sense of self-worth or to become independent and self-reliant.

Teachers in the 106 good schools appeared to believe that their schools were quite effective in helping students develop a sense of self-worth. The majority of elementary teachers, 66 percent, thought their schools "always" were effective and 33 percent felt they "often" were effective. Among middle school teachers, 44 percent, felt their schools "always" were effective in fostering a sense of self-worth and 50 percent felt they "often" were effective. Among secondary teachers, 36 percent and 55 percent, indicated their schools "always" or "often" were effective.

Teachers were not quite so positive in their beliefs about how effective their schools were in helping students become independent and self-reliant. Elementary teachers were evenly split, with 48 percent believing their schools "always" and 47 percent believing their schools "often" were effective in promoting independence and self-reliance. Among middle school teachers, 84 percent felt their schools "always" or "often" were effective in achieving this goal, while 81 percent of the secondary teachers so indicated.

Similar perceptions were held by the students. More than 80 percent of the students at all levels believed their schools "always" or "often" were effective in helping students become independent and self-reliant.

All schools hope to foster positive attitudes toward learning and for students to develop study skills. These goals are essential if students are to become lifelong learners. The Good Schools Project sample was no exception to this. Teachers were asked how effective their schools were in developing positive attitudes toward learning. The majority of elementary teachers, 66 percent, thought their schools "always" were effective and 32 percent thought they "often" were effective. The majority of secondary teachers, 50 percent, thought their schools "often" were effective, whereas 41 percent felt they "always" were effective. Middle school teachers were quite evenly split in their responses (47 percent thought their schools "always" were and 46 percent thought they "often" were). Fewer than 10 percent of the teachers at any level felt the schools "seldom" or "never" were effective in helping students acquire positive attitudes toward learning.

Students were asked to what extent their schools taught them how to study. The largest number of secondary students, 46 percent, responded that their schools "seldom" or "never" taught students how to study. At the elementary level 52 percent indicated that their schools "always" taught students how to study, and another 30 percent said that their schools "often" taught students how to study. Among middle school students, 39 percent said "always" and 35 percent said "often" in response to this survey item.

There seems to be a discrepancy in perceptions here about what might be occurring in relation to the above goals. Although teachers believed they were effective in fostering positive attitudes toward learning, fairly large numbers of students did not believe their schools were teaching them how to study. These are slightly different aspects of the concern for helping students continue to learn, of course, but they are not unrelated. If lifelong learning is a societal value, schools must develop both positive attitudes toward it and the skills needed to engage in it. According to the students in this sample, there was room for improvement in the attainment of study skills.

Attainment of Social Goals

Another category of goals included in the surveys was social development: goals which assist students in relating to other people. Most schools included respect for others as a basic goal to be attained. This goal, in some form or another, was usually found within the philosophy, values, or goal statements of virtually all schools. Teachers in these 106 good schools were asked how effective they thought their schools were in helping students develop friendliness and respect toward people of different races and religions. Among elementary teachers, 63 percent thought their schools "always" were effective in achieving this goal and 32 percent felt they "often" were effective. Among middle school teachers, 52 percent thought their schools "always" were effective in achieving this goal and 40 percent felt they "often" were effective. Among secondary teachers, 42 percent thought their schools "always" were effective in achieving this goal and 46 percent felt they "often" were effective. More elementary teachers again thought their schools "always" were more effective than did middle or secondary teachers.

Students were also asked about two goals similar to the above goal: to what extent did their schools teach students to respect the rights of other individuals and groups and to be friendly toward people of different races, religions, and cultures.

The students' responses were comparable to the teachers' responses concerning these goals.

Similar responses by students were given to the goal of being friendly toward people of different races, religions, and cultures. A majority of elementary and middle school students thought their schools "always" were effective in this regard. Secondary students were somewhat less positive, but 73 percent responded "always" or "often" to this survey item.

The schools in the Good Schools Project were addressing the social goals in their classroom practices. The trend set in the previous categories of goals continued here: more elementary than middle and secondary school students and teachers believed their schools "always" helped in attaining these goals. In general, however, the teachers and students in the Good Schools Project sample were concerned that friendliness and respect toward others were goals to be attained in their schools, and the evidence suggested that these schools were attending to these goals.

Attainment of Vocational Goals

Many people believe the schools should help students attain vocational goals—skills which will help them obtain employment as adults. Only teachers were asked about how effective their schools were in helping students acquire vocational skills. As might be expected, 47 percent of the elementary teachers said their schools "seldom" or "never" were effective at this. Forty percent, however, said they "often" were. Middle school teachers responded in a similar fashion. Forty-two percent thought their schools "seldom" or "never" were effective at this goal, but 37 percent thought they "often" were. Among secondary teachers, 48 percent thought their schools "often" were and 32 percent thought they "always" were effective in helping students develop vocational skills. More secondary teachers than middle or elementary teachers believed their schools were effective more often in helping students develop vocational skills.

A General Item: A Chance To Do Well

Teachers were asked to respond to a general item about

learning: "All students have a chance to do well in this school." More than 98 percent of the teachers at every level felt that their schools were effective in helping students achieve this objective "always" or "often"; only 2 percent felt their schools "seldom" or "never" were effective.

Rank Order of Goals

From the foregoing discussion, it becomes apparent that the teachers and students in the schools identified as good were attending to a broad array of goals. Given this dominant trend, the two response modes of "always" and "often" were combined, and the combined responses were then placed in rank order on the basis of the number of teachers and students responding to each goal.

Table 1 presents the combined responses of "always" and "often" for the teachers in relation to each goal. The previously noted trend for elementary teachers to respond more positively than teachers at the other two levels to all goals except vocational skills becomes very apparent.

Overall, there is little deviation in the rank order of teachers' responses at the three levels of schooling. Factual knowledge is a goal which receives considerable attention, and it is ranked higher than those emphasizing critical thinking and reasoning skills, effective expression of opinions, and skills in evaluating information and arguments. Teachers have been criticized in the past for overemphasizing knowledge of facts and not paying enough attention to higher level thinking skills. Although it is clear that the Good Schools Project sample was paying attention to both, the factual knowledge goal appeared to receive greater emphasis as perceived by teachers than the goals involving higher levels of thinking: critical thinking and reasoning skills, effective expression of opinions, and skills in evaluating information.

The personal goals of developing a sense of self-worth and positive attitudes toward learning also received considerable emphasis, according to the teachers. The social goal of friendliness and respect toward people of different races and religions followed closely in the rank order. Vocational skills were lowest for the elementary and middle school teachers, but somewhat higher for secondary teachers. A reasonable generalization, then,

Table 1

Rank Order of Percentages of Teachers Responding Always or Often to Statements Concerning Goal Attainment

Elementary Level Teachers

Goals	% of Teachers
Reading skills	99
Factual knowledge and concepts in the subject area	99
A sense of self-worth	99
Positive attitudes toward learning	98
Independence and self-reliance	95
Friendliness and respect toward people of different races and religions	95
Critical thinking and reasoning skills	94
Effective expression of opinions	92
Skills in evaluating information and arguments	87
Vocational skills	53

Middle Level Teachers

Goals	% of Teachers
Factual knowledge and concepts in the subject area	98
Reading skills	96
A sense of self-worth	94
Positive attitudes toward learning	93
Friendliness and respect toward people of different races and religions	92
Critical thinking and reasoning skills	84
Independence and self-reliance	84
Effective expression of opinions	82
Skills in evaluating information and arguments	75
Vocational skills	58

Secondary Level Teachers

Goals	% of Teachers
Factual knowledge and concepts in the subject area	96
Positive attitudes toward learning	91
A sense of self-worth	91

Table 1 (cont.)

Rank Order of Percentages of Teachers Responding Always or Often to
Statements Concerning Goal Attainment

Secondary Level Teachers	
Goals (cont.)	*% of Teachers*
Reading skills	89
Friendliness and respect toward people of different races and religions	88
Effective expression of opinions	83
Independence and self-reliance	81
Vocational skills	80
Critical thinking and reasoning skills	80
Skills in evaluating information and arguments	79

according to the perceptions of teachers, was that their schools were effective in helping students "always" or "often" attain three of the four categories of goals: intellectual, personal, and social.

There was more variation among students. Table 2 summarizes the students' responses by rank order. As discussed before, for the large majority of students, reading skills appeared to be taught at the elementary and middle school levels. Even at the secondary level 69 percent of the students said they were taught reading skills. The goal of reading for understanding ranked high at all three levels. Although the percentages of students' responses dropped some at the higher levels of schooling, the social goal of respecting the rights of others also ranked high as being taught, in the perception of students. How to study and read for enjoyment were consistently perceived by fewer students as goals that were taught. Although these goals were lowest in the rank order of the students responding "always" or "often" as to whether these goals were taught, there were still large percentages of students who said these goals were, indeed, taught. The other goals varied as to their rank order by schooling levels.

The majority of students at each level of schooling perceived their schools as attending to each goal. Reading for enjoyment and how to study were perceived by the fewest number of students as being taught either "always" or "often."

Table 2

*Rank Order of Percentages of Students Responding Always or Often to
Statements Concerning Goal Attainment*

Elementary Level Students

Goals	% of Students
Reading skills	96
Read for understanding	93
Respect the rights of other individuals and groups	93
Write effectively	88
Friendly toward people of different races, religions, and cultures	88
Independent and self-reliant	87
Thinking and reasoning skills	87
How to study	82
Read for enjoyment	74

Middle Level Students

Goals	% of Students
Reading skills	90
Read for understanding	88
Respect the rights of other individuals and groups	87
Independent and self-reliant	83
Friendly toward people of different races, religions, and cultures	81
Thinking and reasoning skills	79
Write effectively	75
How to study	74
Read for enjoyment	69

Secondary Level Students

Goals	% of Students
Read for understanding	81
Independent and self-reliant	81
Respect the rights of other individuals and groups	77
Thinking and reasoning skills	74

Table 2 (cont.)

Rank Order of Percentages of Students Responding Always or Often to Statements Concerning Goal Attainment

Secondary Level Students	
Goals (cont.)	*% of Students*
Friendly toward people of different races, religions, and cultures	73
Write effectively	72
Reading skills	69
Read for enjoyment	55
How to study	54

Conclusions

Goals for the sample of teachers and students in the 106 schools studied are not restricted to a narrow array. The schools clearly are not neglecting the basic skills or academic achievement which are used to define effective schools (see Chapter 3). The students and teachers both indicate a concern for and efforts toward developing a much broader array than just those basic skills, however. Goals are being addressed in the personal, social and vocational areas, as well as in the intellectual area. Only very small percentages of the teachers indicate that they "seldom" or "never" believe their schools are effective in helping the students acquire any of the goals to which the teachers were asked to respond, but the percentages of teachers responding to "seldom" or "never" increase with the level of schooling. More middle school teachers responded "seldom" or "never" than elementary teachers, and more secondary teachers responded "seldom" or "never" than middle school teachers.

Two interesting observations stand out as special cases to the above conclusions, however. First, slightly less than half of the elementary and middle school teachers say their schools "seldom" or "never" are effective in helping students develop vocational skills. This area of development seems to be more prominent at the secondary level. Still, 40 percent of the elementary teachers and 37 percent of the middle school teachers say their schools "often" are effective in developing vocational skills.

The second special case is that the largest number of

teachers who responded "seldom" or "never" (even though the percentages were under 25 percent) tends to be for the goals reflecting higher thinking abilities: critical thinking and reasoning skills; skills in evaluating information and arguments; and effective expression of opinions. The percentages of elementary teachers who responded "seldom" or "never" tend to be considerably smaller than the percentages for middle school or secondary teachers. This same trend also occurs for one other goal: independence and self-reliance.

In summary, vocational goals, higher level thinking goals, and the personal goal of independence and self-reliance are those which received less attention, according to teachers. But even for these goals, the majority of teachers think their schools are effective in helping students attain these goals either "always" or "often."

In general, more students than teachers say their schools "seldom" or "never" teach these goals. Almost half of the secondary students say their schools "seldom" or "never" teach students to read for enjoyment or how to study. About a third of the students say they "seldom" or "never" are taught reading skills. A number of students seem to be saying that they are taught reading skills (although not so much at the secondary level), but that students are not being taught to enjoy reading. These students are still in the minority, however. Most students think they "always" or "often" are being taught all of these goals.

As with the teachers, the number of students who responded "seldom" or "never" to each goal increases with the level of schooling, and those who responded "always" decreases with the level of schooling. In general, higher percentages of elementary teachers and students consistently respond that their schools "always" help students attain these goals than at the other two levels of schooling. The responses are perceptions, of course, and not actual evidence of attainment of goals. But for some reason, elementary students and teachers have more positive perceptions in relation to goal attainment. This is an area in which future analyses of the data would be beneficial in understanding this consistent trend in the data.

Note

1. Elliot W. Eisner and Elizabeth Vallance, *Conflicting Conceptions of Curriculum* (Berkeley, Ca.: McCutchan, 1974).

8

Classroom Practices

All of the efforts of planning, funding, providing resources, hiring personnel, and developing curriculum are done to affect classroom practices. It is in the classroom that these efforts come to fruition. It is in the classroom that students ultimately receive their schooling. Classroom practices, then, should be the primary focus of educational planning and development. Classroom practices are the heart of schooling.

Activity in any classroom is extraordinarily complex, however. There are interactions between teachers and students and among students. There are formal interactions focused on learning, and there are informal interactions focused much more on the concerns and interests of young people than the formal lessons sometimes are. A variety of learning materials could be in use. There may be several activities occurring simultaneously. The teacher is engaged in instruction, but at the same time is controlling students and managing the classroom. The classroom is seldom quiet and never devoid of activity.

Much is learned in such a setting. The planned curricula at the formal level and the teacher's planning at the instructional level become the operational curriculum through classroom practices.[1] Some of what is planned and intended will become part of the action; part will never become operational, for a variety of reasons. Much that is unplanned finds its way into the operational curriculum—the interactions within the classroom through the classroom practices. Facts, processes, values, beliefs, attitudes, skills, concepts, and generalizations are attained, or not attained, through classroom practices. Clearly, then, any good school would be characterized by exemplary classroom practices. What classroom practices were found in the Good Schools Project sample?

Given the complexity of a classroom, choices must be made within any research study as to what will be included. What classroom practices will be a part of the study and what will be excluded? Some aspects are so pervasive they dare not be excluded: what is being taught; how it is being taught; what are the roles of the teacher and student in learning; what materials are available and used; and how time is used. These aspects, which are fundamental elements of classroom practices, became the major foci for the Good Schools Project.

The data were collected primarily by questionnaries. Teachers and students responded to items on a variety of topics dealing with classroom practices. This chapter reports the major overall trends. All data on classroom practices are summarized in Appendix A.

Subdimensions of Classroom Practices

Items on the questionnaires that dealt with classroom practices clustered into several subdimensions. Because of the emphasis currently being placed on the teaching of thinking skills, several items were asked of teachers and students which had to do with aspects of how critical thinking was being taught. Another subdimension included items about the choices and options students had in their learning processes: how much did students get to select their own materials, activities, and projects? Several items related to students' and teachers' perceptions of how time was spent: what activities accounted for most of the time; whether time was well-organized or wasted; and did students have enough time to complete assignments? A related item asked how much time was expected by teachers and spent by students on homework each day. Evaluation was the focus for another subdimension. Teachers were asked about the relevance and use of tests, while students were asked about their grades and the fairness of them. Students and teachers were also asked about the availability or use of learning materials in general and specifically whether texts were the major source of their work.

Three subdimensions about how teaching and learning occurred were included as items on the questionnaires. One subdimension asked about the extent to which cooperative learning occurred, and another asked about how much individualization was present. A third subdimension focused on specific instructional practices, based upon the perspectives of the students. The items asked about the difficulty and interest of class assignments, the clarity of teachers' expectations, the extent to which classwork was busy work or a waste of time, and whether teachers explained things in terms of what students already knew.

For the very young children in early primary grades, the questionnaire was necessarily shortened and simplified. Young children were asked only one item each on the subdimensions of critical thinking, use of classroom time, homework, clarity of instructional practices, and difficulty of class assignments. The data about young children are reported separately from other student data.

A teacher's view of classroom practices does not necessarily agree with a student's view of that classroom; nor do students within a classroom agree. These differences can be very significant. For example, a teacher may believe that he or she is teaching critical thinking, inquiry, or positive attitudes toward learning, but students may perceive otherwise.

Researchers cannot rely exclusively on teachers' or students' perceptions of what is occurring in the classroom; both must be obtained if the complexity of the classroom is to be understood. For this reason, in the Good Schools Project many of the items in the *Teacher Survey* and *Student Survey* were asked in similar form. The responses from different data sources significantly enrich the understanding of classroom practices. In the following sections, teachers' and students' responses to comparable items will be reported together. When items exist for only teachers or students, they will be clearly identified.

Critical Thinking

There has been considerable emphasis in recent years on developing higher thinking powers—those involving problem solving and critical thinking. From the preceding chapter, it was apparent that, for both teachers and students, the goal of developing critical thinking was addressed at least "often" and for many, "always." Because of the emphasis upon this as a goal for schooling virtually everywhere in the United States, additional questions were asked about specific classroom practices thought to develop critical thinking.

One aspect of critical thinking is learning to question what is being taught and studied. In the Good Schools Project sample, more than half of the teachers at each level of schooling believed they "always" encouraged students to raise questions about what they studied, and well over 90 percent said "always" or "often." Students believed they were encouraged to raise questions about what they studied, but not quite to the extent the teachers did.

Another aspect of critical thinking involves examining different points of view on a topic rather than searching for "the" right answer. In general, the teachers in these good schools thought they encouraged students to do this "often" (65 percent or more of them at each level of schooling responded in this way). More elementary than middle or secondary teachers believed they "always" encouraged students to examine different viewpoints, but, overall, most teachers felt they "always" or "often" encouraged students to examine differing viewpoints.

Similarly, students perceived that teachers encouraged students to examine different points of view rather than to find the right answers. About three-fourths of the students responded "always" or "often" to this item. Somewhat larger percentages of students than teachers, however, believed students "seldom" or "never" were encouraged to examine differing viewpoints.

A related item asked if teachers encouraged students to disagree with their teachers, an even bolder way to encourage critical thinking than examining different viewpoints. Most teachers said they "often" did, but 38 percent at the elementary and middle school levels and 28 percent at the secondary level said they "seldom" or "never" encouraged students to disagree with teachers.

Students were more evenly split across the response modes as to whether they were free to question or disagree with their teachers: roughly a third of the students at each level of schooling answered "always," "often," or "seldom" or "never." At the same time, more students than teachers felt students "always" were free to disagree with their teachers. It seemed that the teacher remained the unquestioned authority in the classroom, yet, for the majority of teachers and students, students were encouraged to question even their teachers in pursuit of a topic at least some of the time.

Students were asked four additional items about aspects of critical thinking. One item asked students if their teachers encouraged them to question what was in the book. As with the item about whether students were encouraged to question or disagree with their teachers, a similar pattern of responses was obtained. About two-thirds or more of the students at every level said they "always" or "often" were encouraged to question what was in the book. Another item asked students if they were encouraged to express their opinions in class. Many students believed they were "always" or "often" encouraged to express their opinions in class (over 75 percent of them with roughly equal percentages in the two response modes).

At least 50 percent or more of the students at each level said teachers "often" asked students to explain how they got an answer, while another 25 percent said they "always" were asked to explain how they got their answers. Most students apparently believed they were being held accountable for how they arrived at their answers.

One item asked students whether they spent a lot of time memorizing things. Schools have been criticized for spending too much time on having students memorize facts rather than learning to think critically or to engage in problem solving. The responses of the students in these good schools suggested that this does not occur as often as it might in some other schools. Less than 20 percent of the students at each level said they "always" spent a lot of time memorizing things, whereas many students said they "seldom" or "never" did (48 percent at the elementary level, 44 percent at the middle level, and 42 percent at the secondary level). Young children in the early primary grades were asked to respond "yes" or "no" to an item on memorization. Sixty-five percent of the young children said "yes" they spent a lot of time memorizing things. At the earliest level of schooling, rote memorization seemed to occur more frequently.

It would appear, then, that most teachers saw themselves as encouraging their students to develop behaviors related to critical thinking. The one behavior that was not encouraged as much as other behaviors was to have students disagree with their teachers, yet about 50 percent of the teachers at each level even did that "often." For most students, too, behaviors related to critical thinking were usually seen to be a part of their classroom experiences. For many students, not a great deal of time was spent on memorization, and most students felt they "always" or "often" were encouraged to raise questions about what they studied, to examine different viewpoints, to question what was in the book, to explain their answers, to express their opinions, and even to question or disagree with their teachers. The sample of teachers in the Good Schools Project perceived that they did foster critical thinking in their classroom practices. For a sizeable minority of the students, even more could have been done to foster critical thinking. Critical thinking was much more a part of the curriculum, however, than memorization of facts, dates, and events for most teachers and students.

This finding was in contrast to the findings from the "Study of Schooling" where conclusions were reached based on extensive classroom observations.[2] If classroom observations had been made in the Good Schools Project sample, the observers' findings might have been different from the perceptions of the students and teachers. But those who live daily in the good schools perceived that critical thinking was, indeed, being taught.

Student Choice Options

In order to become independent learners, most authorities believe that students must have some choices and opportunities for decision making regarding their learning processes. When decisions are always made for students, learning is adult-directed, which restricts options, limits involvement, and reduces opportunities for students to learn how to learn and to pursue their own interests. Several items were asked of teachers and students to determine the extent to which students had choices and options in directing their own learning.

Since curriculum materials have great influence over what students learn, both students and teachers were asked how frequently students had the opportunity to select their materials. Seventy-five percent or more of the teachers said they "seldom" or "never" let students select the curriculum materials they used. Among students, 57 percent at the elementary level, 69 percent at the middle school level, and 79 percent at the secondary level said they "seldom" or "never" had opportunities to select materials.

Students were asked the extent to which they were encouraged to select topics of interest to study, and what chance they had to decide what they studied. Approximately 70 percent of the students at each level said they "always" or "often" were encouraged to study topics that interested them. Most students believed they were encouraged to study topics of interest most of the time, but 25 to 32 percent responded that they "seldom" or "never" were encouraged to study topics of interest. Somewhat surprisingly, on another item, similar percentages of students said they "seldom" or "never" had a chance to decide what to study.

Students did not feel they had much of a choice about the amount of time they spent working on assignments. Sixty-two percent at the elementary level, 69 percent at the middle level, and 71 percent at the secondary level said students "seldom" or "never" had a choice about the time they spent on assignments.

Teachers were asked about the extent to which they let students select the activities and projects in which the students engaged. Among elementary teachers, 67 percent said "always" or "often," while more than 60 percent of middle or secondary teachers said "seldom" or "never" did they let students select learning activities. In a related item, 62 percent of the elementary teachers and 52 percent of the middle school teachers said they "always" or "often" allowed students the options to do projects, such as pictures or models, rather than written assignments, but only 40 percent of the secondary teachers said they "always" or "often" did. Students did not agree with teachers on this item; students perceived less opportunity for choice in their projects than did the teachers. From 61 to 68 percent of the students said teachers "seldom" or "never" let them do projects, such as pictures or models, rather than written assignments.

Elementary teachers reported some student choice or options at least some of the time, but middle and secondary teachers reported considerably less student choice. Not many teachers at any level allowed students much choice in selecting curriculum materials. Students saw themselves having even less choice in their learning. Most students did not perceive frequent choices in what they studied, how much time they spent on assignments, the type of projects selected, or the materials used. More students believed they were encouraged to study topics of interest to them, but the percentages were small.

It would appear that students in these good schools did not have significant decision-making power over their learning. Students perceived even fewer options than the teachers thought they allowed students to have. Materials, time, topics, and activities in the classroom seemed to be teacher-controlled decisions with limited student involvement. This was similar to the report from the "Study of Schooling" that indicated students had little decision-making opportunities in their classes.[3] In that study, teachers were also in charge of the students and the classroom, and teachers made virtually all of the significant decisions for the students as to what, when, and how students learned, at all levels of schooling. This conclusion was supported by observation data and questionnaire data from both students and teachers. Schools in both of these studies, a "Study of Schooling" and the Good Schools Project, were adult-controlled institutions with little opportunities for students to make decisions in their daily lives.

Use of Classroom Time

The importance of the use of time in the classroom as a variable in learning has been highlighted in recent research on effective classrooms and teaching. For example, academic learning time has been identified as a significant variable in student achievement for reading and mathematics at the elementary school level.[4] Because of the significance of time in relation to what students learn, both teachers and students were asked to estimate how time was used in their classrooms. Fifty-six percent of the teachers at the elementary level said classes in their schools "always" were well-organized and little time was wasted, and another 41 percent reported "often" to this item. Middle and secondary teachers had slightly different perceptions, but very few teachers believed that there was much waste of classroom time.

Students had comparable perceptions about the use of classroom time. Approximately 80 percent of the students felt that classes "always" or "often" were well-organized, and about 20 percent felt that their classes "seldom" or "never" were well-organized. In another area, about 50 percent of the students at each level believed that students "seldom" or "never" fooled around a lot in class. For young students, 62 percent said "no" to the item that asked whether students fooled around a lot in classes.

Students responded to items about the allocation of time in two respects: adequate time for assignments and how most of the time was spent. About 50 percent of the students at each level said they "often" had enough time to finish their assignments, but 18 percent of the elementary school students, 32 percent of the middle school students, and 43 percent of the secondary students said they "seldom" or "never" had enough time to finish their assignments.

A majority of students reported that most of their time during the school day was spent listening to the teacher (53 percent of the elementary students, 71 percent of the middle school students, and 76 percent of the secondary students). Much smaller percentages of students, about 12 percent, reported that most of their time was spent in working with others on special projects or in taking tests. Thirty-three percent of the elementary students said most of their time was spent in working by themselves on workbooks or reading, but only 17 percent of the middle and 12 percent of the secondary students responded that they worked by themselves on workbooks or reading.

Generally, students and teachers believed that their time in classrooms was frequently well-spent. Time was usually well-organized, little time was wasted, most of the time "often" was spent on academic activities, most students "seldom" fooled around in classes, most students had time to complete assignments in their classes, and most students reported that most of their time was spent in listening to the teacher.

The common perception is that much time is wasted in schools. The findings of this study of good schools did not support such an observation. Neither did the findings from the "Study of Schooling," although the items in that study were different from those used here. The observation and questionnaire data from the "Study of Schooling" consistently said that most time was spent on instruction, with relatively little time spent on routines of the classroom or in socializing that was not focused on a learning task.[5] Almost 75 percent of classroom time was spent on instruction.[6] It appeared that teachers and students in both of these samples of schools believed that most of their time was spent on learning tasks.

Homework

The National Commission on Excellence in Education has recommended that students spend more time on homework than they currently do.[7] It is believed that extending opportunities to learn through homework will result in greater student learning. Many people support this position, particularly for the older students. A few people caution, however, that time beyond school might be better spent on other types of learning, and that unless the homework is meaningful and challenging, it can be a factor in turning students off to schooling.

Although no questions were asked about the quality of homework within the schools identified as good, teachers and students were asked to estimate how much time students spent on homework each day. Their answers were not dissimilar. Forty-six percent of the elementary teachers, 34 percent of the middle school teachers, and 35 percent of the secondary teachers expected their students to spend less than thirty minutes per day on homework. Slightly more than 50 percent of the middle and secondary teachers, however, expected their students to spend between thirty and sixty minutes per day or more than sixty minutes per day on homework, while only 38 percent of the elementary teachers expected that much time spent on homework.

Students responded to similar items concerning homework. About 50 percent of the students at each level said they spent from thirty to sixty minutes per day on homework. From 17 to 21 percent said they spent more than sixty minutes per day, while 30 percent of the elementary students, 21 percent of the middle school students, and 32 percent of the secondary students said they spent less than thirty minutes. Seventy percent of the young children surveyed said "no" to the item which asked if they did a lot of homework every night.

In summary, the majority of students said they spent an hour or less per day on homework, and this seemed generally to agree with the expectations of most teachers. Teachers did expect students beyond the primary level to do homework each day, and students said they spent time on homework.

Evaluation

An important classroom practice is the evaluation of student learning. The most commonly used form of evaluation is the test. Tests are used to help teachers determine how well students are doing in their classwork and as a basis for feedback to students about their learning. Teachers in the Good Schools Project were asked about the types of tests and examinations they gave. Most teachers believed that their tests accurately represented the goals and objectives of the school. Among elementary teachers, 51 percent believed this "always" was the case, and another 46 percent said that it "often" was true. For middle school teachers, 45 percent said tests "always" represented the goals of the school, and another 53 percent said tests "often" did. For secondary teachers, the figures for "always" and "often" were 40 and 58 percent respectively.

The standardized test score is considered by lay citizens to be the primary criterion of how well the school is doing. Scores on these tests are printed in community newspapers, debated by parents, and monitored by administrators because of the importance attached to them. Teachers are usually less convinced of the importance of standardized test scores, perhaps because they are not as helpful in making instructional decisions as other types of data.

Teachers were asked explicitly how often they used standardized test results for making instructional decisions. Fifty percent of the elementary teachers and 47 percent of the middle school teachers said they "always" or "often" used tests that way. Among secondary teachers, 43 percent said they "seldom" used standardized test results for making instructional decisions and 27 percent said they "never" used standardized test results that way.

Most teachers, however, did use teacher-made tests for making instructional decisions. Between 82 and 92 percent of the teachers at all levels indicated they "always" or "often" did this. Teacher-made tests were used much more frequently for making instructional decisions than standardized test scores.

Students were asked what grades they usually got in school. Slightly less than 50 percent at each level said they received B's. Thirty-four percent of the elementary students said they received A's, whereas 24 percent of the middle school students and only 16 percent of the secondary students said they usually got A's. Nineteen percent of the elementary students, 27 percent of the middle school students, and 36 percent of the secondary students said they usually received C, D, or F grades. The number of students who saw themselves as doing merely passing or failing work increased with the level of schooling. At the same time, 72 percent of the elementary students and 61 percent of the middle school students believed that they "always" got the grades they deserved, whether or not the teacher liked them. Only 40 percent of the secondary students believed they "always" got the grades they deserved; slightly more believed they "often" did. Most students in these schools believed they were doing well in school, receiving A's or B's, and that their teachers "always" or "often" graded them fairly.

Availability of Instructional Materials and Supplies.

Several of the selection committees of the participating Kappa Delta Pi chapters named the availability of instructional materials and supplies as a criterion of a good school. Although the availability of materials and supplies was not identified as a characteristic of effective schools through the research summarized in Chapter Three, most teachers and students agreed that the amount and type of materials and supplies available for assisting the learning processes were important conditions of schooling affecting the quality of their daily lives.

Students in the 106 good schools were asked the extent to which they used different kinds of materials in their classes, e.g., newspapers and photographs. Many students replied that they "seldom" or "never" did (44 percent of the elementary students and 55 percent of the middle and secondary students). About a third of the students at each level replied they "often" did. In the schools identified as good, use of different kinds of materials did not seem to be a common occurrence for about half of the students, but the other half used different types of materials "always" or "often."

Teachers indicated that curriculum materials available to the students in their classes were usually appropriate. Among elementary teachers, 55 percent said curriculum materials "always" were appropriate and another 42 percent said they "often" were. For middle school teachers, 40 percent said curriculum materials "always" were and 52 percent said they "often" were. For secondary teachers, the figures were 36 and 55 percent. This finding was in agreement with the perceptions of teachers in the "Study of Schooling."[8] Many teachers from the "Study of Schooling" agreed that the materials available were generally appropriate for their students, although fewer teachers in schools with large percentages of minority students perceived this. Davis, Frymier, and Clinefelter have suggested that the quality of many of the curriculum materials available to teachers and students is limited on a number of important dimensions.[9] It is possible that lack of teacher sophistication in selecting and evaluating materials may account for this discrepancy.

Most teachers also believed that audio-visual materials and equipment were available when needed. Ninety-two to 98 percent of the teachers said audio-visual materials and equipment "always" or "often" were available and only very small percentages said audio-visual materials "seldom" or "never" were available when needed. Further, 88 to 94 percent of the teachers said that school supplies "always" or "often" were readily available for classroom use.

Most teachers indicated there were no serious problems with the appropriateness of materials or with the availability of audio-visual materials and equipment and school supplies for classroom use.

Use of Textbooks

Heavy reliance upon the textbook as the tool for learning has been documented by a number of different studies. It appeared that the schools in the Good Schools Project were not significantly different in this respect. About 50 percent of the teachers at all levels responded that they "often" used the textbook as the primary source of information. About 30 percent of the teachers, however, said they "seldom" or "never" did. Slightly more students reported a more frequent use of the textbook. Fifty-eight percent of the elementary students, 63 percent of the middle school students and 61 percent of the secondary students said that most of the work in their classes "often" came from the text. Among elementary students, 21 percent said "seldom" or "never" did most of their work come from the textbook, whereas 16 percent of middle and secondary students reported "seldom" or "never."

The text clearly was an important tool in the classrooms of the 106 schools identified as good. Other materials were available, appropriate, and sometimes used, but the text was a major influence. This finding was supported also by the "Study of Schooling." In that study, the text was reported to have a moderate to high influence over what teachers taught in the academic area.[10] There was some variation from subject to subject and among levels of schooling, but the text was clearly an important determinant of what students learned. The textbook, with its assets and limitations, seems to be a fixture of American schooling.

Cooperation in Learning

Schools foster competition among students in a number of ways: organization, sports, grades, tracking of classes, and grouping of students. Some parents and educators believe this is a good introduction to and preparation for a highly competitive world. Many realize, however, that human beings are social animals and must engage in cooperative acts to survive and have quality in their lives. Schools are thus expected to help students learn to cooperate as well as compete. Teachers and students in the Good Schools Project were asked to what extent their schools fostered cooperation in learning.

Teachers were asked whether they encouraged students to work together on topics students were studying. More than half of the teachers at all levels said they "often" did (62 percent at the elementary level, 56 percent at the middle level, and 58 percent at the secondary level). Another 20 percent of the teachers said they "always" did this. Students, however, did not see the same degree of teacher encouragement for students to work together on what they studied. The majority of students reported that their teachers "seldom" or "never" encouraged them to work together (39 percent at the elementary level, 48 percent at the middle level, and 53 percent at the secondary level). Slightly more than a third of the students said their teachers "often" encouraged students to work together on topics they studied, and an additional 9 to 23 percent reported that their teachers "always" encouraged students to work together.

Students were asked in a second item the extent to which they thought there was a lot of cooperative effort among students. More students responded positively to this item. Slightly over 50 percent of the students at each level said they thought there "often" was cooperative effort among students, and an additional 19 to 29 percent reported that there "always" was a lot of cooperative effort among students.

Students seemed to be saying that, even though teachers did not always encourage them to work together, there was frequently cooperative effort.

Teachers were asked a second time about the extent to

which students tutored or assisted other students in their classes. Slightly over 50 percent of the teachers at each level responded that students "often" tutored or assisted other students in their classes, and an additional 8 to 19 percent of the teachers reported that they "always" had students tutor or assist other students.

Cooperation was a frequent phenomenon in these good schools, according to the perceptions of teachers, but not a frequent phenomenon according to students in regard to their school work. There was frequent cooperative effort among students, however, when the item about cooperation was not specifically tied to school work. These schools appeared to have been fostering cooperation as well as competition. This finding was in contrast to a finding from the "Study of Schooling." Little cooperation in learning was found through observation in that study: the probability was less than 10 percent that the students would be found to be working cooperatively together on an assignment.[11]

Individualization

Teachers are expected to individualize the educational program so that students will have their interests taken into account and their needs for learning met adequately. A recent report on an analysis of a sample of curriculum guides concluded that guides frequently exhorted teachers to individualize, but did not often give help to them in doing it.[12] The majority of teachers at each level in the Good Schools Project said they "often" individualized their instruction (64 percent at the elementary level, 61 percent at the middle level, and 54 percent at the secondary level). Additional teachers said they "always" did. However, a good number of teachers—28 percent at the middle level and 38 percent at the secondary level—said they "seldom" or "never" individualized instruction, although only 7 percent of the elementary teachers said they "seldom" or "never" individualized instruction. A slightly different perception occurred when students were asked to what extent everybody worked on the same things in class. Fifty-one percent of the elementary students, 59 percent of the middle school students, and 61 percent of the secondary students said they "often" worked at the same things in class. In the perceptions of most teachers, individualization occurred at least to some extent, yet most students thought they usually worked at the same things in class.

This was a finding which did differ somewhat from other research on the topic. In the "Study of Schooling," it was found that teachers infrequently used objectives, content, materials, or grouping to individualize the work of their students.[13] Elementary teachers, however, tended to use these curricular elements to individualize more often than did teachers at the junior or senior high levels of schooling. In general, however, limited amounts of individualization occurred, according to the perceptions of teachers at all three levels of schooling in the "Study of Schooling."

Instructional Practices

Specific instructional practices have been identified as fostering learning. To the extent that objectives are clear, tasks are of appropriate difficulty, and feedback exists, the students are likely to learn more. Students in the Good Schools Project were asked their perceptions about such classroom conditions. More specifically, they were asked how often five recommended instructional practices occurred.

First, students were asked if what teachers expected students to learn was clear to them. It was clear for the large majority of students at each level. Approximately 50 percent of the students at each level said what they were expected to learn "often" was clear, and, for many of the rest, it "always" was clear. At the early age level, 81 percent of the young children said "yes" to the statement that they usually knew what their teachers wanted them to do.

These findings were in agreement with what was found in the "Study of Schooling." The majority of students included in the "Study of Schooling" sample also said they were clear about what their teachers expected them to do. It was noted, however, that a sizeable minority had trouble in understanding teachers' directions and comments.[14] For a small percentage of students, this was true also in the Good Schools Project sample. If students are to learn in a teacher-controlled environment, as was indicated from data in both of these studies, students must be clear about what is to be learned. If teachers are going to determine the learning tasks for students, teachers must communicate the tasks to students clearly.

Second, students were asked about the quality of their classwork. Most students did not believe their classwork to be busy work or a waste of time. About 25 percent of the students at each level responded that classwork "always" or "often" was busy work or a waste of time, but the remaining students said it "seldom" or "never" was.

Third, students were asked whether their teachers tried to explain things in terms of things students already knew. The majority of students said their teachers "often" did (45 percent at the elementary level, 52 percent at the middle level, and 60 percent at the secondary level). An additional 36 percent of the elementary students, 30 percent of the middle school students, and 22 percent of the secondary students said their teachers "always" did. For most students, teachers tried to explain what students were learning in terms of what they already knew.

Fourth, students were asked how often most of their class assignments were interesting. About 50 percent of the students at each level said class assignments "often" were interesting. At the elementary level, 21 percent said class assignments "always" were interesting, while 27 percent reported that assignments "seldom" or "never" were interesting. At the middle school level, 13 percent of the students said their assignments "always" were interesting, while 40 percent of the students said their assignments "seldom" or "never" were interesting. At the secondary level, only 7 percent of the students said their assignments "always" were interesting, and 45 percent of the students said their assignments "seldom" or "never" were. For a substantial number of students, class assignments held little or no interest, but for more than 50 percent of the students, assignments "always" or "often" were interesting.

Finally, students were asked to indicate how often their class assignments were too hard for them. Approximately 85 percent of the students said their assignments "seldom" or "never" were too hard for them. Young students, too, were asked this item, and 68 percent responded "no." In general, it would seem that class assignments were not too difficult for most students in the 106 schools identified as good.

Most students in the Good Schools Project sample perceived their teachers as following recommended instructional practices. What teachers expected students to learn was clear, their work was not busy work or a waste of time, teachers explained things in terms of things students already knew, and their assignments were not too hard. For a substantial minority of students, however, assignments were not interesting.

Conclusions

The perceptions of teachers and students of classroom practices in the Good Schools Project are quite similar, overall. Teachers and students perceive similar conditions in the classrooms, even though the percentages vary somewhat on similar items between the two data sources.

The following generalizations seem warranted from the data. Classroom practices are frequently directed toward helping students develop critical thinking abilities which are usually considered to be a unique responsibility of the school. The classrooms within the sample are dominated by the teacher. Students generally perceive relatively little opportunity to make decisions about what or how they learn, or about the amount of time they spend on projects. Although teachers perceive more student options than do students, it is clear from the perceptions of both that teachers are in control of the classrooms. The extent to which this aspect of schooling contributes to the goals which teachers and students say are being attained in Chapter Seven must be questioned. Some adult control over children and adolescents is unquestionably necessary, but unless students have some opportunity to make decisions for themselves, they will not be helped in learning how to study, nor are they likely to become independent and self-reliant. Some balance between student choices and adult control must be present if classroom practices are going to foster the wide array of goals to which schools are expected to contribute.

Time in school is not wasted, according to the perceptions of the majority of students and teachers. To students, what is being done in class is organized. Students believe they are engaged in productive activities, although the activities are not always of interest to a significant minority. Most students understand what the teacher expects of them, work is organized, and most have adequate time in class to finish assignments. Most students have approximately thirty minutes to an hour or more of homework per day. Much of the students' time is spent in listening to the teacher. Teachers believe that most of the time is spent on academic activities. Perceptions of the students and teachers in the Good Schools Project seem to agree with some of the consistent findings about effective schools: the academics are emphasized, time is spent on learning, and expectations are made clear.

Teachers perceive they have appropriate materials and adequate supplies to assist them in their teaching, although about half of the students do not think that much variety is used in their classrooms. The text is seen by both students and teachers to be an important source of learning and frequently used. The importance of the text is highlighted by the recommendation for improving texts from the National Commission on Excellence in Education.[15] Clearly, if texts are to be so basic to the learning process, they must be of the highest quality possible. Whether they should be so important is a question which ought to receive careful attention, however.

Most teachers use teacher-made tests to make instructional decisions, and some teachers use standardized tests this way. Further, the tests given usually are felt to represent accurately the goals and objectives of the school.

Most students think that their teachers evaluate students fairly, regardless of whether the teacher likes them. Most students also believe they are doing well in school. The majority of students do not see school as a place where they are experiencing failure or even doing marginal work. It is apparent, however, that higher percentages of middle and secondary students rather than elementary students say they are making C's, D's, or F's.

Teachers believe they individualize instruction much of the time at the elementary level, but less so at the middle and secondary school levels. At the same time, many elementary students think that everybody usually works at the same things in class. It is possible that students do study the same topics, but teachers provide some degree of individualization in the ways the topics are taught: different materials and texts, different amounts of time, or different teaching strategies. Teachers also believe that they encourage cooperative learning, but students are not so clear about this.

Finally, most students think that what they are expected to learn is clear, that their assignments are not too hard for them, and that teachers usually try to explain things to students in meaningful terms.

The Good Schools Project sample appears to be characterized by productive and informed classroom practices. Learning is expected, organized for, and attained by the large majority of students according to the perceptions of teachers and students. This generally seems to be true for all levels of schooling. Yet there is often—too often—a disturbing trend evident in the data. For many of the classroom practices, which most educators would consider to be positive conditions for schools, there is a diminishing number of teachers and students who perceive these positive conditions as existing as the level of schooling increases.

What is it about the middle school and the secondary school that causes more and more students and teachers to perceive that good classroom practices occur less often at those levels of schooling? Perhaps it is the changing characteristics of students or changes in the societal expectations and pressures for schooling at these levels. Perhaps it is due to some factors more directly related to classroom practices: teachers' expectations of students, the ways in which time is organized, different patterns of grouping students for learning, patterns of interaction between students and teachers, or the types of activities and materials used to promote learning. The extent to which these possible factors contribute to this trend can be identified and then they should be studied and corrected. It should not be an acceptable fact that more and more students and teachers report good classroom practices less often as the level of schooling increases.

It is clear that the Good Schools Project sample reflects much of what is generally considered good classroom practices, as seen by both students and teachers. In most cases, the largest majority see such conditions occurring frequently in their classrooms. Yet it is also clear that, even within this sample of carefully identified good schools, there is room for improvement. The schools could become even better.

Such change will not occur easily; it will require continuous study, effort, and resources. All participants in the educative process must examine critically and study what they are doing in and for the school classrooms and why. Without such critical examination, change for the betterment of schools will not occur. This suggests a very fundamental characteristic of good schools: a continuous appraisal of their programs. This will assist all schools—even good schools—to become better in their efforts to provide the best possible education to all their students.

Notes

1. John I. Goodlad, M. Frances Klein, and Kenneth A. Tye, "The Domains of Curriculum and Their Study," in *Curriculum Inquiry: The Study of Curriculum Practice* (New York: McGraw-Hill, 1979), Chapter 2.
2. Kenneth A. Sirotnik, *What You See Is What You Get: A Summary of Observations in Over 1000 Elementary and Secondary Classrooms* (Los Angeles: Technical Report No. 29, Graduate School of Education, Laboratory in School and Community Education, University of California at Los Angeles, 1981).
3. Joyce Wright, *Teaching and Learning* (Los Angeles: Technical Report No. 18, Graduate School of Education, Laboratory in School and Community Education, University of California at Los Angeles, 1980).
4. Carolyn Denham and Ann Lieberman, eds., *Time to Learn* (Washington, D.C.: National Institute of Education, 1980).
5. Wright, *Teaching*.
6. M. Frances Klein, Kenneth A. Tye, and Joyce Wright, "A Study of Schooling: Curriculum," *Phi Delta Kappan* 61 (December 1979):224-47.
7. David P. Gardner et al., *A Nation At Risk* (Washington D.C.: U.S. Department of Education, 1983).
8. Klein, Tye, and Wright, "Study of Schooling."
9. O.L. Davis, Jr., Jack R. Frymier, and David Clinefelter, "Curriculum Materials Used by Eleven-Year-Old Pupils: An Analysis Using the Annehurst Curriculum Classification System," *Journal of Educational Research* 75 (July/August 1982):325-32.
10. M. Frances Klein, *Teacher Perceived Sources of Influence On What Is Taught in Subject Areas* (Los Angeles: Technical Report No. 15, Laboratory in School and Community Education, University of California at Los Angeles, 1980).
11. Sirotnik, *What You See*.
12. M. Frances Klein, *State and District Curriculum Guides: One Aspect of the Formal Curriculum* (Los Angeles: Technical Report No. 9, Laboratory in School and Community Education, University of California at Los Angeles, 1980).
13. Klein, Tye, and Wright, "Study of Schooling."
14. Wright, *Teaching*.
15. Gardner et al., *Nation at Risk*.

9

Interpersonal Relations

When teachers choose to pay attention to interpersonal relations in their schools, they acknowledge that their work is much like farming. In schools, teachers work not within a vacuum, but within a rich, organic environment. In fact, as Stephens has suggested,

> . . . if we must use a metaphor or model in seeking to understand the process of schooling, we should look to agriculture rather than to the factory. In agriculture, we do not start from scratch, and we do not direct our efforts to inert and passive materials. We start, on the contrary, with a complex and ancient process, and we organize our efforts around what seeds, plants, and insects are likely to do anyway.[1]

Within a school, just as within any other social environment, people interact with one another. Students and teachers influence and respond to one another constantly. They perceive, evaluate, and understand one another, and they repeatedly adjust their modes of relating to one another.[2] Paying attention to what happens when people get together allows educators to channel their efforts in ways that are supported by naturally-occurring interpersonal dynamics. At the same time, this enables educators to grab hold of some of those dynamics and to use them effectively to support the kind of behavior they intend for school inhabitants.

Humanistic educators would add another consideration to a rationale for attending to interpersonal relations within a school: understanding how people interact with and influence one another can enable those within a school to create an environment for teaching and learning that is satisfying and meaningful for students or for school personnel. Whether the argument is based on concern with means or ends, the conclusion points to the importance of understanding the nature of interpersonal relations in a school.

The importance and pervasiveness of the issue is reflected in the number of questions in this area asked of students and teachers through the Good Schools Project. Fifty survey items and two interview questions dealt with the dimension of interpersonal relations. The responses given to these are reported in this chapter and in Appendix G.

Conceptual Background

The significance of the responses to these questions can be seen against a backdrop of several fundamental concepts that are threaded through these questions and answers. The concepts include the notion of the school as a social system and the effect of the organizational character, interpersonal influence, affective issues, and the special interpersonal relations problems of secondary schools.

The School Itself

The school is the social arena where students interact with one another as well as with teachers. In the school, students learn behaviors both intended and unintended, cognitive and affective. The patterns of interaction are shaped by the goals teachers and administrators bring with them, as well as by the goals students bring. Their ways of acting and interacting to achieve these goals establish patterns of relating, in some ways common and in some ways unique to each school. Woven through their interactive relationships are attitudes, perceptions, beliefs, motivations, and expectations held not only in reference to others within the environment, but also in reference to themselves.[3]

Within this structure all behaving is done, whether it is the instructional behavior of teachers or the learning behavior of students. By interacting with one another, students and teachers learn what they can expect from one another, and they learn to behave in ways considered appropriate for that setting. People behave differently in different social settings; school inhabitants act differently in schools with different patterns and qualities of relationships.

> The organizational life of the school can com-
> municate powerful and different messages to the
> participants. . . . The school as an institution em-
> bodies a cultural identity with a vibrant life of its
> own. It presents a mini-culture of values, cognitive
> maps, and feelings. . . . It shapes values, attitudes,
> and even personality structures. It influences hopes
> and aspirations; it can cause alienation and self-
> rejection.[4]

The attempt to define the factors that promote an environment conducive to effective behavior in schools has led to the
generation of a variety of school "climate" instruments. These
vary widely in the factors seen as essential. Fox *et al.* use as indicators of a positive school climate the levels of trust, caring,
cohesiveness, respect, high morale, opportunities for input,
school renewal, and continuous academic and social growth.[5]
Halpin and Croft name as factors staffs who have high esprit, high
intimacy, high engagement, and low hinderance; and principals
who show consideration and trust, who promote high production,
and who are low on aloofness.[6] Miles delineates as factors goal
focus, communicative adequacy, power based on competence,
resource utilization, cohesiveness, morale, autonomy, adapta-
tion, and general problem-solving adequacy.[7] Whatever the factors identified, however, the instruments are based on the
assumption that the school environment has a powerful impact
on the behavior of those within it, and the instruments are
designed to underscore the importance of the affective states of
school inhabitants.

Interpersonal Effects

For some time, the concept of the self-fulfilling prophecy
has been popular in the literature of social psychology. Research
has tended to show that expectations influence how the person
holding the expectations interacts with others, as well as how he
or she interprets the action of others.[8] In the late sixties, the con-
troversial *Pygmalion in the Classroom* stimulated debate within

education regarding the question of whether teachers' expectations could function as self-fulfilling prophecies to influence students' outcomes.[9]

In succeeding studies, the importance of the distinction between induced and naturalistic teachers' expectations was recognized.[10] Studies of naturalistic expectations—those that teachers form themselves through interacting with students, examining records, or knowing brothers and sisters—have repeatedly found that teachers do treat students differently, depending upon the expectations the teachers have formed of the students; and that teachers communicate their expectations to students through both obvious and subtle behaviors.[11]

The expectancies communicated are interpreted by students within their own motive structures. Students tend to work diligently in relation to academic learning when they are achievement oriented and perceive that their teachers expect them to do well and will reward them for showing competence. Students who have little achievement motivation and little support or incentive from teachers tend to do minimal work.[12]

At least partly because of differing levels of expectancy, different schools serving very similar student populations can have widely differing achievement outcomes.[13] Some research suggests that teachers and administrators who believe that their attitudes and related behaviors toward students can be conducive to higher achievement are likely to produce higher mean achievement in their schools.[14]

Influence is a dimension of the other sets of relationships existing in the school as well. Teachers report that they are most satisfied with life in school when they feel able to influence the principal's decisions.[15] This satisfaction then carries over into their relationships with students, to whom they are able to provide additional emotional support.[16] The leadership behavior of principals can significantly affect not only school climate and morale, but even student learning.[17] The dynamic pattern of interacting and influencing embraces all the school inhabitants.

Affective Issues

The social system of the school is dense with affective qualities. The sets of relationships among persons and groups within the school are characterized by the feelings they generate, e.g., students and teachers typically feel they are liked by other school inhabitants or they feel they are not.

How these persons feel about how others relate to them affects their behavior within the school environment. Tyler has pointed to the repeated research finding which shows that

> . . . children give more attention to school work, and direct their efforts more continuously when they feel they are respected by the teacher and other children. When they feel rejected, their attention and efforts are more scattered.[18]

Students with more positive academic self-esteem tend to be less disruptive, more persistent, and more involved in learning than those whose academic self-esteem is less positive.[19] Affective characteristics with higher intensity "tend to impell a person to seek out things . . . or to influence a person to behave in a certain way. . . ."[20] That stronger intensity can be either positive or negative.

It is often apparent to teachers that students' affective characteristics are important in the school environment because of their effect on individual learning behavior and because of the influence students exert on one another. Yet how teachers themselves feel about being in school—how they feel they are related to, how they feel about the others with whom they have interactive relationships—is no less important.

The typical ways teachers feel about themselves and others in the school setting are expressed through both subtle and overt behaviors. Their enthusiasm for teaching, for example, affects their students' attitudes toward learning.[21] The beliefs of teachers in their own effectiveness as teachers is directly related to their ability to elicit high achievement in their students.[22]

Secondary Schools ·

Interpersonal relations are necessarily different in secondary schools than they are in elementary schools, simply because the schools themselves are structured differently. Both size and complexity present special problems, as does the developmental stage of students.[23]

High school buildings are usually larger than elementary

school buildings. Student and teacher populations are generally larger, too. Instead of participating in most classes with the same group of peers, students change groups often during the day. High school classes are "loosely coupled" compared to elementary school classes.[24] Students in large schools have fewer opportunities to interact informally with teachers and proportionately fewer opportunities to hold positions of importance and responsibility.[25] The intimacy of a small school is difficult to achieve on this larger scale.

With the increased size of the school, the roles that regular staff members take on are more specialized. In addition to teachers, students, and principal, in the high school there are assistant principals, coaches, counselors, and department chairpersons. This division of labor promotes more individualized approaches to the school. Staff people in these various roles learn to look upon the school from the perspective of accomplishing their own particular task.[26] The purposes of the school become fragmented, at least compared to those of a typical, smaller elementary school.[27] Achieving shared understanding and commitment to unified goals is therefore more difficult.

At the same time, communicating with people in all these various roles takes the time of teachers as well as of students—time that in a smaller elementary school might be spent talking with one another. Working through channels is more complicated than face-to-face communication; distortions of communication are difficult to avoid.[28] Dealing with all this complexity presents a continuing pressure for students and teachers.

In addition to the increased structural complexity of the high school, the intricacies of adolescent development impinge upon the ways students and adults relate to one another. The fundamental developmental issues of conformity and rebellion are worked out in the social context of the school. Teachers' abilities to influence students lessen as peer relations become the dominant influence.[29] Students' attitudes toward academic outcomes become increasingly important, demanding that even more attention be given to peer norms by school personnel concerned with supporting achievement.[30]

Interpersonal Relations in the Good Schools

Because so many aspects of schooling are affected by the state of interpersonal relations, the Good Schools Project was designed to probe the nature of interpersonal relations in the schools that had been identified as good through the work of Kappa Delta Pi chapters. To facilitate interpretation, responses to the fifty survey and two interview questions dealing with interpersonal relations are grouped here into the following sets: those relevant to issues of task support, personal support, inclusion, and respect.

Task Support

Both teachers and students were asked to respond to statements regarding cooperation and support in their school work. Teachers' responses revealed teachers' perceptions and evaluations of their relationships with their peers. Students' responses, by contrast, included references to their peers but focused on their relationships with teachers.

Teachers' Responses: At least 80 percent of all teachers at all levels—elementary through secondary—responded positively (i.e., either "always" or "often") to the majority of items asking about support they received in their work (see Appendix G, Table 1). Those items asked teachers about the presence of someone in the school upon whom they could count for help, the prevalence of cooperative effort among staff members, and help from other teachers and the principal.

Somewhat less positive responses appeared in relation to the two other items in this set. In reference to a statement about how often teachers' accomplishments were recognized and rewarded, only about 70 percent of the middle and secondary level teachers (although 82 percent of the elementary level teachers) responded "always" or "often"; however, nearly half at every level responded "often." In reference to the statement, "Other teachers in this school seek my assistance when they have teaching problems," slightly fewer than half the secondary and slightly more than half the elementary and middle level teachers responded "often."

When teachers in twenty-seven schools were interviewed by Kappa Delta Pi chapter members and asked generally about the state of interpersonal relations, seven sets of teachers made statements specifically about helping and being helped, e.g., "people go out of their way to help one another" or "the principal gives us ideas, helps, listens." Four referred to "work," emphasizing teachers worked well together. Teachers' expectations of students were not mentioned.

Students' Responses: At least 83 percent of students at all levels said that teachers "seldom" or "never" ignored students who were not smart or got angry when students gave wrong answers (see Appendix G, Table 2). At least 70 percent indicated that students "always" or "often" helped one another. Students' perceptions about how often accomplishments were recognized and rewarded resembled those of their teachers: while nearly half said "often," no less than 70 percent said "always or "often." The young children surveyed gave an emphatic "no" response (92 percent) to a statement that the teacher made fun of students when they were wrong (see Appendix G, Table 3).

When students were interviewed about interpersonal relations in their schools, nearly half responded in terms of the expectations teachers had of them, although the teachers themselves had not even mentioned these. Some form of the word "expect" appeared nineteen times among the twenty-seven student interview summaries, and it most often was linked to the word "work," as in "teachers expect us to work hard."

The term "work" occurred even more often than the word "expect" in student interview responses; the term "work" appeared in more than half the reports. When work was not explicitly linked to expectations, students and teachers were said to still work hard, and teachers were said to make students work hard. In seven schools, students talked about teachers' willingness to help, with statements like "teachers are encouraging and helpful," or "teachers don't embarrass students when they need help."

Personal Support

Both teachers and students were asked to respond to a number of items having to do with how school inhabitants cared for, trusted, or affirmed one another as persons. Some questions explored their perceptions of others and some their feelings about the support they themselves experienced.

Teachers' Responses: The great majority of teachers (at least

84 percent at every level) affirmed that teachers "always" or "often" trusted the principal and other teachers, that the principal was concerned about the personal welfare of teachers, that the work of students and awards were prominently displayed, and that "seldom" or "never" did teachers act as if things were more important than people. Nearly as many (at least 79 percent at every level) said that "seldom" or "never" was there an "every person for himself" attitude in their schools.

On the two items having to do with the principal, as well as the two (overlapping) items having to do with trust, elementary level teachers furnished more positive responses than did either middle or secondary level teachers, although all responses were relatively high. No more than 8 percent of the teachers at any level said that teachers "seldom" or "never" trusted each other, and no more than 16 percent said that teachers "seldom" or "never" trusted the principal, or that the principal "seldom" or "never" was concerned about the welfare of teachers. Yet elementary teachers most often responded with "always" (see Table 1).

Table 1

A Summary of Teachers' Always Responses to Selected Items Concerning Other Teachers and the Principal

Survey Item (Item Number)	School Level		
	Elementary %	Middle %	Secondary %
The principal is concerned about the personal welfare of teachers. (89)	64	53	42
Teachers trust the principal. (71)	61	50	37
Teachers trust each other. (12)	44	33	25

When teachers were interviewed about interpersonal relations in their schools, in one-third of the schools teachers more often than the students generalized about the state of relations, using terms such as "open," "positive," "friendly," or "very good." Teachers also spoke more often than did the students about relationships between the various groups in their schools, referring most often—in nearly half of the schools—to their own positive relationships with the principal. In ten of the twenty-seven schools, teachers talked about positive relations between themselves and the students. In seven schools, it was the student–student relationship that was mentioned, in five schools, the student–principal relationship, and in only five schools, the teacher–teacher relationship.

Teachers spoke much less than did the students in terms of groups liking or caring about each other. Each term was mentioned in only one report: "teachers like the principal, students like the teachers, and students like each other" and "the staff is close-knit; they care about each other."

Students' Responses: Students at every level said that "my friends" were the best thing about their schools, with the most emphatic responses coming from middle level (65 percent) and secondary level (63 percent) students. Elementary students were somewhat more divided between "my friends" (55 percent) and "the teachers" (23 percent).

Students did admit that teachers "seldom" or "never" acted as if things were more important than people (at least 71 percent at every level), although students were predictably somewhat less positive than their teachers in response to the same question. Students also appeared to rank teachers' considerations of other teachers high; no more than 8 percent stated that teachers "seldom" or "never" were considerate of each other.

Responses across school levels were unusually uniform in relation to the friendliness of students, with at least 81 percent perceiving that students "always" or "often" were friendly.

The importance of interpersonal relations was reflected in the *Young Children's Survey* by the number of questions asked of young children about their perceptions of relationships. Of all the questions in this area, the young children responded most favorably to a statement about the principal liking the children in their schools: a resounding 98 percent said "yes." They were also positive (90 percent) about the principal trusting students.

The young children affirmed that they liked their teachers (95 percent), and that their teachers really liked young children (94 percent) and trusted students (90 percent).

The young children seemed slightly less convinced about the quality of student–student relationships. Although the young children felt good about themselves (93 percent responding "yes"), fewer seemed certain that they were liked by the other kids in the school (82 percent), or that students were nice to each other (75 percent). Nearly half (45 percent) perceived that students picked on each other a lot.

During the interview process, students in the schools which

were studied in depth commented about being liked by their teachers more often than any other subject. In reports of students' comments, from the twenty-seven schools where interviews were conducted, mention was made thirty-five times of students either being liked by or cared for by teachers.

Students in fifteen schools were reported as describing interpersonal relations in terms of liking or being liked by teachers, using phrases such as "our teachers like us," or a slightly more qualified, "in general . . . the teachers like the students." In only one school was mention made of reciprocity: "we like one another"; and in only one school did students speak of their own active liking of the teachers. Only twice among the twenty-seven schools were statements of disliking noted: "one teacher doesn't like seventh graders," and "students don't like teachers when they yell."

In one-third of the schools, relations between teachers and students were characterized in terms of "caring," either in addition to or instead of in terms of "liking." Students made statements such as "teachers really care about students," "we know they care," or "students thought teachers genuinely cared about them and their feelings."

In only four schools did neither "like" nor "care" appear; in all but one school, however, other positive comments were made about the teacher–student relationship, e.g., "teachers appreciate the students" or "teachers enjoy being with the students." In the one school that stood as an exception, students were reported as saying that "some teachers have their favorites."

Some form of the word "friend" was used by students interviewed in seven of the schools, i.e., teachers were thought to be friends or their relationships were characterized as friendship, except in one of these where teachers were thought to prefer being teachers to being friends.

Inclusion

Whether teachers and students perceived that they and others were part of the whole—whether they felt like they belonged—was the thread drawing together items in this section. Issues addressed included those of knowing others and being known by them, feeling welcome and acting to make others feel included, and experiencing community rather than exclusion, e.g., because of status concerns.

Teachers' Responses: Some of the most positive responses forthcoming from teachers at every level were given in relation to items that concerned inclusion. According to at least 90 percent of the teachers at every school level, new teachers "always" or "often" were made to feel welcome and part of the group, and teachers from one area or grade level respected those from other areas or grade levels. Teachers emphasized their perceptions that teachers were responsive to the needs of parents, at least 97 percent responded "always" or "often." They also consistently affirmed (at least 92 percent at every level) that the principal accurately represented the needs and interests of the staff and students when acting as a spokesperson for the school.

Of all items in this section, teachers were least affirming of the existence of a positive "sense of community" among students, teachers, and administrators. While 92 percent of the elementary teachers did answer "always" or "often" in response to that item, only 80 percent of the middle level teachers and 77 percent of the secondary level teachers responded in such positive terms.

In the twenty-seven schools where interviews were conducted, teachers often spoke of activities that served to promote inclusion, especially that of "socializing." In more than half the schools, teachers volunteered comments about social affairs, get-togethers, and parties after projects were completed or at Christmas. Teachers spoke in five schools of the importance of what happened outside school in determining the quality of interpersonal relations, e.g., of empathy extended outside school or of the willingness to help in times of personal crisis.

The descriptors "close," "cohesive," "harmonious," "comfortable," "family," or "bond" were used by teachers in ten schools, usually in reference to the staff or "the group." In only one school, however, was a direct reference made to the playful relationship commonly associated with community: "teachers share coffee and they laugh. . . . they have a teasing and playful relationship."

Few comments were made about cliques, outcasts, or ingroups. In the three schools where these comments appeared, they were in the negative, e.g., "no outcasts," and "not many ingroups." In three other schools, teachers made a point of telling about their processes of inclusion, e.g., "big sister/little sister program," "buddy system orientation for new teachers," and "newcomers learn to adjust rapidly with the help of other students."

The principal's role in relation to the group as a whole was mentioned by teachers in only one school: "the principal is our common bond." Only one teacher noted an anti-community orientation (a "me-first attitude"), but not once did the term "community" explicitly appear in the teachers' responses.

Students' Responses: Students tended to be more dispersed in their responses than were their teachers in relation to issues of inclusion. While nearly a quarter of the students at every level felt that it "always" or "often" was hard to get to know students, only half as many said that they "seldom" or "never" knew most of the other students in their grades.

Students seemed to think that teachers, by comparison, were easier—or at least no harder—to get to know than other students. Elementary level students were most emphatic in their beliefs that it "never" was hard to get to know teachers (54 percent), while middle and secondary level students were less positive (42 percent and 32 percent respectively).

Fewer than 20 percent at any level thought teachers "always" showed favoritism, although elementary and middle level students seemed slightly more convinced about responding "seldom" or "never" (56 percent and 53 percent respectively) than were the secondary level students (47 percent). Fully half of the elementary level (51 percent) and approximately two-thirds of the middle level (64 percent) and secondary level students (68 percent) felt that teachers acted as if they "always" were right. Despite this, students seemed satisfied in general with the way they were treated by teachers and other adults, at least 80 percent at every level responding "always" or "often."

When students were interviewed by Kappa Delta Pi chapter members, relatively few of these same concerns surfaced. "Favorite" or "pet" was mentioned in only four reports. In two of these schools, students pointed out that favoritism existed; in two, they pointed out that it did not.

Six comments were made by students (but in only four of the schools) regarding a playful relationship, using the words "joke," "laugh," "fun," or "kid around," as in "teachers tell jokes and laugh and join in the singing" or "teachers kid around with us." In three schools, the words "any" or "everyone" appeared, underscoring concern with issues of inclusion: "teachers work with everyone," "they treat everyone the same," and "they do not discriminate against any individual or group of students."

Respect

This final set of survey and interview responses concerned the issue of respect. The two relationships of respect probed were those between teachers and students and between students and students.

Teachers' Responses: Teachers at all levels (at least 96 percent) agreed that teachers "always" or "often" cared about what students thought. At least 93 percent of the teachers at all levels felt that teachers and students "always" or "often" were considerate of one another.

When asked how often students insulted teachers, most teachers at every level responded "seldom." Responses to this item illustrated a common pattern, however, with elementary level teachers responding most positively and secondary level teachers responding least positively (see Table 2).

Table 2

A Summary of Teachers' Responses at Various School Levels

Survey Item (Item Number)	School Level		
	Elementary %	Middle %	Secondary %
Students insult teachers. (54)			
Always/Often	8	14	15
Seldom	61	71	72
Never	31	15	13

When teachers were interviewed about interpersonal relations, they often (in one-third of the schools) used the term "respect," but the target of respect named was most often the principal: "the principal is respected," "the administration is respected," or "the students respect the principal." In only two schools did teachers volunteer comments on the respect teachers had for one another: "teachers respect one another as professionals and individuals," and "teachers get along well and have respect for one another."

Teachers did not speak directly in terms of respect in reference to the relationships between students and teachers nor between students and students, although one teacher did state that there was "mutual respect between students, teachers, and the principal." In one general statement about respect ("principal and staff are helpful and respected"), the giver of respect was obscure; in another (students have "tolerance and respect for others"), the target of the respect given was unclear.

Students' Responses: Students' perceptions differed most strikingly from those of their teachers in reference to the issue of how often teachers cared about what students thought. While 96 percent of the teachers at all levels agreed that they "always" or "often" did, only 86 percent of the elementary, 80 percent of the middle, and 76 percent of the secondary level students thought teachers cared about what students thought.

Students did admit in large numbers (at least 80 percent at every level) that students "always" or "often" were treated fairly. At least 79 percent of students at every level also admitted that students "seldom" or "never" were treated better if they were wealthy or their parents were important.

Their responses to the question of how often students respected teachers illustrated a common pattern running through students' responses, parallel to that appearing in responses of their teachers, i.e., that elementary students were typically most positive and secondary students were typically least positive (see Table 3).

Table 3

A Summary of Students' Responses at Various School Levels

Survey Item (Item Number)	School Level		
	Elementary %	Middle %	Secondary %
Students respect teachers. (26)			
Always	37	18	13
Often	46	53	59
Seldom/Never	17	29	28

At least two-thirds of the students at every level said they believed that students "always" or "often" respected the rights of other students, and at least three-quarters said that students were similarly considerate of one another.

When students were interviewed, they volunteered relatively

few comments implying concern with the issue of respect. In only three reports was the word "respect" explicitly used: twice, elementary students said "teachers respect us"; once, secondary students commented about "mutual respect between students and teachers."

Students made comments that seemed to imply concern with the issue of respect, but these occurred in only six schools: "teachers treat us like people," "teachers think of us as pretty mature; they don't make us feel dumb," "teachers really believe we're good kids," "teachers feel proud of the students," and "they don't look down on us."

Conclusions

The data gathered through the Good Schools Project underscore the significance for educators of several issues.

Teacher–Student Relations

Students act on their perceptions of what teachers think of them, and this is important in how they regard themselves. The feedback students receive about who they are (e.g., "the teachers think we're good kids") contributes significantly to their own self-definition and therefore to their sense of their own ability.[31]

When teachers are respected, students are vulnerable to feeling that teachers might not care what students think. Teachers who may honestly believe they care may be sending a different message to their students. Inside the "multiple realities" of any school—even a good one—some students may be receiving enthusiastically the message that they are liked and cared for, while others are not so sure.[32]

According to Brookover and Erickson

> . . . a considerable proportion of what a student learns is dependent on his decisions to learn. These decisions are dependent on his conceptions of what is appropriate for self and what he thinks he is able to learn. In turn, the student's conceptions of self are acquired in interaction with others in his social system.[33]

If students are forming their perceptions of themselves—including their academic self-concept—through their interactions with important others in the school,[34] then it is crucial
for the learning behavior of students that teachers send positive
messages.

Student–Student Relations

The teacher–student relationship is not the only important
relationship to pay attention to within the school social system,
even for educators who focus primarily on student learning.
Teaching and learning in school do not take place in a dyadic
relationship between teacher and student. Even though teachers
have been trained to teach individuals, they rarely teach them
one at a time. Teachers teach individuals in groups. Learning in
school is not only a psychological but a social event.[35]

The influences from student–student relationships may have
more powerful effects on achievement, socialization, and
development than any other factor, and yet the power of peer interaction is often ignored.[36] If this factor is ignored, its potential
use as a tool to support intended student behaviors is lost to
teachers.

Generally, students in the schools surveyed indicate that
relations among students are good, even if getting to know one
another is not always easy. The young children seem concerned
about how nice students are to one another and worry about kids
picking on one another. These responses, while not strongly
negative, stand out in contrast to the extremely positive
responses in relation to other survey items and interview questions.

Positive relations among students do not happen
automatically, even in good schools. Teachers can, however, influence group dynamics to build relationships of liking, acceptance, and support through means such as creation of opportunities for students to help one another, promotion of interaction among various groups of students, the sparing use of competitive and individualistic learning strategies, and the constructive management of controversies.[37]

Teacher–Teacher Relations

Even in schools regarded by community members as good—where both teacher and student assessment of interpersonal relations appears very positive—teachers seem not to be consulting one another very often about the work of teaching. Approximately half the teachers surveyed indicate that they "seldom" or "never" are asked for assistance with teaching problems. While this statistic implies conversely that the other half perceive they "often" or "always" are consulted, the proportion of those responding in positive terms (i.e., "always" or "often") is strikingly lower than in relation to other items.

The traditional norm of professional autonomy works against teachers asking one another for help in teaching. Yet "the curriculum of a classroom and the constructive use of innovative strategies will suffer if teachers cannot stimulate one another with new ideas and practices."[38]

The persistence of this norm even within schools that seem to evidence high levels of trust and support in other areas suggests its potency. Those educators who discover such a norm existing within their own schools might raise for themselves the question of its effect on their work.

The Secondary School Context

The issues of interpersonal relations in secondary schools are different from those in elementary schools and, in some ways, from those in middle schools. A quick survey of the three tables of Appendix G shows that neither teachers nor students in secondary schools responded as positively to questions about interpersonal relations as did teachers and students in elementary schools.

To interpret this as a simple reflection of how much more difficult adolescents are to teach than young children is to ignore the impact of the school social structure in which both teachers and students are expected to function. The structure of the elementary school is not the same as the structure of the secondary school.

Secondary schools have liabilities that are apparent. At the same time, however, both the stage of development of their students and the typical organization of secondary schools present opportunities to educators interested in supporting intended behavior. Some of the options pursued by secondary schools in the Good Schools Project hint at how the distinctive strengths of adolescence can be directed toward improvement of the quality of life by creative educators sensitive to interpersonal dynamics, e.g., group participation in flood relief or help to families in crisis.

The interpersonal relations inside contemporary schools—elementary, middle, or secondary and public, private, or parochial—are tangled webs of problems and potential. Data in the Good Schools Project suggest that good schools might be distinguished less by the absence of problems than by the ability to make the most of possibilities and by working intentionally with the dynamics that will certainly occur whenever people are gathered together.

Notes

1. John M. Stephens, *The Process of Schooling* (New York: Holt, Rinehart and Winston, 1967), p. 9.
2. *A Dictionary of the Social Sciences,* 1964 ed., s.v. "Interpersonal Relations," by Edmund H. Volkart.
3. Richard A. Schmuck, "The School Organization" in *The Social Psychology of School Learning,* ed. James H. McMillan (New York: Academic Press, 1980), p. 174.
4. Lawrence W. Lezotte et al., *School Learning Climate and Student Achievement: A Social Systems Approach to Increased Student Learning,* Center for Urban Affairs, University of Michigan (Tallahassee, Fl.: Florida State University, 1980), p. 25.
5. Robert Fox et al., *School Climate Improvement: A Challenge to School Administrators* (Bloomington, In.: Phi Delta Kappa, 1974).
6. Andrew W. Halpin and Don B. Croft, *Organizational Climate of Schools* (Chicago: Midwest Administrative Center, University of Chicago, 1963).
7. Matthew Miles, "Planned Change and Organizational Health: Figure and Ground" in *Change Processes in the Public Schools,* ed. R.O. Carlson (Eugene, Or.: Center for Advanced Study of Educational Administration, 1965), pp. 11-36.
8. Thomas L. Good, "Classroom Expectations: Teacher–Pupil Interactions" in *The Social Psychology of School Learning,* ed. James H. McMillan (New York: Academic Press, 1980), p. 80.

9. Robert Rosenthal and Lenore Jacobson, *Pygmalion in the Classroom: Teacher Expectation and Pupils' Intellectual Development* (New York: Holt, Rinehart and Winston, 1968).
10. Jere E. Brophy and Thomas L. Good, "Teachers' Communication of Differential Expectations for Children's Classroom Performance: Some Behavioral Data," *Journal of Educational Psychology* 61 (October 1970): 365-74.
11. Robert Rosenthal, *On the Social Psychology of the Self-Fulfilling Prophecy: Further Evidence for the Pygmalion Effects and Their Mediating Mechanisms* (New York: MSS Modular Publications, 1974).
12. Schmuck, "The School Organization," p. 207.
13. Wilbur B. Brookover and Jeffrey M. Schneider, "Academic Environments and Elementary School Achievement," *Journal of Research and Development in Education* 9 (Fall 1975): 83-91.
14. Wilbur B. Brookover et al., *School Social Systems and Student Achievement: Schools Can Make a Difference* (New York: Praeger, 1979).
15. Harvey A. Hornstein et al., "Influence and Satisfaction in Organizations: A Replication," *Sociology of Education* 41 (Fall 1968): 380-89.
16. Schmuck, "The School Organization," p. 193.
17. Fox et al., *School Climate Improvement*; Neal Gross and Robert E. Herriot, *Staff Leadership in Public Schools* (New York: Wiley, 1976).
18. Ralph W. Tyler, "Assessing Educational Achievement in the Affective Domain," *Measurement in Education* 4 (March 1973): 1-8.
19. Lorin W. Anderson, "Student Involvement in Learning and School Achievement," *California Journal of Educational Research* 26 (March 1975): 53-62; Jacob S. Kounin, *Discipline and Group Management in Classrooms* (New York: Holt, Rinehart and Winston, 1970).
20. Lorin W. Anderson, *Assessing Affective Characteristics in the Schools* (Boston: Allyn & Bacon, 1981), p. 32.
21. Robert B. Phillips, Jr., "Teacher Attitudes as Related to Student Attitudes and Achievement in Elementary School Mathematics," *School Science and Mathematics* 73 (June 1973): 501-07.
22. Jere E. Brophy and Carolyn Evertson, *Learning From Teaching: A Developmental Perspective* (Boston: Allyn & Bacon, 1976).
23. Lezotte et al., *School Learning Climate*, p. 113.
24. Karl E. Weick, "Educational Organizations as Loosely Coupled Systems," *Administrative Science Quarterly* 21 (March 1976): 1-19; Schmuck, "The School Organization," p. 182.
25. Roger C. Barker and Paul V. Gump, *Big School, Small School: High School Size and Student Behavior* (Stanford, Ca.: Stanford University Press, 1964); Leonard L. Baird, "Big School, Small School: A Critical Examination of the Hypothesis," *Journal of Educational Psychology* 60 (August 1969): 253-60.
26. Lezotte et al., *School Learning Climate*, p. 113.
27. Ibid., p. 115.
28. Ibid., p. 114.
29. Good, "Classroom Expectations," p. 117.
30. Lezotte et al., *School Learning Climate*, p. 125.
31. James H. McMillan, "Social Psychology and Learning" in *The Social Psychology of School Learning*, ed. James H. McMillan (New York: Academic Press, 1980), p. 15.
32. Schmuck, "The School Organization," pp. 170-75.

33. Wilbur B. Brookover and Edsel L. Erickson, *Society, Schools and Learning* (Boston: Allyn & Bacon, 1969), p. 16.
34. Anderson, *Assessing Affective Characteristics,* p. 35.
35. Lezotte et al., *School Learning Climate,* p. 15.
36. David W. Johnson, "Group Processes: Influences of Student–Student Interaction on School Outcomes" in *The Social Psychology of School Learning,* ed. James H. McMillan (New York: Academic Press, 1980), p. 125.
37. Ibid., p. 157.
38. Schmuck, "The School Organization," p. 199.

10

Commitment

This chapter focuses on the commitment of staff, students, and parents in the sample of schools studied by the Good Schools Project. In the context of this discussion, the term "commitment" refers to attitudes and beliefs which result in (1) dedication to the school and its goals, and (2) behavior which is motivated by this dedication rather than by the likelihood of extrinsic reward or punishment. Commitment, therefore, can be inferred from behavior and behavior can be either nonverbal or verbal.

The Variable of Commitment

Historical Orientations

Researchers have not always thought of commitment as a significant variable to be examined when attempting to account for a school's success. This lack of interest by earlier researchers can be traced, in part, to the influence of behaviorism on the educational research community. Acknowledging the importance of a construct such as commitment in accounting for educational success is tantamount to endorsing discussions of subjective states in explaining social phenomena. Philosophers such as Carnap, of course, long ago argued that study of subjective states need not automatically be considered unscientific, since mental states can be inferred from observable behavior (including verbal behavior).[1] Many behaviorists, however, have continued to shun any talk of what goes on inside the black box of the human mind.

There is a second, possibly more important, reason why educational researchers have seldom studied commitment as a variable contributing to school success: in the past, educators tended to believe that education's salvation would ultimately be found in altering organizational structures and standard operating procedures, not in altering the subjective states of individuals. Tyack, for example, indicated that the goal of most progressive educators was to develop the "one best system."[2] Educational researchers were to provide a scientific basis for constructing this "one best system" by investigating the linkage between explicit teaching processes, on the one hand, and explicit student learning outcomes, on the other. Cubberley clearly defined the researcher's role in his 1909 publication, *Changing Conceptions of Education:*

> Every manufacturing establishment that turns out a standard product or series of products of any kind maintains a force of efficiency experts to study methods of procedure and to measure and test the output of its works. Such men ultimately bring the manufacturing establishment large returns by introducing improvement in processes and procedure and in training the workmen to produce a large and better output. Our schools are, in a sense, factories in which the raw products (children) are to be shaped and fashioned into products to meet the various demands of life.[3]

Recent Developments

The mechanistic metaphor Cubberley so obviously employs to conceptualize the teaching–learning process has continued to dominate the thinking of many educational researchers throughout this century.[4] It is not surprising, therefore, that researchers have tended to ignore the variable of commitment when studying schools. Recently, however, something akin to what philosophers of science would call a paradigm shift has occurred within the field of educational research.[5] Quite simply, many educational researchers have begun to rethink mechanistic views of education, as well as challenge behaviorists' beliefs that the subjective states of individuals are off-limits to the scientific researcher.

The origins of this paradigm shift and the consequent discovery of commitment as a significant variable in accounting for a school's success are diverse. One impetus to question a "one best system" orientation came from difficulties which emerged when a supposedly "best" system—i.e., a system which was effective in one educational setting—was implemented in other educational settings. Studies of such program implementation consistently showed that successful implementation required program modifications.[6] Anthropologist Spindler has indicated that such modifications should not be surprising, since

> . . . the first law of sociocultural systems—that all such systems (and a program of any kind is a sociocultural system) are adaptations to their environment. We should expect each program to show significant deviation from an initiating model, and from each of the other programs. The questions should not be, "Do they deviate?" or even "How do they deviate?" but rather, "Are they adapting well (functionally) to their respective environments?"[7]

Studies of program implementation have also suggested that commitment functions as an intervening variable linking site specific modifications, on the one hand, with program success, on the other. The ability to modify facets of a program, it is hypothesized, creates a sense of ownership of the program among program participants, and this sense of ownership generates the sort of dedication which motivates participants to behave in ways which will make the program successful.[8]

Researchers who have studied school program effectiveness have made similar discoveries. The evaluation of Project Follow Through, a planned variation study designed to determine which of several approaches to early childhood education is most effective, revealed that the same program had differential effects depending on the context in which it was implemented. A group of researchers commissioned by the Ford Foundation to analyze Project Follow Through data considered the finding concerning differential effects the most significant finding to emerge from the Project Follow Through evaluation. The researchers wrote:

> This finding should be honored widely and serve as a basis of educational policy. Local schools do

seem to make a difference. The peculiarities of in-dividual teachers, schools, neighborhoods, and homes influence pupils' achievement far more than whatever is captured by labels such as "basic skills" or "affective" education.[9]

Once researchers moved beyond labels and systems and began to liberate themselves from the influence of radical behaviorism, the variable of commitment was noticed. School ef-fectiveness studies which contrasted high achieving and low achieving schools, for example, almost invariably identified a school's positive attitudinal climate—what one researcher labeled a school's ethos—as a significant factor in accounting for a school's success.[10]

Commitment in the Good Schools

Given the apparent importance of the variable of commit-ment in creating a good school, it seemed important to assess the degree of commitment present in the schools which made up the Good Schools Project sample. The most efficient means of assessing the degree of commitment in these schools was to ex-amine responses to survey instrument items designed for this purpose. Responses to commitment-related items are summar-ized below. A more detailed presentation of all responses by teachers and students can be found in Appendix F.

Before proceeding, it is important to acknowledge a limita-tion. The assessment of commitment must be made in relative rather than absolute terms. The question is not whether commit-ment does or does not exist in a particular school; rather, the question is whether the level of commitment in a particular sam-ple of schools is significantly higher than the level of commit-ment in other schools. Because data for a sample of randomly selected comparison schools is not available, we can only speculate about the significance of the responses to the commitment-related survey items. Still, the responses to many items, especially those related to staff commitment, are quite dramatic (i.e., the level of commitment seems much higher than would ordinarily be expected), so many judgments about significance, although clearly based on speculation, seem sensi-ble and well-grounded.

Indices of Staff Commitment

The dramatic nature of the findings was most evident in responses to items designed to assess staff commitment. For example, in the Good Schools Project, 97 percent of the elementary level teachers, 94 percent of the middle level teachers, and 95 percent of the secondary level teachers responded "always" or "often" to the item, "Administrators, teachers, and other staff members are working hard to improve this school." Similarly, 99 percent of the elementary teachers, 96 percent of the middle school teachers, and 95 percent of the secondary teachers responded "always" or "often" to the item, "Teachers are proud to work at this school."

A caveat is in order here: staff commitment looked less impressive when items geared to specific behaviors were examined. For example, 41 percent of the elementary level teachers, 51 percent of the middle level teachers, and 45 percent of the secondary level teachers reported spending an average of one hour or less per day on paper grading and planning. Similarly, teachers reported little absence for professional reasons (e.g., 49 percent of the elementary level teachers, 46 percent of the middle level teachers, and 39 percent of the secondary level teachers reported no missed days for professional reasons during the previous year), but comparatively more absence for health and personal reasons (e.g., 20 percent of the elementary level teachers, 22 percent of the middle level teachers, and 12 percent of the secondary level teachers reported missing more than six school days during the previous academic year). Still, responses to most items designed to assess teachers' perceptions of staff commitment revealed relatively dramatic results. These responses are summarized in Table 1.

Students' judgments concerning staff commitment, while not as dramatic as responses on the *Teacher Survey,* still were consistent with the staff members' appraisals of themselves. Ninety-three percent of the elementary school students, 90 percent of the middle school students, and 88 percent of the secondary school students answered "always" or "often" to the item, "Teachers put a lot of time and effort into their work here." Similarly, 72 percent of the elementary school students and 65 percent of both the middle school and secondary school students responded "seldom" or "never" to the negatively oriented item, "Teachers leave the building as soon as possible when the school day ends."

Table 1

A Summary of Teachers Responding Always or Often to Items Concerning Staff Commitment

Survey Item (Item Number)	School Level		
	Elementary %	Middle %	Secondary %
Teachers are proud to work at this school. (31)	99	96	95
The morale of teachers is high. (43)	92	86	80
Teachers maintain high standards for themselves. (63)	98	98	95
Teachers are receptive to suggestions for program improvement. (40)	97	94	92
Teachers try new ideas to improve their teaching. (91)	98	94	93
Staff members are flexible; they are able to reconsider their positions on issues and change their minds. (145)	91	86	86
Teachers feel responsible for student learning. (92)	99	97	96
The staff is task oriented; jobs get completed and there is little wasted time. (119)	97	94	91
The principal encourages teachers to try out new ideas. (147)	93	86	86
I participate in professional development activities outside of the school. (122)	80	76	76
The principal shares new ideas with teachers. (78)	95	87	86
Administrators, teachers, and other staff members are working hard to improve this school. (59)	97	94	95
Rules and red tape in this school make it difficult to get things done. (69)	14	23	28

Table 1 (cont.)

A Summary of Teachers Responding Always or Often to Items Concerning Staff Commitment

Survey Item (Item Number)	School Level		
	Elementary %	Middle %	Secondary %
Teachers are not responsible for what happens at this school; too many factors are beyond their control. (105)	19	24	28
People in this school complain about things, but are reluctant to do anything about them. (158)	26	38	47
Teachers put in extra time and effort to improve this school. (70)	97	90	91
I plan to teach until retirement. (46)	80	73	74
Teachers support school policies and procedures. (137)	99	97	98
Our faculty meetings are worthwhile. (141)	90	81	77
Teachers spend time after school with students who have individual problems. (144)	55	58	82

Students' responses to items designed to assess whether teachers liked to work in their schools, whether teachers helped out with student activities, and whether teachers and administrators worked hard were consistent with the students' responses just discussed.

Possibly the most surprising aspect of data related to staff commitment was the similarity between different levels of schooling. To be sure, more diversity existed when the two positive responses, "always" and "often," were examined. For example, for the item, "Teachers feel responsible for student learning," 73 percent of the teachers in the elementary schools responded "always" and 26 percent responded "often"; 50 percent of the teachers in the middle schools responded "always" and 47 percent responded "often"; and only 38 percent of the teachers in the secondary schools responded "always" while 58 percent said "often."

These findings were balanced, however, by the fact that on a few items secondary teachers fared best, and middle school teachers fared better than elementary school teachers. For example, while only 6 percent of the elementary school teachers indicated they spent more than ten hours per day on school-related activities, 8 percent of the teachers in the middle schools and 12 percent of the teachers in the secondary schools reported expending more than ten hours of effort daily. Similarly, while 48 percent of the students in the elementary schools responded "seldom" or "never" to the item, "Teachers spend time after school with students who have individual problems," only 27 percent of the students in the secondary schools responded by choosing one of the two negative responses. The same pattern could be seen when examining responses to items concerning time spent on co-curricular activities and time spent helping students after school hours.

Some of the secondary teachers' responses on certain items might be attributable to item bias, of course. With respect to the item on after-school help, for example, it could be argued that elementary teachers who generally work with a smaller number of students in self-contained classrooms could more easily give individual help to students during the school day and, therefore, would not normally need to spend time after school with students who had individual problems. Still, the positive responses and, even more, the low percentage of negative responses to staff commitment-related items was surprising given recent reports by national commissions which portray American secondary schools in particular as being in a state of crisis.

Indices of Student Commitment

Indices of student and parent commitment were less dramatic and, at times, suggested greater disparity between elementary, middle, and secondary school levels. Responses, however, were still very positive at all three levels of schooling.

Responses to certain items designed to assess student commitment, in fact, were quite positive. For example, 86 percent of the students in the elementary schools indicated their schools were a good place in which to be. The percentages at the middle and secondary levels were 78 and 80 respectively. Responses were even more positive at each of the three levels when students were asked whether the work done in school was important to them. A similarly positive picture was provided when teachers were asked to assess students' school spirit. Even at the secondary level, 60 percent of the teachers responded "always" to the item, "Students have a lot of school spirit," while only 25 percent responded "seldom" or "never." Teachers and students also agreed that there was considerable student participation in co-curricular school activities. (As might be expected, participation was lowest at the elementary level.)

As might also be expected, young children were quite positive when responding to items on a special survey instrument administered to first and second graders designed to gauge student commitment. The vast majority of students responded affirmatively to the following items: "I like to come to school" (82 percent); "This is a good school" (96 percent); "The kids in this school really like the school" (86 percent); and "I am proud of this school" (93 percent).

Balancing the positive findings reviewed above were responses which suggested that student commitment in the sample schools might be a bit more modest. For example, 55 percent of the secondary level students, 47 percent of the middle level students, and 32 percent of the elementary level students admitted to watching the clock and counting the minutes until school ended. Also, approximately one-fifth of the students at all levels indicated they believed that luck contributed more than hard work to success in school.

Indices of Parent Commitment

Probably the most disparity between levels of schooling was apparent in teachers' responses to items designed to assess teachers' perceptions of parent commitment. It is important to note, of course, that the data suggested that parent commitment was high at all levels of schooling. While it was probably not surprising that 93 percent of the first and second graders in the sample responded affirmatively to the statement, "My parents think this is a great school," it is also worth noting that, even at the secondary level, 79 percent of teachers responded "always" or "often" to the item, "Parents encourage and support teachers' efforts." It is also worth noting, however, that while 47 percent of the elementary level teachers responded "always" to the item, "Parents support school activities," 25 percent of the middle level teachers and only 18 percent of the secondary level teachers responded in like manner. The same pattern was evident when responses to the item, "Parents support school rules," were examined (36 percent elementary, 23 percent middle, 15 percent secondary).

Disparities between levels of schooling were most dramatic when respondents were asked about specific activities which questionnaire developers believed could be considered indices of parental commitment. Table 2 summarizes these data.

It is interesting to speculate whether the activities described in most of the items included in Table 2 might be causes as well as indices of parental commitment. Certainly many theories (not to mention common sense) have suggested that active involvement in an organization's activities often leads to commitment to that organization and its goals. If this equation is correct, the absence of parents in middle and especially secondary schools may help explain the lower parental commitment and, more generally, the lower public regard these schools command. It is possible, of course, that item bias is once again a factor: while it seems perfectly appropriate for parents to serve as tutors for their elementary age children's peers, the tutor role may be inappropriate for parents during the socially sensitive adolescent school years. The key questions are: (1) Are the kinds of involvement described in Table 2 appropriate for all levels of schooling? (2) If not, are other avenues for meaningful involvement available to parents? (3) If not, can alternative avenues for parental involvement be developed?

Development of High Level Commitment

Ultimately, we were not simply interested in whether high levels of commitment existed among participants in good schools; we were also interested in the factors which *caused* these high levels of commitment to develop. Descriptive data, of course, cannot provide definitive answers to causal questions. Such data, however, can suggest possibilities. One possibility—the relationship between parental involvement in school activities and parental commitment—has already emerged

Table 2

A Summary of Teachers Responding Always or Often to Items Concerning Parent Involvement in Specific School Related Activities

Survey Item (Item Number)	School Level		
	Elementary %	Middle %	Secondary %
Parents serve as teacher aides in this school. (55)	56	37	9
Parents work in the school library. (72)	49	26	5
Parents come to school to discuss their children's problems. (85)	92	83	63
Parents tutor students at this school. (95)	44	20	5
Parents make sure their children do their homework. (146)	81	53	38

from an analysis of the survey data. In this section, the qualitative interview data were used to generate hypotheses about causal factors related to the development of commitment within a school. Four hypotheses emerged when the interview data were examined and when particular emergent variables were considered in terms of the frequency and intensity with which these variables were mentioned.

Positive Belief Systems

One thing that was apparent when the interview data were examined was that, in the vast majority of schools where interviews were conducted, those interviewed believed their schools were special, and the interviewees could readily articulate the characteristics which made their schools special. To be sure, these characteristics were often expressed in terms of the most glittering of generalities. One teacher, for example, when asked whether the school was a good school, responded in a way which was typical of many responses:

> Yes. It offers a challenge to students. It inspires. Students grow academically, spiritually, socially. The whole caring and cooperation and support of

administration [is important]. Teachers are encouraged to be creative. It's a joy to come here
every day.

Despite the level of generality (or possibly because of it), the
schools' positive belief systems often appeared to generate a
religious fervor within many schools. One principal even resorted
to religious imagery when responding to the interview question,
"How involved with their jobs are people in this school?" He
answered, "The people who work here have the same dedication
as a clergyperson. Their profession is children, and their personal
goals are based on children succeeding." Similarly, a secondary
school student at another school in the survey talked of his
school as one which "has a lifted spirit."

Sociologists have often indicated that negative beliefs can
become self-fulfilling prophesies.[11] If negative belief systems can
socially reconstruct reality to conform to a priori expectations, it
seems likely that positive attitudes and beliefs can do the same.

The Principal's Leadership

Simply indicating that commitment is high because people
connected with a school believe a school is good begs the causal
question, of course. At the very least, a follow-up question must
be asked: What caused this belief to come into existence?

Recent studies of effective schools almost invariably identified the principal's leadership as a significant factor in a
school's success, and there was some indication that a school's
attitudinal climate—what one researcher has labeled a school's
ethos and what has been referred to here as a positive belief
system—might be an important mediating variable between the
principal's actions and school success.[12] The interview data from
the Good Schools Project strongly supported the proposition that
the principal was a significant factor contributing to school success. The most frequently mentioned explanation for a school's
success, in fact, was the principal's leadership.

There was also some evidence to support the proposition
that the principal contributed to school success by motivating
staff, students, and community. The evidence was less
compelling here, however, possibly because the interview ques-

tions did not specifically probe for the source of the principal's impact.

One thing the data did speak to unequivocally was principal variation. Indeed, although interviewees in almost every school attested to the importance of the principal, the verbal picture sketched by interviewees differed greatly as one moved from one school to another. In one school, the principal appeared warm and supportive. In the next he or she might be more formal in dealings with staff. Sometimes the principal led by example and model. At other times, instructional leadership appeared more direct and directive.

Disparity in principals' leadership styles was possibly most apparent in the interview data from one school where the teachers talked about the present and former principals. Each principal was quite different, and each principal's contribution to the school was quite different. While the former principal was described as an instructional leader whose creative ideas continued to influence the school long after he left the principalship, the current principal was not instruction-oriented but was more concerned with guidance and discipline. Both principals, however, were credited with contributing greatly to the school's success.

Thus, the interview data tended to support the hypothesis that the principal's leadership was an important contributor to school success. The data also suggested principals' leadership styles and substance vary greatly. Whether the establishment of commitment always functions as an intervening variable between a principal's actions and a school's success remains an open question.

Team Relationships

The interview data also suggested that the feeling of being part of a team might contribute to the development of commitment among members of a school's staff. This variable, in fact, was second only to the principal's leadership in terms of the frequency with which it was mentioned by interviewed staff members.

As was the case with the principal's leadership variable, team relationships looked different from school to school. At times team relationships were formal and part of a school's organizational structure. In one school, for example, the emphasis was on a shared management system, a system which extended to staff committees hiring new staff members. More frequently, the sense of being a part of a team emerged informally and appeared to be rooted more in a school's informally established ambiance rather than in its formal organizational structure. In one middle school, for example, the teachers indicated that the principal made most of the decisions, but they also indicated that a sense of teamwork existed in the school nonetheless, because "teachers support [and] help each other" and because there is "little or no politics."

If team effort was as important as the Good Schools Project interview data suggested it was, it is interesting to speculate about the impact of policy proposals which would reward individual faculty members (e.g., merit pay). It is also interesting to question what implications the findings on teamwork have for in-service education programs and university-based degree programs, most of which are currently geared to developing the skills of individual staff members rather than to developing the staff as a collective.

Excellent Physical Facilities

Another factor mentioned frequently as contributing to a school's success was the school's physical plant. A neat and attractive physical plant seemed especially important to parents and students. (One group of interviewers marveled that virtually every student interviewed mentioned their school's cleanliness as a reason their school was good.) In some schools, the school's facilities were cited by all groups as a source of their schools' "goodness." At least in some schools, an especially good physical facility seemed to serve as a sort of monument which symbolized community interest and support. It is likely that the physical plant, when viewed in this way, will generate reciprocal interest and support (i.e., commitment) from students and staff.

In one sense the finding concerning the importance of a school's physical plant was surprising because empirical studies consistently have indicated that facilities have no impact on school achievement. Viewed from another perspective, however, the finding was not surprising at all. Businesses invest dearly in establishing facilities which project an image of success and inspire confidence. Such investments suggest a commonsense linkage between impressive physical facilities and accomplishment even though empirical research has failed to confirm that such a linkage exists. The canons of construct validity require that, when a major failure in prediction occurs, it is the criterion measure (in this case, standardized achievement test scores) and not commonsense wisdom which needs to be called into question.[13]

One caveat is in order here: while the data suggested that excellent facilities normally contributed to a school's success, the data also clearly indicated that the existence of excellent facilities was not a necessary condition for establishing a successful school. In one inner city school, for example, virtually everyone interviewed mentioned the school's dilapidated physical condition. The school's physical condition certainly created problems, especially in generating parent support. Many parents who were interviewed, for example, indicated that they initially did not want their children to attend the school because of the image the school's physical condition conveyed.

Many of the problems caused by a less than adequate physical plant, however, had been overcome by a resourceful principal and staff. Many of the parents who did not originally want their children to attend a particular school were now among the school's most enthusiastic supporters. Also, local businesses began to provide financial support for the school. Indeed, the very fact that the school was successful in spite of the less than adequate physical plant appeared to be a source of considerable pride among many members of the school community.

The Need for Further Study

Obviously the hypotheses discussed above, as well as other possible causal relationships, deserve further study. While totally new studies are needed (especially to determine the relationships between principal leadership, levels of commitment, and school success variously defined), there is still a considerable amount of information related to causal factors resulting in commitment to be mined from the Good Schools Project data. Correlational analysis of survey data, for example, can indicate whether teachers who feel they have a significant role in school decision making will exhibit greater evidence of commitment. Similarly, correlational analysis can provide evidence to enlighten discussion of the hypothesized linkage between parent involvement in school activities and parental levels of commitment.

The qualitative data can also be analyzed through correlational analysis. In this chapter, the qualitative data have been used as qualitative data have traditionally been used, i.e., they have been used to develop hypotheses. It is expected that subsequent analyses of these data will translate general linguistic description of frequency to numerical measures and that the interview data, like the survey data, will be used as evidence to help support or refute hypotheses that have been generated here and elsewhere concerning the causes of commitment within a school context.

Notes

1. R. Carnap, "Logical Foundations of the Unity of Sciences" in *The Nature and Scope of Social Science,* ed. L. Krimerman (New York: Appleton-Century-Crofts, 1969).

2. D. Tyack, *The One Best System* (Cambridge, Ma.: Harvard University Press, 1974).

3. E. Cubberley, *Changing Conceptions of Education* (Boston: Houghton-Mifflin, 1909), p. 338.

4. See, for example, E.L. Thorndike, "The Contribution of Psychology to Education," *The Journal of Educational Psychology* 1 (1910):5-12; T. Good, J. Biddle, and J. Brophy, *Teachers Make a Difference* (New York: Holt, Rinehart and Winston, 1975); N. Gage, *The Scientific Basis of the Art of Teaching* (New York: Teachers College Press, 1978).

5. See T. Kuhn, *The Structure of Scientific Revolutions* (Chicago: University of Chicago Press, 1962).

6. See, for example, D. Fetterman, "Anthropologists in New Environments: Functioning Within Three Conflicting World Views (Paper presented at the American Educational Research Association Annual Meeting, April 1981).

7. Spindler quoted in Fetterman, ibid.

8. See, for example, D. Mann et al., *Federal Programs Supporting Educational Change, Vol. 3: The Process of Change* (Santa Barbara: The Rand Corporation, 1975).

9. E. House, G. Glass, L. McLean, and D. Walker, "No Simple Answer: Critique of the 'Follow Through Evaluation'," *Educational Leadership* 35 (1968):462.

10. M. Rutter, et al., *Fifteen Thousand Hours: Secondary Schools and Their Effects on Children* (Cambridge, Ma.: Harvard University Press, 1979).

11. See, for example, R. Rist, *The Urban School: Factory for Failure* (Cambridge, Ma.: M.I.T. Press, 1973).

12. See, for example, Rutter et.al., *Fifteen Thousand Hours.*

13. See L. Cronbach and P. Meehl, "Construct Validity in Psychological Tests," *Psychological Bulletin* 52(1955):281-302.

11

Discipline and Safety

Much attention has been focused on an orderly and disciplined environment in the classroom and the school as an important factor in school effectiveness. An orderly and disciplined environment in both the school and the classroom obviously allows more time for learning. Without advocating the return of the hickory stick, school researchers are gaining new respect for educators' efforts to stress a firm discipline policy and to provide a classroom atmosphere that is free from disruption and distractions so teachers can spend more time on cognitive instead of managerial tasks.[1]

As for many of the dimensions of school effectiveness, the principles of good school discipline seem to be deceptively simple: clear and consistent school policies that reinforce the authority of teachers, collective involvement in shared responsibility for learning in an atmosphere of success, and positive support and encouragement for purposive and productive behavior.[2] When an agreed upon standard of behavior and discipline prevails among staff and students, schools can devote less time to keeping order and more time to promoting achievement.[3]

Maintaining order in a classroom is a basic task of teaching. From the beginning of their careers, teachers commonly express concern over how to achieve "good discipline" in their classrooms. Students expect their teachers to be able to keep order and admire those who manage classrooms well. The public considers discipline one of the most serious problems facing schools and sees an orderly school as a "good" school.

Recent studies of teaching effectiveness support this popular belief. Students learn more when more time is spent in productive work rather than in confusion and misbehavior. Effective teachers are also effective managers.[4]

The discipline and safety dimension of the Good Schools Project refers to the perceived reasonableness of school rules and their enforcement procedures, compliance with school rules and regulations, extent to which the school environment is safe and conducive to teaching and learning, and the use of drugs, alcohol, and tobacco. Subdimensions include school rules, rule enforcement, compliance, safety and security, drugs, alcohol, and tobacco, and student behavior.

Related Literature

Research on classroom discipline to date has been sparse. Few research programs have focused specifically on management and organization of classrooms. Kounin's research laid the groundwork for further work in this area by identifying several general characteristics of classroom management that were consistently related to good student behavior.[5] More recently, at the Research and Development Center for Teacher Education at the University of Texas at Austin, a series of studies has been conducted to find out how teachers establish and maintain classroom discipline.[6]

The first of the series of studies, conducted in eight elementary schools, included twenty-eight teachers with different levels of experience. The following year, fifty-one junior high school mathematics and English teachers participated in the study. Data collected in about twenty-five hours of observation for every teacher included detailed descriptive narratives of classroom events and activities, measures of student engagement, ratings of specific teacher behaviors and strategies, ratings of disruptive and inappropriate student behaviors, and logs of the use of class time.

Although some aspects of classroom management varied with students of different ages, similar principles of effective management appeared to operate in both elementary and junior high school classrooms. At the beginning of the school year, effective teachers showed evidence of careful planning and detailed thinking about procedures and student behavior in their classrooms. They planned routines that would help their classes function with a minimum of effort, and they had clear expectations for student behaviors. The effective managers chose a few appropriate rules to govern student behavior in the class and school building and posted the rules in the classroom. These teachers also planned a workable system of consequences—both rewards and penalties—for student misbehavior.

Once school was underway, effective teachers maintained their management system by actively monitoring student behavior and work, by stopping inappropriate behavior quickly, and by using appropriate consequences in a consistent manner. Effective teachers kept students accountable for completing assignments and gave them frequent feedback about their work. These strategies helped teachers maintain task-oriented classes that functioned smoothly throughout the year.

According to Sanford, Emmer, and Clements, school administrators can do much to help teachers establish and maintain good learning environments in their classes.[7] One positive step is for principals to lead their faculties in developing a set of schoolwide rules and procedures. While it does not take the place of a more detailed system of procedures for individual classrooms, this schoolwide consensus provides a framework for teachers as they formulate and teach expectations for student behavior in the classes. Wide involvement of school faculty and staff in choosing school rules and procedures is advised.

Phi Delta Kappa Commission on Discipline

The Phi Delta Kappa Commission on Discipline identified exemplary schools where discipline was not a significant problem. Based on a review of data regarding each school's demographic and program characteristics, commission members found several distinguishing features of schools with effective discipline practices. Five of these features have been discussed by Lasley and Wayson.[8]

First, all faculty members and students were involved in problem solving. Schoolwide problems were the responsibility of all who worked in and used the school. Discipline codes in exemplary schools tended to be developed by many students, teachers, and administrators, and students were given meaningful ways of being involved in the leadership of the school.

Second, the school was seen as a place in which to experience success. High rates of success were important for student academic and social growth. Success contributed to positive student self-esteem, which in turn translated into positive student behavior.

A third feature of exemplary schools was focusing on causes rather than symptoms in problem solving. Teachers and administrators tended not to define problems in terms of specific student behaviors, such as fighting; rather, they looked at student behavior as symptomatic of other problems. Excessive student fighting, for example, might be caused by overcrowded school conditions.

Fourth, the schools in the Phi Delta Kappa study focused on rewarding rather than punishing behavior. Punishment was used by teachers and administrators as a last resort, and only after rules and procedures had been clearly communicated to students. These schools did not concentrate their efforts on formal rule enforcement or punishment programs. Instead, these schools engaged in a wide range of activities to enhance students' self-esteem; they used award days, positive messages to parents, and special programs to recognize student accomplishment.

Fifth, the principal was seen as a strong leader. The principals described in the Phi Delta Kappa study played a prominent role with regard to discipline. They were a source of constant positive strength.

Safe School Study

Between February 1976 and January 1977, administrators, teachers, and students from a representative sample of 4,000 elementary and secondary schools were asked to respond to questions about stealing, vandalism, and physical attacks in public schools. Later, 642 junior and senior high schools selected from the original sample were visited by interviewers. The results were reported in *Violent Schools—Safe Schools: The Safe School Study Report to Congress.*[9] Investigators found that size and impersonality of a school were related to school crime. Large schools had greater property loss through burglary, theft, and vandalism, and they also had slightly more violence. Investigators also found that the more students a teacher taught, the greater the amount of school violence. Findings related to systematic school discipline suggested that students' perceptions of tight classroom control, strictly enforced rules, and the principal's firmness were associated with low levels of student violence. Additional findings suggested that student crime resulted when students perceived rules to be arbitrarily enforced by an unnecessarily punitive staff. Finally, investigators found student violence to be higher in schools where more students said that they could not influence what happened to them.

Effective Schools Research

A synthesis of the research literature on effective schools suggests indicators of effective schools that have low incidence of violence and vandalism and few discipline problems.[10] Student indicators of an orderly environment can be grouped into two clusters: perceptions of discipline procedures, and participation in school affairs. In effective schools, students perceive that discipline procedures are fair and are applied equally to all. Effective schools also elicit high student participation; students are involved in a wide variety of activities.

Teachers can enhance the orderly environment of a school through their skills in instruction and classroom management.[11] In instruction, the teacher's use of time is important; teachers who maximize their allocated time by beginning lessons promptly have fewer discipline problems. It is reported also that teachers who give homework and provide rewards or reinforcement for actual achievement have fewer discipline problems.

The classroom management questions suggest ways discipline is handled by teachers in effective schools. For example, in classrooms with few behavior problems, teachers use punishment but avoid humiliation and violence toward students, and they tend to handle discipline problems themselves. Positive rewards and praise outnumber negative reinforcements. Teachers with fewer discipline problems also tend to be more available to students to talk about personal and academic problems.

The principal, too, has an important role in creating an orderly environment.[12] The principal's role revolves around creating a consensus about the school rules among staff and students, then administering these rules in a firm but fair manner.

Survey and Interview Data

Data from the Good Schools Project yielded various types of information about discipline and safety in schools identified as good by experienced educators in local communities. The following discussion represents an attempt to organize, report, and discuss both the survey and interview data.

School Rules

Much attention has been focused on school and classroom rules as an important factor in school discipline. When rules are made by the people involved and when they are clear and reasonable, there tend to be fewer "discipline problems." Data from the Good Schools Project yielded information about both students' and teachers' perceptions of school rules.

Students at each level of schooling responded to two items designed to yield information about their perceptions of school rules. When asked about the reasonableness of school rules, 85 percent of elementary level students, 79 percent of middle level students, and 72 percent of secondary level students reported that rules "always" or "often" were reasonable. However, when students were asked if they had a voice in making classroom rules, 47 percent of elementary school students, 68 percent of middle school students, and 81 percent of secondary school students responded that they "seldom" or "never" had a say. When young children were asked if they had too many rules at their schools, 69 percent indicated "no" and 31 percent indicated "yes."

Teachers also were asked to report their perceptions of the reasonableness of school rules. Ninety-nine percent of elementary and secondary school teachers and 98 percent of middle school teachers indicated that school rules for students "always" or "often" were reasonable in response to one item about school rules.

In the interview data, school or class rules were mentioned in fifteen schools. In two of these cases, countywide discipline codes were mentioned. It was reported that, in these schools, rules and expectations were clearly defined and understood by those who enforced them and those who followed them. School codes of conduct or school rules were mentioned in five cases.

Again, it was reported that rules were clearly defined and understood by everyone in the school and that school staffs evaluated and revised rules at appropriate intervals. The total staff worked as a team to enforce the schoolwide rules and to communicate expectations to students. Clearly-stated classroom rules were mentioned in eight cases. It was reported that rules were carefully and openly developed, clearly announced or posted, firmly enforced, and consistently applicable to everyone. In two of these cases, student participation in rule making was cited.

Rule Enforcement

Determining the extent to which student misbehavior was dealt with firmly and swiftly, the extent to which rules were fairly enforced, and the extent to which students knew the consequences for breaking rules contributed to our understanding of school discipline. Our purpose was to investigate procedures used in good schools and to raise appropriate questions. Accordingly, we asked questions about rule enforcement to students and teachers.

Students were asked to respond to two items about rule enforcement. Seventy-eight percent of the elementary level students, 81 percent of middle level students, and 83 percent of secondary level students indicated that student misbehavior "always" or "often" was dealt with firmly and swiftly. Additionally, 92 percent of all students reported that they "always" or "often" knew the consequences for breaking rules. When young children were asked to respond to the item, "My teacher is too strict," 21 percent said "yes" and 79 percent said "no."

Teachers also were asked to report whether or not student misbehavior was dealt with firmly and swiftly. Ninety-one percent of elementary level teachers, 82 percent of middle level teachers, and 88 percent of secondary level teachers reported that misbehavior "always" or "often" was dealt with firmly and swiftly in response to one item about rule enforcement. Teachers were asked to respond to two additional items dealing with fair enforcement of rules and how often teachers reported a student to the office for disciplinary action. Ninety-seven percent of elementary level teachers, 88 percent of middle level teachers, and 91 percent of secondary level teachers reported that rules for students were fairly enforced. Eighty-one percent of elementary level teachers, 66 percent of middle level teachers, and 78 percent of secondary level teachers "seldom" or "never" reported a student to the office for disciplinary action.

It was reported in the interview data from thirty-one schools that in twenty-five schools the focus was on rewarding rather than punishing behavior. Punishment was used by teachers and administrators as a last resort, and only after rules and procedures had been clearly communicated to students. In other words, the professionals in these good schools did not concentrate their efforts on formal rule enforcement or punishment programs. Instead, these professionals engaged in award or honor days, verbal praise, positive messages to parents, and special programs to recognize student accomplishments.

When punishment was necessary, several forms were used. The forms of punishment mentioned were: withdrawal of privileges, writing of sentences, isolation, detention, suspension, contacting of parents, and corporal punishment. The most frequently cited form of punishment used was the contacting of parents; this was cited in twelve cases.

In twenty cases, it was reported that teachers handled rule enforcement and any "discipline problems" themselves. Students rarely had to be sent to the office for disciplinary reasons.

Compliance

Determining the extent to which students obeyed school rules and regulations and the extent to which students attended class regularly contributed also to our understanding of discipline in the identified good schools. Accordingly, we asked several questions of teachers and students.

Students responded to three items concerning compliance. These data showed that most students at all levels reported compliance to school rules and regulations. Eighty percent of elementary level students, 71 percent of middle level students, and 67 percent of secondary level students indicated that students "always" or "often" obeyed school rules and regulations. Ninety-five percent of elementary level students, 98 percent of middle level students, and 99 percent of secondary level students reported that they "always" or "often" were expected to attend class regularly and to be on time.

Teachers also reported student compliance to school rules and regulations and that students attended class regularly and were punctual. Ninety-seven percent of elementary level teachers, 94 percent of middle level teachers, and 93 percent of secondary level teachers reported that students obeyed school rules and regulations. Ninety-eight percent of elementary level teachers, 95 percent of middle level teachers, and 92 percent of secondary level teachers reported that students attended class regularly and were on time.

Safety and Security

School effectiveness has been linked with low amounts of violence and vandalism. Our purpose was to investigate the extent to which students and teachers in the identified good schools perceived their environment as safe and to investigate the incidents of violence and vandalism in these schools.

Students responded to a variety of items to determine the extent to which their schools were safe. In response to the item "I feel safe at this school," 87 percent of elementary level students, 78 percent of middle level students, and 83 percent of secondary level students reported that they "always" or "often" felt safe. Twelve percent of elementary and middle school students and only 7 percent of secondary school students indicated that teachers "always" or "often" were physically assaulted in their schools. Thirty-five percent of elementary level students, 48 percent of middle level students, and 37 percent of secondary level students said that students "always" or "often" fought with each other. In response to whether students damaged or stole school property, 15 percent of elementary level students, 24 percent of middle level students, and 26 percent of secondary level students reported that students "always" or "often" damaged or stole school property. Young children responded to the item, "This school is a dangerous place to be." Eighty-nine percent said "no" and 11 percent said "yes."

Teachers also responded to a variety of items about safety and security. Ninety-seven percent of elementary level teachers, 96 percent of middle level teachers, and 90 percent of secondary level teachers reported that their school buildings and school grounds "always" or "often" were safe. Only 2 percent of elementary and secondary school teachers and 3 percent of middle school teachers said that students "always" or "often" physically assaulted teachers. Fourteen percent of elementary level teachers, 16 percent of middle level teachers, and 12 percent of secondary level teachers indicated that students "always" or "often" fought with each other. Teachers responded to two additional items about damaging and stealing school or students' property. Seven percent of elementary level teachers, 14 percent of middle level teachers, and 25 percent of secondary level teachers said that students "always" or "often" damaged or stole school property. Twelve percent of elementary level teachers, 17 percent of middle level teachers, and 31 percent of secondary level teachers said that students "always" or "often" damaged or stole other students' property.

Drugs, Alcohol, and Tobacco

Data from the Good Schools Project yielded information about both students' and teachers' perceptions of the use of drugs, alcohol, and tobacco.

Students at all levels of schooling responded to three items designed to yield information about student violation of rules on smoking and students' use of drugs and alcohol. When asked about violation of school rules on smoking, 12 percent of elementary level students, 25 percent of middle level students, and 49 percent of secondary level students reported that students "always" or "often" violated the rules. Five percent of elementary level students, 17 percent of middle level students, and 41 percent of secondary level students indicated that students at their schools "always" or "often" used drugs. Percentages for alcohol use were somewhat higher. Seven percent of elementary level students, 23 percent of middle level students, and 60 percent of secondary level students indicated that students at their schools drank alcohol.

Teachers responded to the same three items about drugs, alcohol, and tobacco. Three percent of elementary level teachers, 9 percent of middle level teachers, and 39 percent of secondary level teachers reported that students "always" or "often" violated school rules on smoking. One percent of elementary level teachers, 6 percent of middle level teachers, and 29 percent of secondary level teachers said that students in their schools "always" or "often" used drugs. Two percent of elementary level teachers, 7 percent of middle level teachers, and 50 percent of secondary level teachers said that students in their schools "always" or "often" drank alcohol.

Student Behavior

It has been reported that effective managers spend a considerable amount of time, especially during the first several weeks of school, helping students learn how to behave in their classrooms and in their school.[13] Data from the Good Schools Project yielded additional information in this regard.

When students responded to the item, "In this school, we are taught how to behave properly," 91 percent of elementary level, 82 percent of middle level, and 68 percent of secondary level students indicated that this "always" or "often" occurred. Twenty-five percent of elementary level students and 27 percent of middle level and secondary level students reported that their teachers "always" or "often" were more concerned that students kept quiet than that they learned.

When teachers responded to the item, "Students are taught how to behave properly so they can benefit from academic activities," 97 percent of elementary level teachers, 92 percent of middle level teachers, and 87 percent of secondary level teachers indicated that this "always" or "often" occurred.

The comment cited most often in the interview data dealt with student behavior. In thirty-one schools, teachers, administrators, parents, and other school personnel said that the students were well-behaved.

Summary

Overall, students and teachers had very similar perceptions about discipline and safety in their schools. Both students and teachers felt that school rules for students were reasonable, that students obeyed school rules and regulations, that students were taught to behave properly, and that student misbehavior was dealt with firmly and swiftly (see Table 1). It was interesting to note, though, that 65 percent of the students reported no voice in making rules.

Students and teachers felt that their schools were safe, and

Table 1

A Summary of Teachers and Students Responding Always or Often to Selected Statements Concerning Discipline and Safety

Survey Item (Item Number)	School Level		
	Elementary %	Middle %	Secondary %
Rules for students are reasonable.			
Teachers (131)	99	98	99
Students (18)	85	79	72
Student misbehavior is dealt with firmly and swiftly.			
Teachers (87)	91	82	88
Students (54)	78	81	83
Students obey school rules and regulations.			
Teachers (149)	97	94	93
Students (30)	80	71	67
Students are taught how to behave properly.			
Teachers (107)	97	92	87
Students (53)	91	82	68

they reported few incidents of violence and vandalism. There was also close agreement regarding the use of drugs, alcohol, and tobacco, which did not seem to be a serious problem in these schools.

Conclusions

The data reported and discussed in the foregoing pages suggest several themes about the nature of discipline in the schools sampled for this study. The themes are not new, and they suggest that in these good schools "discipline" is not a major problem and that the schools, for the most part, are free of violence and vandalism. An examination of items 161, 162, 171, and 172 in the *Teacher Survey* (see Appendix O) indicates that discipline and students' use of alcohol and drugs are significantly less of a problem today than five years ago. (Please refer to Chapter Fourteen for a more in-depth discussion of these items.)

Emphasis on Rewarding Rather Than Punishing

The schools sampled for this study seem to focus on rewarding rather than punishing behavior. Interview reports indicate that punishment is used by teachers and administrators as a last resort, and only after rules and procedures are clearly communicated to students. The schools do not concentrate their efforts on formal rule enforcement; rather, they use awards, positive messages to parents, and special assemblies to recognize student accomplishments.

Effective Disciplinarians

The teachers sampled in this study are able to maintain discipline in their classes; they spend little time punishing students. Additionally, teachers handle any discipline matters themselves and rarely send students to the office for disciplinary action.

Reasonable Rules and Fair Enforcement

In the schools sampled in this study, rules are perceived as reasonable and fairly enforced, but the majority of students in these schools have no voice in making the rules. This fact is contrary to most of the literature, which suggests that when rules are made by the people involved, there are fewer discipline problems. Might there be even fewer discipline problems in these schools if students were more involved?

Few Incidents of Violence and Vandalism

There is very little violence and vandalism in these schools. Responsible factors likely include: rules are reasonable; rules are fairly enforced; and the emphasis is on rewarding behavior.

Perhaps the most significant finding is that there is no single recipe for success. These schools appear to be successful because teachers, administrators, and students work in a variety of ways to create a positive school atmosphere; there are no simple solutions to achieving good discipline in schools.

Notes

1. W.W. Cooley and G. Leinhardt, "The Instructional Dimension Study," *Educational Evaluation and Policy Analysis* 2 (1980): 7-25.
2. Thomas J. Lasley and William W. Wayson, "Characteristics of Schools with Good Discipline," *Educational Leadership* 40 (December 1982): 28-31.
3. M. Rutter et al., *Fifteen Thousand Hours: Secondary Schools and Their Effects on Children* (Cambridge, Ma.: Harvard University Press, 1979).
4. Walter Doyle, *Classroom Management* (West Lafayette, In.: Kappa Delta Pi, 1980), p. 3.
5. Jacob S. Kounin, *Discipline and Group Management in Classrooms* (New York: Holt, Rinehart and Winston, 1970).
6. Julie P. Sanford, Edmund T. Emmer, and Barbara S. Clements, "Improving Classroom Management," *Educational Leadership* 40 (April 1983): 56-60.
7. Ibid.
8. Lasley and Wayson, "Characteristics of Schools."
9. U.S. Department of Health, Education, and Welfare, *Violent Schools—Safe Schools: The Safe School Study Report to Congress, Volume I* (Washington, D.C.: Government Printing Office, 1978).
10. David A. Squires, William G. Huitt, and John K. Segars, *Effective Schools and Classrooms: A Research-Based Perspective* (Alexandria, Va.: Association for Supervision and Curriculum Development, 1983).
11. Ibid.
12. Ibid.
13. Edmund T. Emmer, Carolyn M. Evertson, and L. Anderson, "Effective Management at the Beginning of the School Year," *The Elementary School Journal* 80 (1980): 218-28.

12

Support Services and Facilities

The support services and facilities dimension refers to the perceived adequacy of school support services and to the condition and use of the school building. Subdimensions include library services, secretarial services, worthwhileness of inservice programs, pleasantness and cleanliness of the school, and use of the building.

School resources, support services, and facilities do affect the educational experiences of students, although according to summaries of the effective schools research, they, when independent of other interventions, are not powerful enough to affect school outcomes. Resources and facilities are tools that can be effective or ineffective, depending upon the educators who utilize them.

Of the subdimensions included in this dimension, only inservice is featured in the effective schools research. Successful schools typically provide their staffs with frequent opportunities for inservice training and development.[1]

Survey Data

Data from the Good Schools Project yielded various types of information about support services and facilities in schools identified as good. The following discussion represents an attempt to organize, report, and discuss the survey data.

Library Services

Teachers at each level of schooling responded to two items designed to yield information about teachers' perceptions of library services. Ninety-four percent of elementary level teachers,

90 percent of middle level teachers, and 84 percent of secondary level teachers indicated that library services "always" or "often" met the needs and interests of students. Additionally, 93 percent of elementary level teachers, 85 percent of middle level teachers, and 83 percent of secondary level teachers reported that library services "always" or "often" met the needs of teachers.

Secretarial Services

Teachers responded to one item about secretarial services. Ninety-two percent of elementary and middle level teachers and 76 percent of secondary level teachers reported that adequate secretarial services "always" or "often" were available.

Worthwhileness of Inservice Programs

When asked to respond to one item about worthwhile inservice programs, 83 percent of elementary level teachers, 69 percent of middle level teachers, and 65 percent of secondary level teachers indicated that inservice programs "always" or "often" were worthwhile.

Pleasantness and Cleanliness of the School

Teachers were asked to respond to two items about the pleasantness and cleanliness of the school. Ninety-eight percent of elementary level teachers and 91 percent of middle level and secondary level teachers reported that their school buildings "always" or "often" were pleasant places to be. When asked about the cleanliness of the school, 95 percent of elementary level teachers, 93 percent of middle level teachers, and 92 percent of secondary level teachers said that their school buildings and grounds were kept clean.

Ninety-four percent of the young children responded "yes" and 6 percent responded "no" to the item, "This school is nice to be in."

Use of the Building

When teachers in these good schools responded to the item, "Teachers and students are allowed to put things on the walls in this building," 93 percent of elementary level teachers, 86 percent of middle level teachers, and 82 percent of secondary level teachers indicated that this "always" or "often" occurred. Teachers responded to one additional item in this subdimension. Ninety-nine percent of elementary level teachers, 97 percent of middle level teachers, and 96 percent of secondary level teachers reported that furniture and equipment "always" or "often" could be rearranged as desired.

Conclusions

The data reported in the foregoing pages suggest that, in the schools sampled for this study, library and secretarial services are adequate and that inservice is worthwhile. The schools are pleasant and clean places in which to be, and teachers and students are allowed to put things on the walls and rearrange furniture as desired.

While facilities and resources are not featured in the summaries of the effective schools research, they do seem to be important to the persons in the identified good schools. Perhaps facilities and resources are more important to good schools than to effective schools.

Note

1. Willard R. Duckett, Don L. Park, David L. Clark, Martha M. McCarthy, Linda S. Lotto, Leonard L. Gregory, Jack Herlihy, and Derek L. Burleson, *Why Do Some Urban Schools Succeed? The Phi Delta Kappa Study of Exceptional Urban Elementary Schools* (Bloomington, In.: Phi Delta Kappa, 1980).

13

Decision Making

Introduction and Background

Many decisions must be made in schools. Such decisions range from the formulation of the budget and management of the school to deciding on a specific instructional activity for an individual child. Our interest here is on school level decisions—decisions that affect the school in general and across time. These decisions include, for example, those that relate to policies, curriculum and development, selection of instructional strategies, hiring, and assignment and evaluation of personnel. Our major focus here is on teachers' perceptions of their own involvement and that of the principal in decision making. Attention is also given to teachers' perceptions of student and parent involvement, as well as to students' perceptions of their own involvement.

Decision making is one of the dimensions which contributes to the school milieu. The school milieu is seen as shaping the nature of learning opportunities that are provided and how they are interpreted in the daily school experiences of teachers and students.

The decision making role of various parties may influence learning opportunities directly or indirectly. For example, if teachers are not involved in the selection of instructional materials to be used in their classes, this may detract from the opportunity for students to learn. Not being involved in the selection of instructional materials may also affect the feelings that teachers have about their jobs or schools. These feelings, in turn, may influence the daily job performances of the teachers.

The way in which teachers are involved in decision making varies a great deal from school to school. In some schools, teachers are provided with textbooks selected by other people. The teacher may have some choice in terms of specific instructional activities, but no involvement in decisions about content, sequencing, pace, and testing. The teachers may also have no involvement in decisions about discipline, instructional policies, or personnel placement and evaluation. In many schools, teachers appear to have autonomy, but are pressured to conform to organizational norms.[1] Teachers are held accountable, but have little to say about what they do.

Results of a recent survey suggest that many principals see group decision making as desirable, but do not have confidence in or trust their teachers.[2] The principals see the teachers as wanting power and as being interested in their own welfare, not that of children. If this is true, some principals view the involvement of teachers in decision making as an adversarial, non-cooperative series of confrontations.

Ideally, we envision schools in which all of those who have a stake in the outcomes of decisions have some share in the decision making. While both individuals and positions (e.g., the principalship) would retain authorities and responsibilities, there would be an atmosphere of trust and communication in which issues and problems could be discussed openly and dealt with humanely and rationally at all times. Goodlad suggested that such schools would exhibit high levels of dialogue, decision making, action taking, and action evaluations.[3] When issues arise in these schools, teachers and principals would discuss and research the issue, unite in the decision making process, and then make decisions. Conway concluded that his findings support the view that participatory management "is to be expected rather then suspected."[4]

In many cases where teachers have the opportunity to be involved, they do not get involved. One reason for this is that, while potential benefits are high and costs low, they may feel that their involvement will have little influence on decisions.[5] Shared decision making in these cases is viewed as a formality or an attempt to create the illusion of teacher influence. Similarly, teachers may want to be involved in decision making with regard to instruction but not management.[6] Flynn has described the involvement of a total teaching staff in decision making.[7] He reports that the staff improved their communication, felt that they and other staff were more influential in decision making, and developed a new method of problem solving which became an integral part of the method of the school. He later decided that involvement of the total staff was too impractical. He then formed a decision making body composed of department chairmen, two head teachers, the principal, and the assistant principal.[8]

It has been suggested that the existence of participative decision making in schools and other organizations is related to the structure of the organization and to the characteristics of the leader. It appears that there will be more involvement in decision making in less centralized organizations in which the leader is supportive and facilitative. When participation is high, people are more satisfied with their jobs, more committed to their jobs, more loyal, more understanding of the issues involved and of the decision making process, and more likely to perceive the organization as successful or effective.

In the Good Schools Project we have tried to answer the following questions:

1. How do teachers view decision making in their schools with regard to staff involvement, procedures, and outcomes?

2. How do teachers view their decision making roles in ten specific areas?
   a. How often are they involved in each of these?
   b. How often do they think they should be involved?
   c. Does their desired level of involvement in each of these match their actual level of involvement?

3. How do teachers view the decision making involvement of the principal, parents, and students?

4. How do students view the involvement of students in school decision making?

Teachers' Views of School Decision Making

In general, the teachers in the Good Schools Project sample were quite positive about the decision making process (see Table 1). The majority of the teachers responded "always" or "often" when asked how often they had control over their jobs; when asked if schoolwide problems were identified and acted upon cooperatively by administrators, teachers, and other staff; when

Table 1

A Summary of Teachers Responding Always to Statements Concerning the School Decision Making Process

Survey Item (Item Number)	School Level		
	Elementary %	Middle %	Secondary %
Staff			
Schoolwide problems are identified and acted upon cooperatively by administrators, teachers, and other staff. (115)	52	40	31
People in this school do a good job of examining alternative solutions to problems before deciding what to do. (136)	46	30	22
The staff evaluates its programs and activities and attempts to change them for the better. (117)	51	37	29
Procedures			
When a problem arises in this school, there are established procedures for working on it. (88)	49	38	44
Control and Outcomes			
Overall, I have control over how I carry out my job. (128)	58	51	50
It is difficult for teachers to influence administrative decisions regarding school policy. (154)	9	11	9
Our efforts to solve schoolwide problems are successful. (49)	32	18	13
Other			
Teachers' unions or associations should bargain about curriculum and teaching materials. (100)	12	14	13

asked if alternative solutions to problems were examined before deciding what to do; when asked if there were established procedures for working on problems; and when asked if efforts to solve schoolwide problems were successful. The majority also felt that it "seldom" or "never" was difficult to influence administrators' decisions regarding school policies. The majority of the teachers also felt that teachers' unions or associations "seldom" or "never" should bargain about curriculum and teaching materials. While all responses were quite positive, in every instance elementary teachers were more positive and secondary teachers were less positive (see Appendix C).

Teachers' Involvement in Selected Areas

Teachers were asked how often they participated in making decisions in each of ten decisional situations, and how often they thought they should participate in making the decisions in each area (see Table 2). The ten decisional areas were adapted from items developed by Alutto and Belasco.[9]

Actual Involvement

The teachers in these good schools tended to be "always" involved in: establishing classroom discipline policies, determining appropriate instructional methods and techniques, and resolving the learning problems of individual students. Fewer teachers "always" were involved in evaluation of their own job performances, in selecting textbooks, and in establishing general instructional policies. Few teachers were involved in determining faculty assignments, evaluating the performance of other teachers, hiring new teachers, or selecting administrative personnel for the school.

In general, the actual involvement in decision making in these activities decreased as school level went up. For example, 67 percent of the elementary teachers but only 50 percent of the secondary teachers indicated that they "always" were involved with establishing classroom discipline policies. There was little difference in the decision making involvement of teachers at different school levels with regard to: selecting administrative personnel, hiring teachers, evaluating the performance of teachers, and determining faculty assignments. In each case, very few faculty "always" were involved at any school level. Involvement in decisions about selecting textbooks increased with school

Table 2

A Summary of Teachers' Perceptions of Whether They Always Do and Should Participate in Specific Decisions

Survey Item (Item Number)	School Level					
	Elementary		Middle		Secondary	
	Do %	Should %	Do %	Should %	Do %	Should %
Establishing classroom disciplinary policies (185/195)	67	75	55	65	50	61
Determining appropriate instructional methods and techniques (184/194)	55	67	47	56	46	56
Resolving learning problems of individual students (183/193)	54	64	34	45	30	42
Selecting textbooks (182/192)	40	58	38	50	45	60
Evaluating your own job performance (190/200)	40	57	39	56	34	47
Establishing general instructional policies (186/196)	33	47	27	40	24	36
Selecting administrative personnel to be assigned to the school (189/199)	2	9	1	8	2	9
Evaluating the performance of teachers (188/198)	2	4	1	4	4	7
Determining faculty assignments in the school (187/197)	4	8	4	6	4	11
Hiring new teachers in this school (181/191)	1	5	2	6	4	8

level. Forty percent of the teachers were involved in decisions about selecting textbooks at the elementary level, while 45 percent were involved at the secondary level.

Desired Involvement

The majority of the teachers at each school level thought that they "always" should be involved in decisions about determining classroom discipline policies, determining instructional methods and techniques, and selecting textbooks. The majority of the elementary and middle level teachers thought that they "always" should be involved in establishing general instructional policies and evaluating their own job performances, while only 47 percent of the secondary level teachers felt this way.

A majority of the elementary level teachers but not the middle and secondary level teachers felt that they "always" should be involved in resolving learning problems of students. With the exception of decisions about selecting textbooks, in each case the desire to be "always" involved in these kinds of decisions decreased as school level went up. About the same percentages of elementary level (58 percent) and secondary level (60 percent) teachers thought they "always" should be involved in selecting textbooks, as compared to 50 percent of the middle level teachers.

Very few (4 percent to 11 percent) of the teachers at each school level thought that they "always" should be involved in decisions regarding the selection of administrative personnel, determining faculty assignments, hiring new teachers, and evaluating the performances of teachers. While the desire to be involved in the selection of administrative personnel differed little across school level, the desire for involvement in the other three decisions was highest at the secondary level. The major differences were between elementary and secondary level teachers. For example, 11 percent of the secondary level teachers, 6 percent of the middle level teachers, and 8 percent of the elementary level teachers thought that they "always" should be involved in decisions about determining faculty assignments.

Discrepancy Between Actual and Desired Involvement

It may be that the actual level of involvement in decisions and the desired level of involvement were less important than whether teachers were involved at the level they wanted to be. An inspection of the data in Table 2 reveals that, at each school level and for each type of decision, a larger percentage of the teachers thought that they should be involved (at various levels) than were involved. To explore this issue further, we created a discrepancy score between desired (should) level of involvement and actual (do) level of involvement. This produced three groups: those whose level of involvement was less than desired; those whose

Table 3

A Summary of Teachers Who Feel They Have the Right Amount or Not Enough
Participation in Specific Decisions

Survey Item (Item Number)	School Level					
	Elementary		Middle		Secondary	
	Not Enough %	Right Amount %	Not Enough %	Right Amount %	Not Enough %	Right Amount %
Establishing classroom disciplinary policies (185/195)	13	85	16	81	20	78
Resolving learning problems of individual students (183/193)	15	82	21	76	24	73
Determining instructional methods and techniques (184/194)	16	82	20	75	17	80
Establishing general instructional policies (186/196)	27	70	30	69	30	67
Selecting textbooks (182/192)	31	67	30	67	26	72
Evaluating your own job performance (190/200)	34	64	32	64	33	63
Evaluating the performance of teachers (188/198)	32	65	39	58	37	61
Determining faculty assignments in the school (187/197)	40	58	41	54	44	52
Hiring new teachers in this school (181/191)	40	59	40	59	45	53
Selecting administrative personnel to be assigned to the school (189/199)	51	47	51	47	50	47

level of involvement was *exactly* right (no discrepancy), and those whose level of involvement was more than desired.

Very few teachers were more involved than they thought they should be. The most dramatic case was that 5 percent of the middle level teachers felt that their involvement in determining instructional methods and techniques was too frequent. As can be seen in Table 3, a sizeable percentage (60 percent or more) of

the teachers at each school level had the right amount of involvement in seven of the ten types of decisions. Small percentages
(13 to 24 percent) of teachers wanted more involvement in resolving learning problems of individual students, determining instructional methods and techniques, and establishing classroom
disciplinary problems. The biggest discrepancies were found in
selecting administrative personnel for the school, hiring new
teachers, determining faculty assignments, evaluating the performances of teachers, evaluating their own job performances, and
selecting textbooks. Although the majority of the teachers had
some involvement with selecting textbooks, evaluating their own
job performances, and evaluating the performances of other
teachers, they wanted more involvement. Few teachers had involvement in hiring administrators or teachers or in assigning
other teachers. Teachers wanted more involvement.

The percentage of teachers who wanted more involvement in
determining instructional methods and techniques, establishing
general instructional policies, evaluating their own job performances, and selecting administrative personnel for the school
did not differ substantially across school levels (e.g., 16 percent
of the elementary level teachers and 17 percent of the secondary
level teachers wanted more involvement in determining instructional methods and techniques). A higher percentage of elementary level teachers (31 percent) than secondary level teachers (26
percent) wanted increased involvement in selecting textbooks. In
each of the remaining decision areas, a higher percentage of
teachers at the secondary level than at the elementary level
wanted more involvement. These areas included: hiring new
teachers, determining faculty assignments, evaluating performances of teachers, resolving learning problems of individual
students, and establishing classroom disciplinary policies.

The Principal's Involvement

Over 60 percent (61 to 98 percent) of the teachers at each
school level felt that the principal "always" or "often" trusted
them to use their professional judgments on instructional matters, saw that decisions were carried out, made the important
decisions, encouraged teachers with leadership abilities to move
into leadership roles, sought out teachers' suggestions for improving the school, and accepted staff decisions even if he or she

Table 4

*A Summary of Teachers Responding Always to Statements Concerning the
Principal's Involvement In and Orientation Toward Decision Making*

Survey Item (Item Number)	School Level		
	Elementary %	Middle %	Secondary %
The principal trusts teachers to use their professional judgment on instructional matters. (114)	68	61	54
Once decisions are made, the principal sees that they are carried out. (50)	63	50	41
The principal encourages teachers with leadership abilities to move into leadership roles. (120)	43	35	27
The principal makes the important decisions in this school. (76)	35	41	31
Administrators seek out teachers' suggestions for improving the school. (56)	30	28	20
The principal accepts staff decisions even if he or she does not agree with them. (81)	17	16	13

did not agree with them (see Table 4). In general, these percentages went down as school level went up. In other words, fewer secondary level teachers than elementary level teachers indicated that the principal "always" or "often" did these things.

The differences between percentages of elementary and secondary level teachers who indicated that the principal "always" did these things were more dramatic. The majority of the teachers at each school level felt that the principal "always" trusted teachers to use their professional judgments on instructional matters. The majority of the elementary and middle level teachers but less than half of the secondary level teachers felt that, once decisions were made, the principal "always" saw that they were carried out. Few teachers (2 to 9 percent) indicated that the principal "seldom" or "never" trusted their judgments or failed to carry out decisions that had been made.

Less than half of the teachers at each school level indicated that the principal "always" encouraged those with ability into leadership roles, made the important decisions, sought their suggestions for improvement, and accepted staff decisions with which he or she did not agree. One-fifth of the middle and secondary level teachers indicated that the principal "seldom" or "never" encouraged those with leadership abilities into leadership roles. One-fourth or more of the middle and secondary level teachers (and one-fifth of the elementary level teachers) indicated that the principal "seldom" or "never" sought out teachers' suggestions for improving the school. About one-third of the middle and secondary level teachers (and one-fourth of the elementary level teachers) indicated that the principal "seldom" or "never" accepted staff decisions if he or she did not agree with them.

Students' Involvement

Both teachers and students were asked how often they thought students had a chance to change things. Less than a majority of each responded "always" or "often" (see Table 5). Teachers at the secondary level (52 percent) were more likely to respond this way than their counterparts at the elementary level (41 percent) and middle level (34 percent). The opposite occurred for the students. Similar percentages of secondary level students (33 percent) and middle level students (34 percent) felt they "always" or "often" had a chance to change things, while 43 percent of the elementary level students felt this way.

Both teachers and students were asked whether the students participated in the development of policies, procedures, and programs. While the majority of the students at the elementary level (67 percent), middle level (68 percent) and secondary level (62 percent) responded that this "always" or "often" was true, less than a majority of the teachers at the elementary level (41 percent) and middle level (36 percent) responded "always" or "often." The majority of the students at the elementary level (68 percent), middle level (57 percent) and secondary level (54 percent) reported that teachers "always" or "often" listened to students' suggestions for program changes. In general, as school level went up, teachers believed that students were more involved with school decision making. For students, however, as school level went up, they were less likely to believe that they were involved in school decision making.

Parent and Community Involvement

In general, the teachers felt that parents and community

Table 5

A Summary of Teachers and Students Responding Always or Often to Statements Concerning the Frequency of Students' Involvement in School Decision Making

Survey Item (Item Number)	School Level		
	Elementary %	Middle %	Secondary %
In this school, students have a chance to change things they don't like.			
Teachers (116)	41	34	52
Students (17)	43	34	33
Students participate in the development of school policies, procedures, and programs.			
Teachers (143)	41	36	55
Students (21)	67	68	62
Teachers listen to our suggestions for program changes.			
Students (97)	68	57	54

Table 6

A Summary of Teachers Who Report That Parents Are Always or Often Involved In School Level Decision Making

Survey Item (Item Number)	School Level		
	Elementary %	Middle %	Secondary %
In this school, parents and community organizations work with school personnel to identify and resolve schoolwide problems. (86)	80	62	60
Parents are important members of school committees and advisory groups. (140)	89	72	68

organizations worked with school personnel to identify and resolve schoolwide problems (see Table 6). Elementary level teachers (80 percent) were more likely than middle level teachers (62 percent) or secondary level teachers (60 percent) to indicate that this "always" or "often" occurred. Teachers were more likely to indicate that parents were important members of school committees and advisory groups. Over 80 percent of the elementary level teachers and over two-thirds of the middle and secondary level teachers indicated that this "always" or "often" occurred.

Summary

The teachers in these schools are generally quite positive about the decision making process in their schools and their involvement in it. They feel that they have control over how they carry out their jobs. They feel that the staff does a good job of identifying problems, examining alternatives, evaluating programs and activities to improve them, and the staff are successful in solving problems. Teachers also feel that they can influence administrators' decisions regarding school policy.

More teachers are involved in instructional decisions than in managerial decisions, but more teachers want involvement in instructional decisions than in managerial decisions—in fact, very few teachers (11 percent or less) think they "always" should be involved in managerial decisions. There is no discrepancy between the actual and desired level of involvement in instructional decisions for two-thirds or more of the decisions. Discrepancy rates for managerial decisions indicate that, while these teachers do not "always" want to be involved in these types of decisions, teachers do want to be involved more often than they are.

The teachers feel that the principal trusts them to use their professional judgments on instructional matters and to see that decisions are carried out, but teachers are less likely to feel that the principal encourages those with ability into leadership roles, makes the important decisions, seeks their suggestions for improvement, and accepts staff decisions with which he or she does not agree.

Fewer teachers believe that students can change things they do not like or are involved in the development of school policies. The majority of the students indicate that they "always" or "often" participate in the development of school policies and that teachers listen to students' suggestions for program changes. The majority of the students, however, do not think they have a chance to change things they do not like. While few teachers indicate that parents "always" are involved in the identification and resolution of schoolwide problems or "always" are important members of school committees, many of these teachers think that parents "often" are involved in these things.

In many of these schools the teachers have a very full involvement in the decision making process. We do not know at this point how teacher involvement in decision making in these schools is related to principals' characteristics, school characteristics such as size of enrollment, or teachers' characteristics. We also do not yet know how this involvement is related to job satisfaction or job performance. We suspect that further research on these data will corroborate the findings of other studies. We believe that appropriate involvement in decision making is necessary and beneficial. Further analyses will be done to explore the relationship between teacher decision making at the school level and instructional decisions at the classroom level, interpersonal relationships in the school, teachers' job commitments, and a host of other variables which have not been studied extensively by other researchers.

Notes

1. A. Lieberman, "Political and Economic Stress and the Social Reality of Schools," *Teachers College Record* 79 (December 1977): 259-67.
2. J. Sweeny, "Principals vs. Teachers," *Phi Delta Kappan,* April 1980, pp. 565-66.
3. John I. Goodlad, *The Dynamics of Educational Change: Toward Responsive Schools* (New York: McGraw-Hill, 1975), pp. 97-99.
4. James A. Conway, "Power and Participatory Decision Making in Selected English Schools," *The Journal of Educational Administration* 16 (May 1978): 80-96.
5. Daniel L. Duke, Beverly K. Showers, and Michael Imber, "Teachers and Shared Decision Making: The Costs and Benefits of Involvement," *Educational Administration Quarterly* 16 (Winter 1980): 93-106.
6. Allan M. Mohrman, Jr., Robert A. Cooke, and Susan Albers, "Participation in Decision Making: A Multidimensional Perspective," *Educational Administration Quarterly* 14 (Winter 1978): 13-29.
7. C. Wayne Flynn, *The Principal as an Organizational Consultant to His Own School* (Ph.D. diss., University of Oregon, 1971).
8. C. Wayne Flynn, "Collaborative Decision-Making in a Secondary School," *Education and Urban Society* (February 1976): 172-82.
9. Joseph A. Alutto and James A. Belasco, "Patterns of Teacher Participation in School System Decision Making," *Educational Administration Quarterly* (Winter 1972): 27-41.

14

History: Change over Time

Historical Features of Successful Schools

Schools, like other social institutions, are not autonomous. They are an integral part and reflection of their setting and past. Neither are schools static. Although critics and reformers bemoan the slow, uneven pace of school change, schools are dynamic entities that do change over time.[1] Yet, with few exceptions, the recent effective schools literature has tended to examine schools in isolation, out of their context of community setting and history.[2] For the most part, we have been offered snapshots rather than motion pictures.[3]

A major assumption underlying the Good Schools Project has been that neglect of the dynamics of schooling, and the sociohistorical contexts in which schools are embedded, limits our understanding of schooling and how schools might be improved. Even a rich description of the characteristics and the operation of good schools, including identification of patterns of beliefs and practices that distinguish them from other schools, would not provide enough information to help others improve their schools. Also needed is knowledge about how good schools came to be so that their experiences might benefit others.

The schools we studied are successful schools, successful because they are perceived by people in their communities to be good. How have these schools come to be as they are now? What can be learned from the experiences of these good schools that might be helpful to improvement efforts elsewhere?

In considering history as an important dimension of schooling, we are not looking for lessons to be learned in the sense of universal recipes for success. Rather, we see history providing perspective on present situations and suggesting possibilities for the future. In examining the history of good schools, we have looked for clues as to how the dimensions of classroom practices, school milieu, and instititutional–community context have developed to their present state. Historical elements were identified in the course of analyzing responses to open ended interview questions about school history, teacher survey items about potential school problems five years ago and today, and available school documents.

In contrast to longitudinal or documentary studies, we have tried to glimpse the recent history of these good schools retrospectively, primarily through the perceptions and recollections of the school principals, teachers and other school personnel, students, and parents. While the school history offered here is fragmentary, it does offer insight into how these schools have become or managed to remain successful.

School Problems Then and Now

Consistent with the assumption that schools are dynamic entities that change over time, we sought to identify teachers' perceptions of school problems "five years ago" (1978) and "today" (1983) in order to determine the extent and direction of any changes. Given the particularly strident recent criticisms of public schooling and the wide media coverage it has received, it would not be surprising to find that teachers, even those in good schools, perceive more problems now than previously. It also would not be surprising to find that teachers perceive the recent past more favorably than they perceive their present situation.

A section of the *Teacher Survey* (Appendix O, items 161-180) asked teachers to respond "always," "often," "seldom," or "never" to a list of ten potential school problems in terms of the extent to which each was a problem five years ago and the extent to which each is a problem today. Their responses are presented by school level in Appendix H, Table 1.

First, it is clear that even good schools are not without problems, from the teachers' point of view. Across school levels in our sample, the mean percentage of teachers perceiving each potential problem as "always" or "often" existing at their schools ranged from 3 to 59 percent five years ago and 3 to 53 percent today. However, relatively few potential problems were seen as "always" or "often" a problem by more than one-third of the teachers.

Five years ago, only class size was seen as "always" or

"often" a problem by more than one-third of the elementary teachers. Middle and secondary teachers identified additional problems. More than one-third of these teachers identified discipline, financial support, and parental support, as well as class size, as "always" or "often" a problem. Secondary teachers also cited students' use of alcohol and drugs, getting and keeping good teachers, and administrative leadership as a problem. Discipline and students' use of alcohol and drugs were seen as the most serious secondary school problems, with more than half the secondary teachers perceiving these two items as "always" or "often" a problem.

Today, only financial support is seen as "always" or "often" a problem by more than one-third of the elementary teachers (class size was cited by 33 percent). More than one-third of the middle school teachers identified financial support and class size as "always" or "often" a problem (parental support was cited by 33 percent). As before, more problems were identified by the secondary teachers: students' use of alcohol and drugs, getting and keeping good teachers, and parental support, as well as financial support and class size. However, only financial support was cited as "always" or "often" a problem by more than half the teachers.

With the exception of financial support, which has increased as a perceived problem, teachers see these potential problems as about the same or less of a problem at their schools today compared to five years ago. The most dramatic changes are evident at the secondary level, where the percentage of teachers perceiving discipline, students' use of alcohol and drugs, and administrative leadership as "always" or "often" a problem declined by more than fifteen points in each case. Today, for example, 22 percent of the secondary teachers see discipline as "always" or "often" a problem, compared to 53 percent five years ago.

Although the survey results were descriptive, not explanatory, a relationship among teachers' perceptions of fewer problems with administrative leadership, discipline, and students' use of alcohol and drugs seemed likely. Better leadership may have been a factor in reducing discipline and alcohol–drug problems. However, fewer discipline and alcohol–drug problems as a result of other factors may have influenced teachers to see administrative leadership more favorably. Supporting the former interpretation, the interview data to be presented in the following section suggested that key administrators have made a positive difference in many of these schools.

The tentative picture emerging from these results was one of schools holding their own or getting better despite financial problems. Improvement, as indicated by a decrease in the percentage of teachers perceiving potential problems as "always" or "often" a problem at their schools, was particularly evident at the secondary level. The secondary level results suggested that a number of these schools might be turn-around schools, i.e., schools that have undergone dramatic and positive change in recent years. The interview data shed some light on this possibility.

Before turning to the interviews, it is interesting to compare the teachers' ranking of school problems five years ago and today with the rankings of a national sample of adults surveyed by the annual Gallup poll of the "Public's Attitudes Toward the Public Schools" (see Table 1).[4]

Granted that differences between the two surveys temper any comparison of results, there are some noteworthy parallels and discrepancies between the ranking of teachers in good schools and the public at large. While both surveys rank financial support high on the list of problems, discipline, not financial support, is the number one school problem from the perspective of the general public. The public also ranks problems with students' use of alcohol and drugs, curriculum, and academic standards higher than do the teachers. Teachers see parental support as more of a problem than does the public. Overall, there is less evidence of change during the past five years in the public's perceptions of school problems than in the teachers' perceptions of conditions at their own schools. Public attitudes, especially negative ones, change slowly, and the public has become so accustomed to bad news about schools that evidence of improvement may not be readily accepted.

Routes and Hurdles to Successful Schooling

Perceptions and recollections of school history were obtained by means of open ended interviews with the school principal, teachers and other school personnel, students, and parents at thirty schools. In general, these schools were more representative of schools across the nation than was the larger sample of schools.

A systematic content analysis of the interview responses

Table 1

Teachers' Ranking of School Problems Compared to Gallup Polls *

School Problem	Elementary		Middle		Secondary		Gallup** 1978 1983	
	Five Years Ago	Today	Five Years Ago	Today	Five Years Ago	Today	1978	1983
Discipline	2	3	1	2	2	9	1	1
Students' use of alcohol and drugs	10	10	10	10	1	4	2	2
Financial support	2	1	3	1	3	1	2	3
Time students spend riding the school bus	8	5	7	6	10	7	2***	9***
Curriculum	6	7	9	9	9	9	2	3
Academic standards	6	7	8	8	8	6	2	3
Getting and keeping good teachers	8	6	5	5	5	4	7	6
Class size	1	2	2	2	3	2		
Administrative leadership	4	7	5	6	5	8		
Parental support	4	4	4	2	5	2		8

 * Teachers' ranking based on percent of "always" plus percent of "often" responses; less than 2 percent difference scored as a tie

 ** For equivalent items rated as a problem by more than 5% of Gallup respondents

 *** Phrased as "integration/busing" in Gallup poll

relevant to school history was undertaken by this author and a graduate student.[5] Over a period of three months, we read through more than 500 interviews, identified themes, developed and refined categories of responses, and noted similarities, differences, and patterns within and across schools. What follows is a summary of that analysis.

As with other interpretive accounts of the dimensions of good schools, this account of history should be treated as a consideration of possibilities to be elaborated, refined, and tested against the experience of other schools. The data were fragmentary and selective, dependent on what people were able and willing to tell us in the interviews, and what we perceived to be relevant.

Diversity was readily apparent with and across schools and interviews. For example, interviewees differed in their interpretation of what counted as history. While there were very few discrepancies in perceptions among groups interviewed within a school, some aspects of school history were more salient to one group than another. For example, parents more often mentioned school desegregation than did teachers. More striking was the seeming lack of awareness of school history. With the exception of one elementary school that had just celebrated its fiftieth anniversary, most interviewees' knowledge of the history of their schools did not go back more than ten or fifteen years. Most interviewees evidenced a present orientation, a concern with the immediate situation of the school. For many, history was not at all salient, and they had very little to say.

Interview responses relevant to school history fell into five thematic categories: tradition; continuity; local events; people; and other.

Tradition referred to the school's reputation, i.e., to feelings and beliefs about the school. Interviewees' comments such as "it's always been a good school" and "people move here because of the school" were classified as tradition.

Continuity referred to actual school conditions, such as the stability of the staff or community. Interviewees' comments such as "teachers tend to stay here because it's such a good place to teach" and "we've only had three principals in twenty-eight years" were classified as continuity. The continuity category also included interviewees' comments regarding prior discontinuity, such as "the school was a real problem institution before the present principal arrived. He really turned the school around" and "five years ago I would not have wanted to send my kids to this school—today I'd be glad to."

Local events referred to events in the local community or school district directly involving or affecting the school. Frequently mentioned events included institutional–organizational changes such as reorganization and desegregation.

The fourth category, people, referred to individuals and groups seen as playing a key role in the school's history. Administrators, particularly present and previous principals, were most often mentioned as significant to the school's being what it is today.

The "other" category included less frequently mentioned aspects of school history. We had anticipated an "external events" category, including societal factors and movements that impinge upon the schools, such as legislative mandates (e.g., minimal competency testing) and pressures for "basics." However, interviewees in only two schools mentioned external events, and these were classified as "other" along with such things as university ties (two schools) and continued openness to new ideas (four schools).

The aspects of school history mentioned most often involved key people and local events. Tradition and continuity were mentioned next most often by interviewees. Key people were not only most often mentioned, but were also seen as most important in the school's history. While the head custodian was cited in one school, the students in another, parents in a third, and the teaching staff in several others, present and previous administrators, particularly principals, were most often cited as playing a key role in the school's history.

The perceived importance of the principal was consistent with the findings of recent school effectiveness research. However, what it is about the principal that makes a difference remains elusive in that literature as well as here. In the Good Schools Project's interviews, principals were lauded for bringing or pulling people together, for "smooth" management of the school, for successfully solving problems, and occasionally for encouraging new ideas and supporting innovation. What is generally assumed to constitute leadership was clearly implied here, although no particular leadership style was indicated.

It may be that the interviewees' perceptions of the principal's importance, and their lack of specificity regarding his or her accomplishments, is a function of the principal's role. Like the U.S. president, the school principal is a formal, recognized, and usually operating chief executive of an organization. The visibility of principals and presidents brings them credit and blame for organizational conditions, both successes and failures, for which they may be only partially or not at all responsible. Their salience may lead observers to attribute power and importance out of proportion to their actions and influences.

School Level Differences

School level differences were evident, both in the frequency that the various aspects of school history were mentioned and in their perceived importance. While people were frequently mentioned and perceived as important across elementary, middle, and secondary school levels, local events were more often mentioned and considered important in the history of the middle and secondary schools. School district reorganization was mentioned in five of the seven middle schools and desegregation in three. This was not surprising, given that many middle schools often were established during the last two decades as part of a school district desegration plan. Local events mentioned in six of the seven secondary schools were more diverse, including the construction of new facilities and tornado damage to a school building, as well as reorganization and desegregation.

Tradition was mentioned in only one middle school, perhaps because of the relative newness of middle schools and their relatively turbulent recent history. Although tradition was mentioned in all of the secondary schools, it was not seen as a particularly important factor. In contrast, tradition was mentioned in twelve of the sixteen elementary schools, and it was seen as most important or second in importance in seven schools. Continuity was mentioned in two-thirds of the elementary schools but only two middle and three secondary schools. Prior discontinuity was noted in two elementary and two middle schools. Overall, the histories of the elementary schools seemed to be serene and marked by a relative continuity and a tradition of competence or excellence, compared to the histories of the middle and secondary schools. Tradition may well be self-sustaining insofar as a school's good reputation tends to attract teachers, parents, and students who value and act in such a way as to maintain that reputation.

Conclusions

A major pattern emerging from both the survey and interview data is that these good schools have not been without problems. They are schools where problems have been anticipated or identified and acted upon with expectations of success, and where changes have been seen as resolving problems and improving school conditions. Would-be crises such as school desegregation or consolidation seem to have been viewed as challenges to be confronted and dealt with. For example, with one exception, desegregation seems not to have been a major problem in these schools. Interviewees often said with considerable satisfaction and pride that desegregation had gone smoothly in their schools. Without exception, the local events mentioned by interviewees were significant changes (e.g., movement of an elementary school into a former high school building) or potential crises. Yet, even where local events were seen as most important or second in importance in the school's history, tradition or continuity often were mentioned (in four of the five elementary and all five secondary schools, but in only one of the six middle schools).

Success in one situation seems to have provided impetus to further efforts. Thus, not only have immediate problems been resolved, but there have been long range positive effects in terms of self-confidence in facing the future and coping with challenges to school success. This success orientation is a positive illustration of what Rutter and his colleagues termed "ethos," the values and actions that come to characterize a school's functioning as a social organization.[6] It also reflects the "sustaining characteristics of a productive school culture" identified by Purkey and Smith in their review of the effective schools research. These process variables, which develop over time from within a school, include collaborative planning and collegial relationships, a sense of community, and commonly shared clear goals and high expectations.[7]

A second major pattern is that of schools getting better. School improvement is evident in both the survey and interview data. Discipline, for example, is perceived as much less of a problem today than five years ago, particularly in the secondary schools (see Appendix H, Table 1). Interviewees' comments suggest that four of the thirty schools (one elementary, two middle, and one secondary school) might be described as turn-around schools. After reaching a low point during the past ten years, these schools were able to change, to turn themselves around to the point where they are now considered successful by people in the schools and in the local community. In addition to the four turn-around schools, five schools (two elementary, one middle, and two secondary schools) were described as continuing to improve. Thus, good schools include not only those perceived as always having been good, but also those perceived as getting better. They resemble schools that Heckman describes as "renewing," i.e., schools that resolve their own problems and maintain staff-designed improvement processes that enable them to cope with continuing change.[8] It should be encouraging to all concerned that these good schools have not led charmed lives. Most have faced and dealt constructively with challenge and change, with hard times as well as good ones.

Neither of these patterns—problem resolution and improvement—is attributable to only one of the identified themes or aspects of school history. Multiple, interrelated factors comprise the history of these successful schools. Thus, while people, especially principals, are cited most often as responsible for how the schools came to be, we would not subscribe to a "great principal theory" of successful schooling. It would have little explanatory power. It would also grossly oversimplify the complexity of school history and present circumstance.

Within and beyond these patterns, we found considerable diversity of school experiences. There are different routes to becoming a good school. There is no one best system or path to successful schooling.

Notes

1. Paul H. Mattingly, "Structures over Time: Institutional History," in *Historical Inquiry in Education,* ed. John H. Best (Washington, D.C.: American Educational Research Association, 1983), p. 34.

2. The ahistoricism and decontextualization of much of the effective schools research has also been noted in some of the more thoughtful recent reviews of this literature. See, for example, Donald E. Mackenzie, "Research for School Improvement: An Appraisal of Some Recent Trends," *Educational Researcher* 12 (April 1983):5-16; Stewart C. Purkey and Marshall S. Smith, "Effective Schools: A Review," *Elementary School Journal* (1983):427-52.

3. Notable exceptions to the school snapshot literature include the "portraits" of exemplary secondary schools by Sara Lawrence Lightfoot and Philip W. Jackson in *Daedalus,* Fall 1981; also, see Alan Peshkin, *Growing Up American: Schooling and the Survival of Community* (Chicago: University of Chicago Press, 1978).

4. George H. Gallup, "The 15th Annual Gallup Poll of the Public's Attitudes Toward the Public Schools," *Phi Delta Kappan* (September 1983):33-47; Stanley M. Elam, ed., *A Decade of Gallup Polls of Attitudes Toward Education 1969-1978* (Bloomington, In.: Phi Delta Kappa, 1978).
5. I am indebted to Jane Holahan, University of Pittsburgh, without whose assistance this analysis and interpretation of the interview data could not have been accomplished.
6. Michael Rutter et al., *Fifteen Thousand Hours: Secondary Schools and Their Effects on Children* (Cambridge, Ma.: Harvard University Press, 1979).
7. Purkey and Smith, "Effective," pp. 444-45.
8. Paul E. Heckman, *Exploring the Concept of School Renewal: Cultural Differences and Similarities Between More and Less Renewing Schools* (Los Angeles: A Study of Schooling, Technical Report No. 33, Graduate School of Education, Laboratory in School and Community Education, University of California at Los Angeles, 1982).

15

Educators as Inquirers

From its inception, the Good Schools Project was designed to serve two purposes. One purpose was to collect descriptive data about a sample of good schools. The second purpose was to involve members of Kappa Delta Pi in the research project in meaningful ways, i.e., involving members in the kinds of problem-solving activities in which researchers engage. Most of this book has been devoted to reports related to the first purpose. The second purpose has not yet received attention. This chapter is designed to add at least a modicum of balance by focusing on member involvement.

This chapter will be divided into three parts. Part one provides a rationale for wanting to involve members of Kappa Delta Pi in the research project. Part two describes specific procedures designed to involve members in the project. Part three focuses on the results of having educators function as inquirers in the Good Schools Project.

The Rationale

The Good Schools Project research committee's reasons for promoting the meaningful involvement of Kappa Delta Pi members can be communicated best by briefly chronicling changing conceptions of the role of educational research in influencing educational practice. The traditional view of the relationship between research and practice was expressed by E.L. Thorndike, in 1910, in the inaugural issue of *The Journal of Educational Psychology*:

A complete science of psychology would tell every fact about everyone's intellect and character and behavior, would tell the cause of every change in human nature, would tell the result which every educational force—every act of every person that changed any other or the agent himself—would have. It would aid us to use human beings for the world's welfare with the same surety of the result that we now have when we use falling bodies or chemical elements. In proportion as we get such a science we shall become masters of our own souls as we now are masters of heat and light. Progress toward such a science is being made.[1]

The view articulated by Thorndike continued to dominate the educational research community's thinking throughout most of this century.[2] Even the absence of definitive research results did not generally inhibit most researchers' enthusiasm for a natural science-based conception of educational inquiry. Researchers could simply console themselves (and quiet impatient critics) with the fact that educational research was a young science which needed time to mature.[3]

Recently, however, educational researchers have begun to reassess the foundations of their field. In 1975, for example, Cronbach, a major figure in the area of research methodology, declared that the natural sciences do not provide an appropriate model for inquiry into social phenomena because social phenomena are far more complex than physical phenomena. Part of this complexity, according to Cronbach, results from the fact that culture is dynamic; therefore, generalizations which hold at a certain place and time will not necessarily hold in another context. Cronbach wrote:

> The trouble, as I see it, is that we cannot store up generalizations and constructs for ultimate assembly into a network. It is as if we needed a gross of dry cells to power an engine and could only make one a month. The energy would leak out of the first cells before we had half the battery completed. So it is with the potency of our generalizations.[4]

Other major figures in the field of educational research have reached much the same conclusion.[5] This conclusion, however, does not imply that research is unimportant. It simply suggests that the function of research is different than was once thought. Weiss, after studying how policy makers used evaluation results, defined the contribution of research to practice by distinguishing between problem solving and problem setting. Traditionally, Weiss argued, it was thought that research would provide the answer to problems such as which one of multiple educational means could most efficiently and most effectively accomplish particular educational ends. The newer view, however, pictures the contribution of research quite differently. In Weiss' words, the role of research is to provide "powerful labels for previously inchoate and unorganized experiences . . . to help mold officials' thinking."[6]

Research, in other words, functions as a heuristic rather than a recipe that can be applied and reapplied indiscriminately in situation after situation. Put another way, the new view of science suggests that researchers cannot do practitioners' thinking for them; rather, as practitioners confront and attempt to control the various educational settings in which they work, each practitioner must be his or her own inquirer and must adjust and consistently update the multiple heuristics which are part of each individual's response repertoire. Only if this is done will an individual be able to respond appropriately to an ever dynamic environment.

The view that each practitioner must ultimately be his or her own researcher has certain implications for researchers who hope their work will help practitioners act more intelligently. These implications might best be clarified if the image of researcher-as-teacher is employed to characterize the researcher's role. There are various kinds of teachers. Some teachers teach by disseminating information. This is the pedagogical role the researcher-as-teacher has traditionally played. There are also teachers, however, who are as concerned with process as they are with the dissemination of content. Inquiry-oriented science teachers, for example, involve their students with observing, classifying, hypothesizing, and experimenting, because they believe inquiry-oriented teaching most effectively teaches content and because they believe learning about the inquiry process by participating in that process is a worthwhile goal in and of itself.

Researchers who want to be teachers and who use inquiry-oriented science teachers as their pedagogical models will not simply disseminate findings to practitioners. Rather, they will attempt to engage practitioners in the research project itself in meaningful ways. Like the science teachers described above, these researchers will do this for two reasons. First, they will do this because they believe engagement in process will lead to a better understanding of the eventual findings. Second, they will do this because they believe the development of inquiry skills is a worthwhile goal, in and of itself, and that such development is best accomplished through involvement in inquiry. The researchers on the Good Schools Project research committee wanted to function as teachers, and they took the inquiry-oriented science teacher as their pedagogical model. Therefore, early on they decided to involve the practitioners and practitioners-to-be who are members of local Kappa Delta Pi chapters in the research project in meaningful ways.

Procedures for Involving Members

It is one thing to decide to involve members of local Kappa Delta Pi chapters in meaningful ways; it is quite another thing to find ways of doing this. The qualitative data collection process appeared to be the best access route to meaningful involvement in the research project. Although chapter members would facilitate the administration of the survey instrument, most significant intellectual activity, which related to the survey component of the study, occurred before and after data collection (i.e., during the related activities of conceptualization and item writing on the one hand and data interpretation on the other). Qualitative research is simply a more refined, more self-conscious, and more self-critical version of the process used by ordinary people to make sense of everyday life. Data collection, conceptualization, and data analysis are intertwined and must occur in the field to a much greater extent than is the case with quantitative study.[7] Some sense of structure had to be provided to the members of the local chapters that were going to engage in qualitative field work. The research committee, after all, wanted to use the qualitative data that members of local chapters collected. Furthermore, most Kappa Delta Pi members were neophytes when it came to doing qualitative research, and they required direction on how to proceed.

The research committee's solution to these problems was to

construct a "workbook" of sorts. The "workbook" contained a series of open ended interview questions and possible follow-up probes for interviewing teachers, administrators, parents, and students, with blank spaces below the question probes for note taking. It was hoped that the "workbook" would provide: (1) enough structure so data would be usable and (2) sufficient latitude for chapter members to formulate hypotheses on the basis of the interviewees' initial responses and then for local chapter members to formulate follow-up questions on the basis of their hypotheses. The interview questions for teachers, students, parents, and additional school personnel were either identical or nearly identical to the principal's interview procedures and questions which are reproduced in sections I, II, III, and IV of Appendix L.

Even more important than the "workbook" was the General Summary Booklet, which asked all the data collectors jointly to summarize and analyze the data each data collector had gathered. Although the research committee members hoped they might be able to use this summary booklet as a kind of index of the information recorded in interview "workbooks," the summary booklets were developed primarily to give local chapter members an opportunity to analyze critically the information they had collected. The procedures and questions from the General Summary Booklet relating to parent interview data are reproduced in Table 1. Table 2 contains the procedures and questions from the General Summary Booklet relating to the interviewers' general impressions of the schools they studied.

Results

The data on the effects of having educators and educators-in-training function as inquirers in the Good School Project were somewhat limited. A tremendous amount of data was collected as part of the study, but it did not seem reasonable to collect extensive data on the data collection process itself. Thus, a systematic study of the study was not part of the Good Schools Project design.

The evidence that exists on the impact of actively involving members of Kappa Delta Pi in the execution of the study came from two sources: (1) members' self-reports of their opinions about their involvement in the project that were written in response to the final question in the General Summary Booklet

Table 1

*Procedures and Questions from the General Summary Booklet Relating to the
Analysis of Parent Interview Data*

Procedures

If all parent interviews have been conducted by the same person(s), the following procedures should be followed:

1. The individual or pair should review the interview notes and tapes.

2. For each question that was asked during the interviews:

   (a) consider whether things about the responses were similar or different.

   (b) take note of anecdotes, illustrations, and examples which tell a lot about the school.

3. The responses for each question along with key anecdotes should be summarized on the following pages. Make sure to note instances where the persons interviewed disagreed with each other.

If parent interviews were conducted by different individuals or pairs of individuals as recommended in the "Instructions for Conducting Interviews," the following procedures should be followed:

1. The team captain should schedule a team review meeting so members of the team can share information about the interviews with each other.

2. Before this meeting, each person or pair of individuals who conducted the interviews should review their notes and tapes and prepare a brief summary of responses to each question. Include anecdotes, illustrations, and examples which the person being interviewed used.

3. At the meeting the team captain should assign a note taker and then follow the procedures listed below:

   (a) for each question asked during the interview, have each person who conducted the interviews share his/her findings, including anecdotes, illustrations, and examples.

   (b) after each individual has shared his/her findings, discuss whether the responses were similar or different.

   (c) decide on anecdotes, illustrations, and examples which tell a lot about the school.

Procedures (cont.)

4. As soon as possible after the meeting, the team captain should complete this section of the booklet using the notes taken during the meeting as a reference.

Questions

1. How did parents respond to question 1? That is, what did parents say when asked to sum up the school in a phrase? (Please indicate whether parents tended to view the school in similar or different ways.) Also, record several anecdotes, illustrations, or examples which parents told that seem to reveal a lot about parents' perceptions of the school.

2. Summarize parents' responses to question 2. That is, did parents think theirs was a good school? What reasons did they give to support their answers? What examples, illustrations, or anecdotes were shared in responding to this question which seemed especially revealing?

3. How did parents respond to question 3? That is, what did parents cite as reasons that people would judge this school as good?

4. How did parents respond to question 4? That is, did they think the school was different from other schools? If so, what differences did they describe? (Make sure you include specific examples and illustrations parents used to clarify generalizations.)

5. What did parents say about the school's history? What events and people did they talk about? Did parents generally tell the same story? If not, how might differences be accounted for?

6. What did parents say about teaching methods in this school?

7. Did parents indicate different things are learned in this school than in most schools? If so, what things were talked about? (Make sure to include parents' examples and illustrations.)

8. What did parents say about decision making in the school? Tell which people or groups were identified as decision makers and the kind of decisions each group or individual normally makes? Make sure you include examples cited by the parents.

9. What did parents say about discipline and student behavior in this school?

10. What did parents say about school/community relations?

11. What did parents say when asked about beliefs which influence the education of children in this school?

12. What did parents say when asked about job involvement? Be sure to include specific examples cited by parents.

13. How did parents characterize relationships in the school? What anecdotes and examples did they share when responding to question 13?

14. What other things did parents say about the school?

15. Please record below personal impressions of those who were involved with parent interviews.

Table 2

Procedures and Questions from the General Summary Booklet Relating to the Analysis of Interviewers' General Impressions

Procedures

After all meetings have been completed, the team captain should answer the following questions. If for some reason a team approach was not used and all interviews were conducted by one individual or a pair of individuals, the questions should be completed by that person or pair of persons.

Questions

1. Did different groups (e.g., teachers, parents, students, administrators) see the school in the same way? Explain:

2. Describe, in detail, how those of you who studied the school perceived the school.

3. Did the people who studied the school see the school in the same way as those interviewed? Explain:

4. Describe the people who conducted the interviews (i.e., How many people were involved? How old were they? Did they volunteer? etc.).

5. Describe the reactions of those who studied the school to being involved with the study (e.g., What did they learn? What parts of the study did they enjoy and what did they not like? Would they recommend that others engage in a similar project? etc.).

(see question 5, Table 2); and (2) the products produced by members of Kappa Delta Pi, including the remainder of the General Summary Booklet. These sources suggest the following generalizations about the effects of trying to involve educators in a nationwide study.

First, only a small percentage of chapters participated in the study at all, all participating chapters did not choose to complete the qualitative portion of the study, and not all of the chapters that participated in the qualitative portion of the study completed the General Summary Booklet. Research in general, and qualitative research in particular, requires considerable amounts of time. This fact was mentioned by virtually every chapter that completed the General Summary Booklet.

Second, the completed interview "workbooks" and General Summary Booklets that were returned to the Good Schools Project research committee indicated that chapters varied with respect to the care and seriousness with which they approached this project. In a few instances, only one sentence or phrase was recorded as a response to an interview question. Similarly, in certain instances there was no evidence that an attempt had been made to compare and contrast the responses of various subjects.

Third, materials from most chapters suggested that considerable care was given to the project, but in at least two instances these results might have been evidence more of members' willingness to fulfill an obligation rather than of members' engagement in the kind of learning experiences the research committee had envisioned when the project was conceptualized. The team captain of one local research effort stated explicitly in response to the final question in the General Summary Booklet concerning reactions of those involved in the project: "I think the process was viewed more as a service than a learning experience for members." The team captain at another chapter made similar comments about members' reactions:

> They considered it a part of their professional responsibility to Kappa Delta Pi, so they did the job to the best of their abilities. They spent many hours checking materials, summarizing, and meeting with the committee to complete the summary report. They did not like the amount of time consumed with the project; they liked the feeling of satisfaction that they had completed the job they set out to do.

Fourth, the evidence suggested that, in the majority of chapters participating in the qualitative portion of the project, members benefited by participating in the project in ways envisioned by the research committee and in ways the committee had not initially considered. The research committee, for example, had envisioned that participants would have an opportunity to engage in the kinds of critical thinking which, if transferred to participants' classroom practices, would make these participants better educators. There were indications that critical thinking occurred. There were indications, for example, that interview data were not always accepted at face value. Two undergraduate students, in summarizing their parent interview data, for instance, cautioned that their summary might not be representative of the opinions of all parents of children in the school that had been studied, since the sample of parents which the principal had provided did not seem nearly as diverse as the sample of students that had been interviewed. Similarly, other individuals reported having prior assumptions and biases exploded. One chapter, for example, reported that, as a result of participating in the study, chapter members had learned that "rural education can be excellent." Similarly, a student in another chapter who studied a highly successful urban school in a poor, largely black section of the city reported that she "would definitely recommend similar projects to others," because she now "better understands that community location does not determine the school," since the school her chapter studied was "contrary to stereotype."

One result of participation the committee had not envisioned was the inspirational effect which several participants reported. One team captain, for example, wrote of her group's reaction to participating in the project.

> We loved it and wished that others could have and
> would have been involved—running into that much
> enthusiasm would do them good. . . . I told the prin-
> cipal that I wish my group were as enthusiastic as
> his is.

The inference that growth occurred as a result of members participating in the process was also supported by testimonial evidence gleaned from responses to the final question in the General Summary Booklet. This question was designed to elicit members' reactions to participating in the project. The vast majority of these responses were positive, and many of these positive responses alluded to the learning that had occurred as a result of participating.

Some of the most enthusiastic testimonials came from retired educators who are members of alumni chapters of Kappa Delta Pi. Two such members wrote:

> We would recommend that others participate in
> this type of project, particularly those currently
> engaged in teacher education and those who are ac-
> tive members of local boards of education.

Similar enthusiasm was expressed by a seventy-four year old, who is a retired university administrator, former school principal, and professor of educational administration, and who is now serving in an adjunct professor role. He wrote:

> I am in schools several times each year for various
> assignments (accreditation teams, advisory council
> activities, etc.). This effort was decidedly the most
> satisfying and productive. The carefully structured
> instruments and directions played a major role.

Two graduate student members of Kappa Delta Pi were also
positive, but they tempered their enthusiasm with an important
cautionary note:

> We also learned much about interviewing as a form
> of data gathering. . . . We are both of the opinion
> that quantitative measures, by themselves, are *not*
> sufficient for determining *anything* about schooling
> or education. We would, therefore, recommend
> projects similar to this which attempt to match data
> with impressions. We feel that what we have done
> here is valuable to us and may be of value to the
> people at. . . [the school]. However, we cannot ex-
> press an honest enthusiasm for our role in the Good
> Schools Project until we see what, ultimately, is
> produced from our involvement here in Texas and
> can determine to what extent that work reflects
> both our findings here and our impressions of
> . . .[the] project as a whole.

Conclusion

The final comments above remind us that the Good Schools
Project was indeed designed to serve two purposes: to produce
good, usable research findings and to aid in the professional
development of educators who participated in the project. The
research committee chose to emphasize the first goal, yet there
is evidence that the second purpose was also accomplished to
some extent. Whether the second purpose might have been better accomplished by a research effort which was less national in
scope and less product oriented remains an open question.

Notes

1. E.L. Thorndike, "The Contribution of Psychology to Education," *The Journal of Educational Psychology* 1 (1910):6.
2. See, for example, N. Gage, *The Scientific Basis for the Art of Teaching* (New York: Teachers College Press, 1978); T. Good, J. Biddle, and J. Brophy, *Teachers Make a Difference* (New York: Holt, Rinehart and Winston, 1975).
3. See, for example, A. Rubin and M. Timpane, eds., *Planned Variation in Education* (Washington, D.C.: Brookings Institution, 1975).
4. L. Cronbach, "Beyond the Two Disciplines of Scientific Psychology," *American Psychologist* 30 (February 1975):123.
5. See, for example, P. Jackson, "The Promise of Educational Psychology," (Invited Address for Annual Meeting of the American Psychological Association, August 26, 1977).
6. C. Weiss, "Policy Research in the Context of Diffuse Decision Making," *Journal of Higher Education* 53 (1982):622.
7. For a relatively concise discussion of the differences between qualitative and quantitative inquiry, see J. Spradley, *Participant Observation* (New York: Holt, Rinehart and Winston, 1980), Chapter 3.

16

General Summary

The purposes of the Good Schools Project were four: to identify good schools throughout Ameria; to study those schools
carefully; to determine what made it possible for those schools to
develop over time; and to make inferences that would be useful
to people who want to make their own schools better.

Local chapters of Kappa Delta Pi formed committees of experienced, competent professionals to solicit nominations and
establish criteria for schools that were thought to be good in their
own communities. Using their own criteria, these local committees
finally identified 132 schools as good, and those schools were invited to participate in the Good Schools Project.

Reasonably complete sets of data were collected from 106
schools identified as good. These data sets included responses to
survey instruments from more than 3,200 teachers and 28,000
students, along with extensive interview data from each building
principal. In addition, more than 500 hours of interview data were
collected from students, teachers, parents, and others in 30 of
the 106 schools. Finally, achievement data were collected from
83 schools.

All data were aggregated, by school, according to the following conceptual dimensions: curriculum perspectives; goal attainment; classroom practices; interpersonal relations; commitment; discipline and safety; support services and facilities; decision making; and change over time. Previous chapters have
reviewed these data sets, according to each conceptual dimension, and complete descriptive information about the responses
to each survey item is reported in Appendices A through I.

In this chapter, a general summary of what these data seem
to mean is set forth in terms of six organizing constructs: comparisons; outsiders' perceptions; insiders' perceptions; grade
level differences; relationship to other studies; and the work yet
to be done.

Comparisons

There is a story, perhaps apocryphal, attributed to James Thurber regarding his response to the question: "How is your wife?" Thurber answered, so the story goes, "Compared to what?" Throughout this project the research committee wanted "typical schools" or "poor schools" or "other schools" with which to compare the "good schools" that had been identified and studied.

This study was begun with the explicit intention of being descriptive. The basic purpose was to describe *what is* rather than *what ought to be.* Because each member of the research committee was an experienced professional, however, the tendency persisted to compare *what is* with *what ought to be,* in terms of each person's own values and beliefs. The earlier chapters each reflect some of that bias, though a conscious effort was made to minimize or make explicit such a bias as much as possible. Wherever possible, comparisons were limited to other research studies, but the reader will undoubtedly detect instances in which personal beliefs or conventional wisdom can be discerned. Since the basic data are reported in detail in the appendices, readers are encouraged to study those tables and make their own interpretations.

Outsiders' Perceptions

One of the unique aspects of the Good Schools Project was the development and use of locally defined criteria for identifying schools as good. Typically, researchers have articulated criteria that previous research or authority or practice suggested were defensible in identifying schools as good. Because such typical approaches often resulted in extremely narrow and limiting conceptions of what makes a school good, the Good Schools Project research committee wanted to use a different approach.

In effect, competent and experienced professionals were asked to develop criteria that they felt were appropriate and defensible for identifying schools as good. The assumption of the Good Schools Project research committee was that such an approach would "open up" the criterion problem and allow the intelligence and wisdom of many able and experienced professionals to come to bear on the question. Some persons will critize such an approach. They will argue, in effect, that without predetermined criteria, local school people made poor decisions about which schools were good. The Good Schools Project research committee felt otherwise. The committee was confident that the schools identified as good in this study were actually good schools.

Futhermore, the information generated from the process for establishing the criteria produced a view of good schools that was only dimly perceived before. By asking competent and experienced professionals to identify schools that they felt were good in their own communities—according to criteria that they had developed for themselves and justified to themselves—the Good Schools Project research committee had really posed the question: How do school people define a "good school?" In other words, how do those professionals who are outside a given school perceive that school as good?

From the data reported in this study, outsiders saw the 106 schools in this study as good because the programs, people, and processes in those schools were good.

First, balance and richness of curricular offerings were seen as characteristics of the schools that were identified as good. Flexibility and variety were seen in programs. Goals were clear. Expectations were high. Achievements were valued.

Second, ousiders saw the 106 schools in this study as good because the processes in those schools were good. Students and staff worked hard. Opportunities for involvement were extensive. Acceptance of personal diversity was apparent, and recognition of attempts to adapt to individual differences was evident.

Third, students, administrators, teachers, and others in the schools were seen as good people. They were dedicated, caring, competent persons. They liked one another. They worked together effectively. They created ways of working in which the uniqueness and integrity of each person was valued. They communicated well among themselves and with those beyond the school. There was a spirit of acceptance and enthusiasm evident in their relationships day by day.

In summary, the outsiders who identified the 106 schools as good thought the schools were good because the people and the quality of life within the schools were good. The criteria used suggested that professionals in education have a broad conception of schooling that encompasses much more than academic achievement, per se, or strong administrative leadership. Those factors were important but insufficient by themselves to result in a school being seen as good.

Insiders' Perceptions

In all, more than 31,000 persons who knew that their schools had been identified as good responded to various survey questions about their schools. More than 400 different questions were posed. As least six summary statements seem warranted regarding the way those 31,000 persons saw their own schools: the excellent quality of human relationships that prevailed; the reasonableness that existed between expectations and standards; the breadth and balance of opportunities; the positive commitment that existed toward learning and toward the school; the positive direction in which the school was moving; and the realistic but helpful approach taken toward the routine, day-to-day activities within the school. Each of these six summary statements is elaborated below.

Human Relationships: The data in this study document and dramatize the point that these schools were good places in which to be and work each day. Students liked the teachers. Teachers liked the students. Students related to each other in positive ways. Administrators were seen in exceptionally positive terms. Parents were accepted as important members of the schooling teams.

There was a minimum of physical confrontation or violence and a maximum of harmony. The people in the schools felt safe and secure. Vandalism was almost nonexistent. Rules were reasonable and fairly enforced. There was evidence of the use of drugs, alcohol, and tobacco but the problems seemed manageable.

Students and staff looked forward to going to school each day. People trusted one another. The quality of human interactions was characterized by richness, openness, honesty, and confidence. People came together and stayed together and worked together to make their schools better places in which to be.

Expectations and Standards: The goals and expectations in these schools were clear and acceptable. In a sense, goals had been both clarified and ratified. Students and staff were clear about what they were trying to do, and all agreed that the intentions were being pursued.

The goals and expectations in these schools were learning oriented, but they were also broadly conceived rather than narrowly focused. Reading, writing, and factual knowledge were important objectives for these schools, but so were problem solving and critical thinking, developing a sense of self-worth, and respecting people who were different.

Not only were the goals in these schools clear and acceptable, but the ways in which the goals were realized were seen as reasonable. For example, homework was required, but moderately. Students worked, but they also played. Teachers taught, but they did so with compassion and concern, and they struggled to recognize and honor the individual variations that existed among their students.

There was very little unilateralism evident among the professionals who worked in these good schools. These professionals were not arbitrary or capricious in their expectations of students. They were not unforgiving in their demands. They were not inflexible or unyielding in their assessment of students' achievements. They recognized that teaching and learning are long-term ventures, and they seemed to tug and pull rather than yank or try to drag their charges along. They were less interested in failing students than they were in passing students on to more and better opportunities to learn.

Opportunities: Programmatically, these schools offered opportunities for students to broaden and deepen their horizons. There was both a range and balance among course offerings, classroom activities, teaching methods, evaluation procedures, extracurricular events, socializing opportunities, relationships within the community, and relationships with different people within the school.

Again, these opportunities seemed to be characterized by diversity and breadth rather than uniform requirement. The people in these good schools seemed committed to expanding and enriching their students' opportunities rather than restricting and limiting what those young people ought to do.

Commitment: The students and staff in these good schools felt strongly and positively about what was going on inside the schools and were committed to the purposes, programs, policies, and people involved. Students and staff believed that what they were doing was worthwhile and meaningful.

Parents were strong supporters of these schools. Many parents participated directly in school activities as aides or tutors. Most encouraged and supervised their children's homework, met with teachers to discuss particular problems, and supported the school in other ways. It also was obvious that the professionals in the schools worked to involve parents in a variety of ways.

Teachers and administrators in these schools were hardworking, open to suggestions, and generally responsible people. They were committed to success, to improvement, and to fostering a spirit of cooperation and collegiality that would enable all of those within the school to make it a good place to be and learn.

Direction of the School: The 106 good schools in this study were not perfect, but they were moving in that direction. The schools had problems, but the people in the schools generally recognized those problems, then mobilized their energies, intelligence, and skills to ameliorate or overcome the problems.

More important, perhaps, the people in these schools seemed to be oriented towards possibilities rather than problems. These people had a way of shifting their attention from difficulties and dilemmas to potentialities and challenges. The people in these schools were goal oriented; they wanted their schools to become better at doing what these people were trying to do—help students learn.

Several of the schools in this study were ordered by the courts to desegregate. These schools did, but the experience did not weaken them. It seemed to make them better. The people in the schools converted what others saw as a problem to what these people saw as a possibility.

In certain instances, some of these schools were able to establish a tradition for themselves as "good" or "getting better." Just how this came about was not always clear, but the idea of establishing precedent or creating history as a way of assuring continued improvement was evident, nonetheless.

A Realistic But Helpful Approach: The professionals who worked in these schools were oriented toward the positive, but these professionals were realistic in their approaches. They were not "dreamy-eyed." They did not always do what so-called experts in the field suggested, but these professionals did make decisions, took actions, confronted problems, created possibilities, and generally moved from where they were to where they wanted to be.

For example, teachers in these good schools apparently were participating in the decision-making process at a level at which they felt both comfortable and satisfied. It was evident that these teachers wanted involvement in decisions that pertained to instruction, but they did not generally want to participate in managerial-level decisions. Teachers felt that students should have some opportunities to exercise personal choice, but within a fairly narrow framework of predetermined options selected by the teacher.

The principals in these schools played an important role in making their schools good, but there was great variety in the approaches that individual principals used. In other words, there was no "one best way" of providing leadership. The principals developed strategies and styles of working that were unique to their own personalities and circumstances. However, in every instance these administrators had developed ways of coodinating their preferences with the people they worked with and the community they served.

Pragmatic, trial-and-error efforts, coupled with intelligence and sensitivity to surroundings, evidently made it possible for these building principals to reject "canned" solutions and, instead, to create "homemade" but relevant ways of dealing with the problems these principals confronted. Furthermore, these principals seemed to have done these things in ways that inspired confidence.

Grade Level Differences

The Good Schools Project research committee began this study with a commitment to identify good schools, wherever they might be and, then, to describe those schools carefully and completely so that others might be able to benefit from those descriptions. The intentions of the committee from the outset were to describe, not to compare.

However, within the sample of 106 schools identified as good there were 70 elementary level schools, 15 middle level schools, and 21 secondary level schools. Even a cursory examination of the data suggested that there were important differences among these schools, according to the grade levels served.

Some of the differences among these good schools by grade level lines have been described in previous chapters. Other differences are described in this chapter. No tests of the statistical significance of differences between means or percentages have been accomplished as of this writing. The concern here was to highlight, in a general sense, what seemed to be important variations between the responses of teachers and students, according to the grade levels involved.

Three response patterns seemed especially evident. In one pattern, the general tendency was for a sizeable majority of elementary level teachers or students to respond "always," somewhat fewer middle level persons to respond "always," and still fewer secondary level persons to respond in that same manner. For example, assuming that "always/often,"

Table 1

Percent of Teachers Responding Always, Often, Seldom, or Never to a Statement Concerning the Extent to Which Parents Work in the School Library

Survey Item (Item Number)	School Level		
	Elementary %	Middle %	Secondary %
Parents work in the school library. (72)			
Always/Often	49	26	5
Seldom	22	21	15
Never	29	53	80

"seldom," and "never" constituted a continuum, Table 1 portrays this first pattern clearly for one item to which teachers were asked to respond. The general slope is from higher percentages of agreement with "always" among elementary level teachers to lower percentages among secondary level teachers. This example illustrates only one pattern of response, however.

A second pattern would be one in which there were no basic differences according to grade level.

A third pattern would be the opposite of pattern number one. That is, the general tendency would be for a sizeable majority of secondary level teachers or students to respond "always," somewhat fewer middle level persons to do the same, and still fewer elementary level teachers or students to respond that way. The slope of agreement would be reversed from that reflected in Table 1.

Differences Among Teachers

Roughly 40 percent of the teachers' responses in this study corresponded to pattern one. Another 40 percent corresponded to pattern two, and the remaining 20 percent fell into pattern three. These are crude approximations, but they suggest one way in which there are differences among teachers according to grade level.

Pattern One: In studying those items where more elementary level teachers responded "always" than secondary level teachers, differences in at least four areas seemed to be evident: classroom practices; staff morale; involvement of parents; and feelings about the building and grounds.

In the area of classroom practices, elementary level teachers felt that they were more effective in achieving the goals of the school, had more materials available, made more options available to students, and placed greater emphasis on the academic than did their secondary level counterparts.

The morale of elementary level teachers seemed to be higher than the morale of secondary level teachers. The elementary level teachers seemed to sense a greater spirit of cooperation among their colleagues; faculty and inservice meetings were seen as more worthwhile; and there was a general sense of well-being, not quite so evident among secondary level staff.

As might be expected, the frequency and extent of parent involvement was also much higher at the elementary level than at the secondary level.

Finally, the sense of satisfaction with the workplace itself seemed to be much higher among elementary than secondary level teachers. The building was seen as more pleasant, more attractive, and the walls and other aspects of the building were used more frequently to display students' and staff work.

Middle level teachers were generally somewhere in between the elementary and secondary level teachers on almost every item in these four areas.

Pattern Two: In studying the many items in which there were almost no differences apparent according to grade level, four areas emerged: beliefs about curriculum; decision making; pressure on students to achieve; and dependence on the textbook as a primary source of instruction.

Beliefs about curriculum reflected the extent to which people felt that certain objectives or goals were important and how people defined subject matter, to themselves and to their students. Whereas there were consistent differences between the way elementary, middle, and secondary level teachers perceived the effectiveness with which goals were *achieved* (elementary teachers thought they were more effective), there were almost no differences among teachers in terms of their indications of the *importance* of different goals for schools to try to achieve.

In the area of decision making, few differences were evident that related to school level. Decisions about selecting instructional materials, hiring staff, disciplining students, and the like were almost all seen in a comparable way by teachers at different levels.

Likewise, most of the teachers in the 106 schools in this study indicated about the same amount of pressure on students to achieve, regardless of grade level served. Typically, teachers felt that there were moderate pressures placed on students, but there were few differences.

Finally, about three-fourths of the teachers in this study indicated a general dependence on the textbook as a primary instructional source, but there were few differences according to grade level.

Pattern Three: In approximately 20 percent of the items used in this study, secondary level teachers responded "always" or "often" more frequently than the elementary level teachers. Two kinds of items seemed evident: age-related and responsibility-related.

Among the age-related items, there was, as one might expect, increased evidence of vandalism and drug, alcohol, and tobacco use among older students than among younger students, according to their teachers' perceptions.

Several items that reflected responsibility seemed to differentiate secondary from elementary level school teachers. Secondary level teachers indicated that they spent more time—during school and after school—working with students in various ways than did elementary level teachers. However, secondary level teachers also indicated that they felt they had less control over what they were doing than elementary level teachers.

As stated before, none of the differences indicated here have been tested statistically, but the patterns seem important.

Differences Among Students

Pattern One: In approximately a third of the instances, elementary level students responded "always" more frequently than secondary level students to the questions on the survey. Two areas were apparent: relationships with other people and goals and expectations.

Although the general pattern of human relationships evident in all of the schools studied was positive, elementary level students had even more positive perceptions of those around them than secondary level students. Elementary level students liked and respected their teachers, thought their teachers were fair and considerate, and thought their teachers cared about the students. Further, the elementary level students also felt more positively toward the other students in their schools than did the secondary level students.

Elementary level students felt that there were high expectations for them to achieve, and that they actually did achieve the goals that had been set for them by the teachers in their schools. Secondary level students felt the same way, but to a slightly lesser degree.

Pattern Two: Elementary and secondary level students tended to have comparable patterns of agreement in four areas: discipline and safety in the school; teacher encouragement of students to disagree; limited choices available to students; and teachers' fairness. Approximately half of all the students' responses fell into pattern two.

There were few differences among students according to grade level regarding the reasonableness of rules, what happened when rules were broken, or safety within the school. Students generally felt very safe and secure, and they understood and accepted the rule structure that existed.

Students in these 106 schools felt that teachers encouraged students to disagree, to express their own opinions, to examine different points of view, and to challenge such things as the textbook.

There was general agreement among students across grade levels that they had little choice of subject matter topics or instructional materials. Further, much school work was seen as uninteresting.

There was also general agreement among students regarding whether teachers showed favoritism, got angry, and the like. The consensus was "no."

Pattern Three: In two areas, secondary level students tended to indicate "always" more frequently than elementary level students: use of drugs, alcohol, and tobacco by students and perception of the school as a necessary but not particularly interesting place to be. About a sixth of the responses fell into pattern three.

As might be expected, secondary level students acknowledged that students more frequently used drugs, alcohol, and tobacco than elementary or middle level students.

In another vein, secondary level students were generally committed to graduating from high school, but they also felt that teachers made few efforts to individualize instruction to meet the students' unique needs. Further, secondary level students, more than elementary level students, admitted to being clock watchers and claimed that classwork was more often a waste of time.

Relationship to Other Studies

Is there any relationship to what we have learned about good schools and other studies of especially successful institutions? We began this report by outlining some of our concerns regarding the tendency of many researchers to focus on the pathological or problematic aspects of human endeavor. Our focus was on *good* schools, successful institutions. In previous chapters, specific findings from the Good Schools Project have been compared to previous research. In this section, emerging generalizations from the Good Schools Project data base will be held alongside some of the generalizations that Peters and Waterman report about corporations that have been especially successful over a fairly long period of time.[1]

It can be argued that comparing schools to corporations is an inappropriate comparison. That may be true. But schools, like corporations, are social institutions. Both involve people working together to achieve human purposes in a structured, organized way. Both have been studied primarily in terms of bureaucratic theory, and both have been carefully scrutinized and severely criticized in recent years. Acknowledging the problems with such a comparison, we still felt it might be worthwhile.

The generalizations that follow should be seen as tentative, however, and not definitive. As more data analyses become available, these generalizations may represent streams of thought that ought to be pursued. For the time being, though, these generalizations should be interpreted cautiously and carefully.

Peters and Waterman cite eight attributes that characterize excellent, innovative companies.[2] From our data about good schools we will try to generalize in terms of those eight attributes.[3]

1. *A Bias for Action*: Outstanding corporations are characterized by the fact that they "get on with it." They act; they are not forever planning. Whereas most corporations are meticulous in appointing committees, considering alternatives, and proceeding carefully into the future, the best companies have a way of moving quickly and decisively, capitalizing upon the creative insights of a few persons, usually within a few weeks.

The data from the Good Schools Project do not relate very well to this point, so no useful comparisons seem possible here. The questions in the survey concerning decision making, for example, asked about who was involved and in what decision making areas, but almost no questions pertained to the quality of decisions in relation to time and action.

2. *Close to the Customer:* People in outstanding corporations learn from the people the corporations serve. They listen, intently and regularly. There is an obsession with providing service and quality to the customer.

The data from the Good Schools Project suggest that teachers and administrators do "pay attention" to the students and parents in these schools. The professionals are concerned. They invite parental involvement. They care about the students. They want students to learn, to achieve, and to participate. Most school people would *say* that such things are important; professionals in these good schools *believe that such things are important*, and *act* on that belief.

3. *Autonomy and Entrepreneurship*: Innovative companies foster many leaders and innovators throughout the organization. They do not try to hold everyone on a tight rein. They encourage risk taking.

The schools in the Good Schools Project seem to have some of these qualities, too. The evidence in this project is modest, but there are clear signs that experimentation is encouraged and not simply "allowed." Administrators have confidence in their staff members; teachers work at fostering autonomy among students.

4. *Productivity Through People*: Excellent companies treat the rank and file as the root source of quality and productivity. They respect the individual. Every worker is seen as a "source of ideas, not just acting as a pair of hands."

This principle is clearly evident in the Good Schools Project data. People are important. Teachers' ideas are heard. Students' concerns are honored. There is a definite commitment to make the school function effectively by using the talents and the contributions of all who are involved.

5. *Hands-on, Value-driven*: Every excellent company is clear on what it stands for, and its values permeate the entire corporation. Philosophy is translated into achievement, and resilient companies (i.e., those that have lasted and prospered over the years) are those that have clarified and adhered to their beliefs.

The people in the schools in the Good Schools Project are also clear about their beliefs. Learning is important. People are important. Achievement is important. Involvement is important. Furthermore, the people in good schools act on those beliefs. They are committed to converting goals and values into practice.

6. *Stick to the Knitting*: Excellent companies stay reasonably close to the business they know. Mergers are almost unheard of. They tend not to diversify; not to take on new commitments in areas in which they have little experience or expertise.

There is little in the Good Schools Project data that relates to this point. It may be that good schools have worked to maintain a tighter focus—to resist the demands to "do this, do that" that are often urged on schools—but that cannot be discerned from the data available.

7. *Simple Form, Lean Staff*: The underlying structural forms in the excellent companies are elegantly simple. The matrix arrangement is seldom used. Organizational structure is extremely stable. Top level staff members are few in number.

The data from the Good Schools Project are difficult to relate to this principle. The fact is, most schools are characterized by simple form and lean staff, but this principle probably applies because of historical rather than conscious factors. Furthermore, even though this principle is in evidence, it seems inappropriate to make too much of the point. It is certainly not "causal" in any real sense of that term. The fact that schools as institutions are often enmeshed in much larger "systems," however, compounds the problem. The "school," as we have studied it, corresponds to a "plant" that is a part of a larger corporation, but no attempt was made in the Good Schools Project to sort out the entanglements that may very well exist between the school building and the school district. In all probability, much that is not "lean and simple" in schools' operations may be directly attributable to district level demands and functions, but there are few data on that point in this study.

8. *Simultaneous Loose–Tight Properties*: Excellent companies are both centralized and decentralized. Typically, these companies have pushed autonomy down to the shop floor, but they are fanatic centralists around the few core values they hold dear.

Good schools are very much like the outstanding corporations in relation to this principle, it seems. Schools that have been identified as good are characterized by unanimity regarding goals, but there is latitude among the staff regarding methods and practices.

By way of summary, then, the concepts of organizational theory that have been highlighted by Peters and Waterman as characteristic of outstanding corporations seem generally to apply to schools. However, the data from the Good Schools Project were not collected from that theoretical perspective, so the data relate more in a marginal than direct way. It should be pointed out, though, that no direct reversals were apparent. Future studies might lean more directly on Peters and Waterman's theory and generate more direct comparisons. For the time being, it seems sufficient to suggest that the Good Schools Project data and the successful corporations data are more consistent than inconsistent. Additional research remains to be done.

Work Yet To Be Done

The time line for the Good Schools Project was about three years. The research committee was appointed in the Fall of 1981, and this report will be published during the Spring of 1984. Considering the fact that hundreds of people participated in identifying schools and collecting data, those of us who have had responsibility for coordinating this project feel good about all that has been done. However, there is much more that we can do and should do, if we hope to understand what good schools are like and what makes them that way.

At least three different kinds of research studies and two different kinds of action projects are apparent to the research committee: intensive studies; achievement studies; correlational
studies; chapter involvement projects; and dissemination
projects. Examples of each of these are outlined below.

Intensive Studies: During the course of this project 106 good
schools were identified. Would it be possible to reduce this
number to a much smaller set of schools that might be studied intensively? For example, certain items on the *Teacher Survey* or
Student Survey could be specified and then an item analysis, by
school, would sort out schools on those particular variables.
Other ways to reduce the number of schools could be employed.
Intensive, on-site studies of those few remaining schools would
be particularly revealing.

Achievement Studies: Achievement data from 83 of the 106
good schools are readily available. Those data should be analyzed. Conversion to some type of a common "score" (i.e., the
scores now available represent various grade levels and different
testing instruments) would allow direct studies of achievement,
as well as correlational studies of various kinds. For example, do
schools which have higher "scores" on certain survey items (e.g.,
teachers' expectations) actually have higher achievement scores?
Or, do schools which report more vandalism have lower levels of
achievement?

Correlational Studies: Given the huge data base available,
multiple regression, path analysis, and factor analysis-type
studies could be and should be accomplished. For example,
would the conceptual dimensions used in this study "fall out" as
factors if factor analytic studies were accomplished? Such
studies would do much to support or refute the theoretical basis
that has been utilized and should provide insights into the
theoretical dimensions of good schooling.

The most promising correlational studies, however, would
be to carefully analyze the interview data and then to correlate
those data with survey item data, school by school.
Methodologically, such approaches could bridge the typical
quantitative/qualitative dichotomy and open new vistas for
researchers and other students of schooling.

Chapter Involvement: Everything that has been accomplished in the Good Schools Project thus far has been accomplished because Kappa Delta Pi counselors and members
met and worked together to make this project a reality. The ques-

tion now is: "Are there other ways in which chapters can work with the Good Schools Project data to help themselves and help the schools?" For example, could chapters sponsor inservice meetings with local school people to study the results of the Good Schools Project? Could other schools be encouraged to use the survey instruments to collect data in their schools and then compare the results with the findings of the Good Schools Project? Could seminars or "brown bag lunches" be held on college campuses for graduate students or college faculty members to discuss the results of the project?

Dissemination: In one sense, the Good Schools Project has been completed. This monograph is evidence of that fact. In another sense, much remains to be done. If the findings reported here have any utility at all, they ought to be shared more widely. Videotapes, periodical publications, seminars, inservice sessions, college courses, and other ways of sharing information might be developed. The Good Schools Project research committee has shepherded the project along this far, and the committee hopes to do more. Since the project was a Kappa Delta Pi venture, though, it may be that other people within the society will become interested and think of creative ways and means to share the results with others. The research committee hopes so.

Summary

This chapter has summarized why those who identified the 106 schools in this study felt those schools were good, how the students and teachers and others in those schools felt about their schools, and how their perceptions of their schools varied according to grade level. In addition, the findings in the Good Schools Project were compared in a general way to one study of successful corporations, and the research and action projects that might be accomplished in the future were described briefly. In the last chapter, implications from this study will be described.

Notes

1. Thomas J. Peters and Robert H. Waterman, Jr., *In Search of Excellence: Lessons from America's Best Run Companies* (New York: Harper and Row, Publishers, 1982).
2. Ibid., Chapter 1.
3. Ibid., Chapters 5-12.

17

Toward Good Schools: An Epilogue

The research committee's final discussions about Kappa Delta Pi's Good Schools Project reviewed the central assumptions of the study, drew and assessed inferences from the data, and projected some generalizations about the future of schooling in the United States. This final section presents in highlight fashion some major implications its author gleaned or developed from these discussions and from the project itself.

The Goal: Good Schools

Every person associated with the Good Schools Project is impressed with the importance of good schools. Faith in the power of education is strengthened by testimonials given by faculty and students about their schools. Our fears for the future had been increased by uncertainties about the quality of education in many situations, but are now somewhat lessened by knowledge of widespread interest in the quality of schooling in the United States.

In the early 1980s, education has been a major matter in the news, in political campaigns and issues, and in public and private funding. Major studies of educational goals, programs, and problems have received much attention in the media. In all these concerns and activities there is the search for better education for more people because of the recognized power of good education in the lives of individuals and in the character of American society.

There are different opinions, of course, as to what is considered good education. The traditions of American democracy almost mandate variety in the goals and practices in American institutions, but the traditions also mandate opportunity for all. The Good Schools Project has produced no complete, universal, or magic formula for good education. However, characteristics of schools considered good have been identified, and schools seeking to become better can find in this text descriptions of these characteristics for study and perhaps emulation.

Our clearest conclusion, though, is that there is universal belief in the power of good schools to improve the human condition. The goal of maintaining *good* schools—as widely as possible for as many as possible—was the focus of this study, and this goal is the guide for the future that is herein accepted and projected.

The Role of Kappa Delta Pi

Kappa Delta Pi's sponsorship of the Good Schools Project was a forward-looking step for an honor society in education. Historically committed to excellence in education, Kappa Delta Pi has taken, through this project, a significant step towards involving its members and its funds in school improvement. It is regrettable, but not surprising, that only a small number of chapters, less than 10 percent, did participate, with a correspondingly low representation of the membership.

But Kappa Delta Pi can help greatly in the further search for good schools and in efforts to increase the numbers and quality of good schools. In the first place, Kappa Delta Pi is helping to do this by publishing this report, and earlier ones, and by continuing its support of additional publications and other forms of dissemination. In the second place, Kappa Delta Pi can lend its support to the Good Schools Project research committee and other representative groups which may seek large-scale funding of research and development projects for school improvement. In the third place, Kappa Delta Pi's future publications, convocations and conferences, and committee activities can and should reflect the interest in good schools stimulated by this project. Kappa Delta Pi can demonstrate to the profession and to the public how such an organization can maintain a mission focused on the advancement of schools and society, not just the welfare of Kappa Delta Pi members. Finally, the successful experience of many participants in the Good Schools Project should encourage increased participation of chapters and members in further studies.

The Role of a School

The goal of increasing the number of good schools cannot be achieved by Kappa Delta Pi or any other organization external to schools. We can only agree with all of the authors and researchers who insist that the ultimate responsibility for a school's quality rests with the people most directly involved in the school—administrators, faculty, students, parents, and control board members. These people can be greatly influenced by the appropriations for the school and by the community's culture, but within these limitations these persons usually have much latitude in operating good, bad, or indifferent schools.

The task of school leaders in regard to school quality is to keep the goal of becoming or being a good school paramount in all school planning and implementation. The Good Schools Project has not identified any one process or procedure that always brings about school improvement, but there is certainty that local school leadership—administration/faculty group, school/community group, control board/school group, or other combinations of the critical leadership groups—must be permanently and actively involved. The leadership group, however constituted from its critical components, is responsible for setting the directions toward the central goal of becoming (or improving) a good school. There is need for attention to the goal of becoming a good school whenever a school is lagging in its demonstration of such earmarks of a good school as those proposed here. The following checklist has been prepared as a possible departure point for a school's self-assessment or toward a definition of the characteristics of a good school.

Some Earmarks of a Good School

1. The school is part of a *community-wide education program,* with well-defined bridges for cooperation with other schools, school levels, and community educational programs.

2. *School goals* are sufficiently comprehensive, balanced, realistic, and understood, and they permeate the activities of the school.

3. The school has and exercises considerable responsibility for *program planning by its own personnel* within the policies and regulations set by its control group.

4. *School climate* is friendly, good-humored, busy, and members of the school faculty and staff generally regard their work as challenging and satisfying.

5. A variety of *teaching modes and resources* are used as appropriate to instructional purposes.

6. *Student performance* toward all school goals is evaluated as regularly and fully as needed or possible and is generally regarded as satisfactory.

7. *Students participate* fully and enthusiastically in the wide variety of activities provided by the school and community.

8. *Parents and other citizens of the school community participate* fully and enthusiastically in the opportunities provided for their involvement in the educational program.

9. The *library and other learning skills centers* are widely and effectively used by students.

10. The school program provides, at its level, for the *natural progression of learners* from dependent, other-directed learning to independent, self-directed learning.

11. The *school principal* is a generally liked and respected leader who leads and collaborates effectively in school and community projects.

12. The school faculty seeks *continuing renewal and improvement.*

Some Directions Toward the Goal

Eight major ideas about how leaders in school improvement efforts can move toward the goal of good schools have been affirmed by or inferred from this study.

Define the Characteristics of Good Schools

Any school district, parent group, school faculty, or other sponsoring organization seeking to develop or even study good schools needs to prepare a working definition of what makes a school good. As described in Chapter Two, the members of each local chapter selection committee participating in the Good Schools Project developed their own set of criteria. There was value in this process, and other study and research groups may wish to utilize it. There may also be value in research studies and school improvement programs which utilize existing criteria to facilitate comparison and evaluation of schools according to such external criteria. The essential step is the careful development of criteria related to the goals of the study.

This report can be of service to individuals and groups developing such definitions of good schools. Chapter Three presents a summary and discussion of the criteria developed by the local committees of educators set up by the various Kappa Delta Pi chapters participating in the Good Schools Project. Differing from criteria relating largely to quantitative aspects of education, the most numerous of the committee's criteria related to the nature of the school program. Within this category the largest subcategory of criteria had to do with providing for students' needs. A broad, balanced, flexible curriculum, with full recognition of individual differences, was desired, not simply a universal set of graduation requirements. Worth noting, too, are the interests of educators in school climate, with emphasis on such matters as interpersonal relationships and morale. The various other categories are described in Chapter Three, and special note is made of the differences between the criteria suggested in the Good Schools Project and the research on effective schools, especially in the greater breadth of the criteria reported here.

Individuals and groups undertaking studies and improvement programs toward good schools may also find useful the data reported in Chapter Five as to various physical, demographic, and other characteristics of the schools involved. Although the Good Schools Project schools are not compared with other populations, the data raise many speculations about good schools. For example, are good schools smaller, more homogeneous in population, more stable, and freer of vandalism?

Again, the Good Schools Project does not propose universal use of a particular set of characteristics of good schools. It does provide data and inferences that may assist any group wanting to develop such a set.

Continue Research About Good Schools

One Hundred Good Schools may raise more questions than it answers; indeed, this is the hope of the research committee and leaders of Kappa Delta Pi, the sponsoring society. Past attention to the faults, problems, and weaknesses of schools does not seem to have brought about the excellence needed in education. More attention to the characteristics of good schools and the emulation of these characteristics may provide the positive direction needed.

This report suggests many specific needs for research. New studies based on selection of good schools by a set of external criteria as well as continued use of the criteria-formulating process employed in this study may be useful. Additional dimensions for study not included here can be used to broaden the scope of such research. Case studies over time could greatly extend the type of inquiry that is reported in Chapter Fourteen. The roles of various change agents and factors in moving toward better schools is an intriguing area for study.

The process of movement toward better schools also involves the dissemination as well as the identification of ideas and practices of good schools, but what dissemination devices are effective? How are people best involved in implementation? How are innovations evaluated in use? What devices, innovations, and processes relate best to particular goals of improvement? Are there constants—for example, in school organization, financing, buildings, and zoning—that can be relied upon to help produce better quality education?

The author of this epilogue would especially favor intensive studies of individual characteristics of good schools as implied from this Good Schools Project, or as postulated in such lists of characteristics as illustrated earlier in this chapter. For example, school improvement groups could be aided greatly by definitive information on such questions as these:

• How are reading and other learning skills affected by

cooperative educational efforts of a school and such community agencies as a library, television station, and
newspaper?

- What effects, if any, does the identification and continued
discussion and publication of a set of school goals have on
achievement of the goals—for example, school behavior
goals or violation of behavior regulations?
- What measures of school climate are developed and used
in schools considered good, and what explanations are
found of differences between schools?
- What teaching modes and resources are used in teaching
the same units, skills, or concepts in different classrooms
of good schools, and what effects on student learning and
satisfaction can be related to the use of a variety of modes
and resources?
- What methods of evaluating performance in school goals
of an affective nature are used in good schools and with
what results?
- What effects of the use of adult volunteers can be identified, with regard to student achievement, school morale,
and parental support of the school?
- What practices for developing independent study skills
are used at the elementary, middle, and secondary levels
in schools considered good? How does the use of these
practices in the good schools compare with other
schools?
- What differences can be identified between the principals
of schools considered good and other principals on such
factors as: specific preparation for the principalship;
previous teaching experience; quality of any internship or
previous administrative experience; method of selection
of the principal?

With a sample population of schools considered good, there
could be an almost endless list of possible studies identifying
practices in these schools and comparing practices in these
schools with other schools.

The questions for study about good schools are legion. The
approach espoused here is that of utilizing the "good schools"
base in the planning, facilitating, and use of further research.

Involve Educational Organizations

Various types of educational organizations—honor societies, educational foundations, job-related organizations of a great variety, and others—have sponsored, financed, or conducted educational research for many purposes and with varied results. Kappa Delta Pi has exerted significant leadership in demonstrating how such an honor society can evolve, finance, and conduct—through the effort of a research committee—this research on good schools. As suggested earlier, Kappa Delta Pi can and should continue to give such leadership and service in an area uniquely related to the excellence in education for which the organization stands. Other organizations can participate, too.

An organization can provide the human resources essential to research—leadership, performance of tasks however small or large, liaison with the schools needed for inquiry and experimentation, and the writers, speakers, and other disseminators needed to make the results known. The honor societies and educational foundations have relatively broad interests and are not restricted to particular approaches or positions.

The job-related organizations for teachers (by fields and levels), administrators, librarians, counselors, and so forth also can provide needed specificity in research interests. Such organizations can continue individually to study what specific programs and techniques best assure quality education in their members' fields and levels of special interest.

Research is expensive. School budgets have not usually accorded funds for research, except as they are contributed by external agencies. Government funding, once almost lacking, has increased, but not enough to provide for the continuing needs of education in an ever-changing future. Philanthropy of foundations, industries, businesses, and of individuals can help more.

Dissemination and adoption of research findings are especially aided by educational organizations. Such organizations are the greatest producers of educational journals, books, and other educational materials. These organizations can give great impetus to the interest of the nation in good schools through the care and importance accorded journal articles and columns, pamphlets and monographs, and books, as well as videotapes and other audio-visual productions on the nature and characteristics of good schools and the elements thereof.

One interesting possibility is the creation of educational

consortia dedicated to the advancement of quality in schools across the nation. Organizations with similar interests—for example, by field, position, or location—might team together, perhaps enlisting the aid of honor societies, colleges and universities, and groups of schools. Networks have been widely used in educational improvement programs. The suggestion here is to extend such networks, especially for identification of the characteristic features of good schools and the dissemination and extension of such features.

Seek Cooperation of Educators, Citizens, and the Media

As noted earlier, education is an important area today—in news reporting, political campaigns, and public budgets. Much of the space devoted to education in the past decade has been about the reputed failures and shortcomings of education. Negative happenings can be expected in any such broad human enterprise, but quality and success can be publicized, too, as educators, citizens, and the media cooperate for positive results.

The annual Gallup polls of the public's attitudes toward the public schools constitute a case in point. The 15th Annual Gallup Poll results were published in the September 1983 issue of the *Phi Delta Kappan*.[1] Each of the fifteen polls has involved participation of educators, citizens, and educational organizations; the reports have provided useful data as to the status of public opinion on recurrent educational issues. Increasingly, as education has become of greater interest, the press and other outlets also report or comment upon the polls.

Such score cards also are needed on the quality of education in local communities, and Phi Delta Kappa's Dissemination Division provides materials and services to help local communities conduct surveys of their population. A parallel effort might be made by Kappa Delta Pi or some other organization to sponsor polls, case studies, or other types of investigations of progress on achieving the characteristics of good schools—e.g., an annual rating, perhaps by local patrons and citizens, of the status of one or more schools on a "Becoming A Good School" scale. Competitions are possible and could be useful incentives if the bases of comparative ratings are positive.

The need seems especially great for stories in the press and media in general of programs, projects, and classroom activities in local schools which are illustrative of good practice. Could local chapters of Kappa Delta Pi, and perhaps other educational societies and professional organizations, constitute local advisory committees on good schools to advise the media of specific stories, as well as to alert the schools to the types of practices which can be appropriately reported?

The data of the Good Schools Project are consistent, too, with the belief that cooperation of educators, citizens, and the media is essential to providing the financial and other resources needed to maintain good schools. Because this type of cooperation is needed to produce the shoulder-to-shoulder effort required in many communities, Kadelpians and other interested and knowledgeable individuals can be catalysts in organizing local groups for cooperative activity.

Focus on Appropriate Educational Goals

Much controversy over the quality of education seems due to disagreement and confusion as to its goals. Perhaps the reason elementary schools in general are regarded more favorably than secondary schools is that there is more general agreement as to the goals of the elementary school. Is it possible that the lower ratings given secondary schools are actually due to the greater disagreement or, perhaps, less common understanding of secondary school goals? Good schools are best for particular purposes, but they also tend to be better on most purposes than other schools, as well as good on any scale that produces an average.

Continuing efforts to improve the quality of schools should include careful formulation of school goals and ever-faithful adherence to accepted goals in the schools' improvement efforts and evaluation. Goodlad, in his "A Study of Schooling," proposed a list of "Goals for Schooling in the U.S." that were derived from two inquiries included in the study, and he stated that these goals appeared in sufficient frequency in state educational documents to suggest considerable national agreement. Although such a list is not proposed in this report of the Good Schools Project, there is thorough agreement with Goodlad's commentary:

> We are not without goals for schooling. But we are lacking an articulation of them and commitment to them.[2]

Efforts to improve the quality of schools must be directed toward particular needs for improvement, and these needs should relate to educational goals and problems associated with goal attainment. More rather than less effort is essential for our systems of education and our local schools to formulate, adopt, and amend goals that can guide education and help in efforts to improve it.

Differentiate the Roles of Schools and Other Educative Agents

Many educators and citizens believe that the problems of schooling have been multiplied by uncertainty, confusion, and controversy over the respective roles of educative forces and agencies, such as the family and home, church, media, child- and youth-serving organizations, industry and business, the military forces, and others. It is not that the schools avoid cooperation, but the pressure of traditional and legally assigned tasks allows too little opportunity to explore ways of working better and more effectively in cooperative educational enterprises.

The research committee members can envision an "educative community" in which schools take their appropriate role, a comprehensive but not exclusive one. We agree with Goodlad that the "idea has been with us for a long time" and "it may be an idea whose time has come."[3] Drastic steps are needed in many and probably most communities to bring about the cooperative efforts required for genuinely good education. All educative forces and agencies must be involved, if the young are to have the quality of experiences in home, school, and community that influences the development of the citizens that America wants.

We suggest that the community groups at work for developing or improving good schools include in their memberships representatives of the nonschool educative agencies in the community. Such a group may have no voice in coordinating various educative efforts but, in developing school goals, programs, and studies, the group very much needs information on the educative roles of other agencies. A common complaint is that "schools have taken on too much" or, perhaps better, that "schools have been given too much to do." When will schools and their communities start doing something constructive about this problem? Community education advisory councils, school–media planning committees, community-wide reading, writing, and viewing programs, school–home–church programs of education against crime, drug abuse, and similar plagues of modern living are among the types of cooperative endeavors schools can help organize. Kappa Delta Pi chapters and other honor societies and professional organizations might well take leadership in stimulating these cooperative approaches.

Seek Continuity and Progression in Learning

Public school organization, as it exists today, was never conceptualized and implemented as a whole, although some planned communities have been able to begin and build a total organization at one time. In general, though, different grade combinations, student groupings, teaching arrangements, and other organizational features have been added on or substituted for existing plans as necessity or invention indicated. An individual child going through twelve to fourteen years of schooling typically encounters barriers and gaps that interfere with continuous progress in learning.

Ideas and opinions of educators working at different levels vary substantially. As noted in Chapter Sixteen, many of the analyses of students' and teachers' responses reported in this study show differences between those working at the elementary and secondary levels, with those at the middle level usually falling in the middle of the range. For example, middle and secondary level teachers indicated less confidence than elementary level teachers in students' choices of learning activities; elementary level students and teachers viewed goal attainment by their schools more positively than those at the other two levels; elementary level teachers tended to rate interpersonal relations in their schools more positively than did secondary level teachers, with middle level teachers again in between the two. Undoubtedly the maturity and broader experiences and interests of the older students affect both students' and teachers' perceptions, but could it also be that the secondary school tradition and organization have tended to make school–student relations more adversarial at the upper level?

Continuing studies of school improvement can well give major attention to the concept of continuous progress and to all the barriers and gaps which jeopardize its implementation in schooling. Team teaching, individualized instruction, school-within-a-school, and other efforts that promote closer student–teacher relations found in this study may need more study and implementation. Although middle schools developed in the United States during the past twenty years have aimed to improve the transition from elementary to secondary schools, our observation indicates that many middle schools have not yet developed adequate transitional programs. Vertical articulation from school entrance to school exit is a great need in American public education. Islands exist where smoothly flowing tributaries should be joining the mainstreams. Good schools require smooth movement of learners along a continuum—in fact many continuums—rather than up a ladder with many barriers and gaps.

Use the Ultimate Criterion: Lifelong Learning

In the learning society toward which the United States is moving so rapidly, the ultimate criterion of a good school becomes: Does the school help its students become interested and effective lifelong learners? Obviously, school researchers, evaluators, and patrons cannot wait for the answer from extended longitudinal studies, but they can try to identify the factors and practices that relate to the creation of both the will and the skills required for lifelong learning. Present lifelong learners can assist in identifying what helped them; persons who seem to have given up active learning interests may be able to analyze what turned them off; studies of motivation and learning skills in any population may yield clues. More imaginative research, stimulation of practice to embrace the research findings, and stretching of minds are desirable and possible.

The goal of creating lifelong learners is real, not idealistic. Predispositions, attitudes, and behaviors toward learning develop early and are constantly influenced by schools and educative agencies. The indications of too few opportunities for students to engage in self-directed learning activities, of possible undue reliance on single-source textbooks, and of less than desired individualized instruction are enough to suggest the need for more intensive examination of classroom practices and other school experiences.

A Dynamic Goal: Toward Good Schools

We cannot end this epilogue without a wistful acknowledgment that all the research and improvement suggested herein cannot ensure that good schools will remain good. The search commenced by the Good Schools Project for Kappa Delta Pi and all other interested organizations and individuals has to be a permanent one. Knowledge increases very, very rapidly while institutions will require adjustments of types this writer cannot now conceive. The search is indeed the thing. If properly and widely conducted, it may help schools become good and stay good, although different.

Notes

1. George H. Gallup, "The 15th Annual Poll of the Public's Attitudes Toward the Public Schools," *Phi Delta Kappan,* September 1983, pp. 33-47; also see in the same issue Stanley M. Elam, "The Gallup Education Surveys: Impressions of a Poll Watcher," pp. 26-32.
2. John I. Goodlad, *A Place Called School: Prospects for the Future* (New York: McGraw-Hill Book Company, 1984), p. 56.
3. Ibid., pp. 349-57.

APPENDICES A-S

Appendix A

Classroom Practices

Table 1

Percent of Teachers Responding Always, Often, Seldom, or Never to Statements Concerning Classroom Practices

Survey Item (Item Number)	School Level		
	Elementary %	Middle %	Secondary %
Critical Thinking			
I encourage students to disagree with me. (32)			
Always	13	16	18
Often	49	46	54
Seldom/Never	38	38	28
Students are encouraged to examine different points of view rather than to expect that there are right answers. (58)			
Always	26	17	14
Often	65	69	71
Seldom/Never	9	14	15
I encourage students to raise questions about what they are studying. (74)			
Always	63	59	57
Often	34	35	40
Seldom/Never	3	6	3
Homework			
How much time do you expect students to spend on homework each day? (10)			
A. None	16	9	7
B. Less than 30 minutes	46	34	35
C./D. Between 30 and 60 minutes/ More than 60 Minutes	38	57	58
Use of Textbooks			
I use the textbook as the primary source of information. (106)			
Always	17	14	15
Often	52	51	50
Seldom/Never	31	35	35

Table 1 (cont.)

Percent of Teachers Responding Always, Often, Seldom, or Never to Statements Concerning Classroom Practices

Survey Item (Item Number)	School Level		
	Elementary %	Middle %	Secondary %
Evaluation			
I use standardized test results for making instructional decisions. (53)			
Always/Often	50	47	30
Seldom	37	37	43
Never	13	16	27
The tests and examinations I give my students accurately represent the goals and objectives of this school. (98)			
Always	51	45	40
Often	46	53	58
Seldom/Never	3	2	2
I use my own teacher-made tests for making instructional decisions. (109)			
Always	14	26	29
Often	68	63	63
Seldom/Never	18	11	8
Use of Classroom Time			
In this school, most classes are well-organized, and little time is wasted. (38)			
Always	56	34	27
Often	41	61	64
Seldom/Never	3	5	9
Most of the time in class is spent on academic activities. (157)			
Always	37	29	26
Often	61	67	69
Seldom/Never	2	4	5
Individualization			
Teachers individualize instruction. (96)			
Always	29	11	8
Often	64	61	54
Seldom/Never	7	28	38

Table 1 (cont.)

Percent of Teachers Responding Always, Often, Seldom, or Never to Statements
Concerning Classroom Practices

Survey Item (Item Number)	School Level		
	Elementary %	Middle %	Secondary %
Student Choice Options			
I let students select the curriculum materials they use. (93)			
Always/Often	25	19	17
Seldom	58	53	59
Never	17	28	24
I let students select learning activities. (104)			
Always/Often	67	37	36
Seldom	31	54	53
Never	2	9	11
I give my students the option to do projects such as pictures or models rather than written assignments. (121)			
Always/Often	62	52	40
Seldom	31	36	43
Never	7	12	17
Availability of Materials, Supplies			
The curriculum materials available are appropriate for the students in my classes. (97)			
Always	55	40	36
Often	42	52	55
Seldom/Never	3	8	9
Audio-visual materials and equipment are available when needed. (133)			
Always	71	60	51
Often	27	36	41
Seldom/Never	2	4	8
School supplies are readily available for classroom use. (151)			
Always	52	37	35
Often	42	54	53
Seldom/Never	6	9	12

Table 1 (cont.)

Percent of Teachers Responding Always, Often, Seldom, or Never to Statements Concerning Classroom Practices

Survey Item (Item Number)	School Level		
	Elementary %	Middle %	Secondary %
Cooperation and Learning			
Students tutor or assist other students in my classes. (148)			
Always	19	8	11
Often	58	58	54
Seldom/Never	23	34	35
I encourage students to work together on topics they are studying. (61)			
Always	25	21	22
Often	62	56	58
Seldom/Never	13	23	20

Table 2

Percent of Students Responding Always, Often, Seldom, or Never to Statements Concerning Classroom Practices

Survey Item (Item Number)	School Level		
	Elementary %	Middle %	Secondary %
Critical Thinking			
Teachers ask us to explain how we got an answer. (16)			
Always	29	28	25
Often	50	55	57
Seldom/Never	21	17	18
Teachers encourage us to question what's in the book. (28)			
Always	36	39	31
Often	40	37	38
Seldom/Never	24	24	31
Teachers encourage us to raise questions about what we are studying. (41)			
Always	44	50	46
Often	41	37	41
Seldom/Never	15	13	13
Teachers encourage us to examine different points of view rather than just find the right answers. (74)			
Always	30	30	24
Often	49	46	50
Seldom/Never	21	24	26
We are free to question or disagree with our teachers. (80)			
Always	37	37	38
Often	31	33	37
Seldom/Never	32	30	25
We are encouraged to express our opinions in class. (90)			
Always	40	40	35
Often	39	39	42
Seldom/Never	21	21	23
We spend a lot of time memorizing things. (96)			
Always	16	15	13
Often	36	41	45
Seldom/Never	48	44	42

Table 2 (cont.)

Percent of Students Responding Always, Often, Seldom, or Never to Statements Concerning Classroom Practices

Survey Item (Item Number)	School Level		
	Elementary %	Middle %	Secondary %

Student Choice Options

We have a choice about the amount of time we spend working on assignments. (32)

Always	13	9	7
Often	25	22	22
Seldom/Never	62	69	71

Teachers let us select the materials we use in class. (49)

Always	10	6	3
Often	33	25	18
Seldom/Never	57	69	79

We have a chance to decide what to study. (52)

Always	6	4	7
Often	19	16	20
Seldom/Never	75	80	73

We are encouraged to study topics that interest us. (72)

Always	31	27	24
Often	44	41	45
Seldom/Never	25	32	31

Teachers let us do projects such as pictures or models rather than written assignments. (76)

Always	9	7	4
Often	29	32	28
Seldom/Never	62	61	68

Availability of Materials, Supplies

We use different kinds of materials in class, such as newspapers and photographs. (67)

Always	18	12	10
Often	38	33	35
Seldom/Never	44	55	55

Table 2 (cont.)

*Percent of Students Responding Always, Often, Seldom, or Never to Statements
Concerning Classroom Practices*

Survey Item (Item Number)	School Level		
	Elementary %	Middle %	Secondary %
Use of Classroom Time			
How do you spend *most* of your time during the school day? (9)			
A. Listening to the teacher talk with the whole group	53	71	76
B. Working by myself on workbooks or reading	33	17	12
C./D. Working with other students on special projects/Taking tests to see how much I have learned	14	12	12
What we do in class is well organized and little time is wasted. (31)			
Always	33	26	19
Often	49	55	59
Seldom/Never	18	19	22
Students fool around a lot in class. (77)			
Always	13	16	15
Often	29	34	36
Seldom/Never	58	50	49
I have enough time in class to finish my assignments. (81)			
Always	29	14	8
Often	53	54	49
Seldom/Never	18	32	43
Homework			
How much time do you spend on homework each day? (5)			
A./B. None/Less than 30 minutes	30	21	32
C. Between 30 and 60 minutes	53	58	47
D. More than 60 minutes	17	21	21
Individualization			
Everybody works on the same things in class. (24)			
Always	16	25	27
Often	51	59	61
Seldom/Never	33	16	12

Table 2 (cont.)

*Percent of Students Responding Always, Often, Seldom, or Never to Statements
Concerning Classroom Practices*

Survey Item (Item Number)	School Level		
	Elementary %	Middle %	Secondary %
Instructional Practices			
Most of our class assignments are interesting. (34)			
Always	21	13	7
Often	52	47	48
Seldom/Never	27	40	45
Teachers try to explain things in terms of other things we already know. (48)			
Always	36	30	22
Often	45	52	60
Seldom/Never	19	18	18
Class assignments are too hard for me. (57)			
Always/Often	17	16	15
Seldom	51	58	63
Never	32	26	22
What teachers expect us to learn is clear to me. (66)			
Always	42	34	24
Often	48	52	57
Seldom/Never	10	14	19
Most of our classwork is busy work—a waste of time. (91)			
Always/Often	21	23	25
Seldom	30	45	55
Never	49	32	20
Use of Textbooks			
Most of the work in my classes comes from the textbook. (47)			
Always	21	22	23
Often	58	63	61
Seldom/Never	21	15	16

Table 2 (cont.)

Percent of Students Responding Always, Often, Seldom, or Never to Statements Concerning Classroom Practices

Survey Item (Item Number)	School Level		
	Elementary %	Middle %	Secondary %
Evaluation			
What grades do you usually get in school? (4)			
A. A	34	24	16
B. B	47	49	48
C./D. C, D, or F	19	27	36
We get the grades we deserve, whether or not the teacher likes us. (82)			
Always	72	61	40
Often	18	27	45
Seldom/Never	10	12	15
Cooperation and Learning			
Teachers encourage us to work together on what we're studying. (44)			
Always	23	18	9
Often	38	34	38
Seldom/Never	39	48	53
There is a lot of cooperative effort among students. (79)			
Always	29	19	19
Often	54	57	59
Seldom/Never	17	24	22

Table 3

Percent of Young Children Responding Yes or No to Statements Concerning Classroom Practices

Survey Item (Item Number)	Percent of Young Children
Critical Thinking	
We spend a lot of time memorizing things. (25)	
Yes	65
No	35
Use of Classroom Time	
Students fool around a lot in class. (2)	
Yes	38
No	62
Homework	
I do a lot of homework every night. (21)	
Yes	30
No	70
Instructional Practices	
My class assignments are hard. (7)	
Yes	32
No	68
I usually know what my teacher wants me to do. (5)	
Yes	81
No	19

Appendix B

Curriculum Perspectives

Table 1

Percent of Teachers Responding Always, Often, Seldom, or Never to Statements Concerning Knowledge and Student Learning

Survey Item (Item Number)	School Level		
	Elementary %	Middle %	Secondary %
Conceptions of Knowledge and Learning			
What is considered to be true or important changes as conditions change. (142)			
Always	26	18	18
Often	61	64	64
Seldom/Never	13	18	18
Open-ended questions are confusing to students. (112)			
Always/Often	42	54	55
Seldom	49	41	40
Never	9	5	5
It is more important that students learn what is right than to think for themselves. (34)			
Always/Often	36	44	37
Seldom	45	37	43
Never	19	19	20
It is important for students to learn what is in the textbook. (44)			
Always	23	19	18
Often	69	73	70
Seldom/Never	8	8	12
Information is learned primarily so it can be applied to real-life situations. (153)			
Always	37	19	17
Often	59	73	70
Seldom/Never	4	8	13

Table 1 (cont.)

*Percent of Teachers Responding Always, Often, Seldom, or Never to Statements
Concerning Knowledge and Student Learning*

Survey Item (Item Number)	School Level		
	Elementary %	Middle %	Secondary %
Conceptions of Knowledge and Learning (cont.)			
Students learn best when new content and skills are related to their previous experiences. (66)			
Always	64	59	53
Often	34	40	46
Seldom/Never	2	1	1
Students learn best when they begin with discrete skills and information rather than broad ideas. (90)			
Always	20	17	15
Often	55	60	60
Seldom/Never	25	23	25
Content is integrated across subject boundaries to promote learning. (156)			
Always	32	14	9
Often	62	62	62
Seldom/Never	6	24	29
Students learn best when they have some choice in the selection of materials and activities. (101)			
Always	24	15	16
Often	60	61	60
Seldom/Never	16	24	24
Students learn best when a wide variety of activities are provided. (125)			
Always	69	51	43
Often	29	43	51
Seldom/Never	2	6	6
Given the opportunity, students will choose activities that are educationally worthwhile. (139)			
Always	8	5	4
Often	76	61	61
Seldom/Never	16	34	35

Table 1 (cont.)

*Percent of Teachers Responding Always, Often, Seldom, or Never to Statements
Concerning Knowledge and Student Learning*

Survey Item (Item Number)	School Level		
	Elementary %	Middle %	Secondary %
Expectations			
All students are capable of higher-level learning. (52)			
Always	17	14	16
Often	62	55	49
Seldom/Never	21	31	35
Teachers in this school expect students to learn. (102)			
Always	84	73	61
Often	16	26	38
Seldom/Never	0	1	1
If teachers expect students to learn, students will learn. (80)			
Always	41	34	23
Often	53	55	64
Seldom/Never	6	11	13
How important is it for this school to help students acquire each of the following:			
Reading skills (21)			
Always	97	94	91
Often	3	6	8
Seldom/Never	0	0	1
Factual knowledge and concepts in the subject area (22)			
Always	79	70	68
Often	20	28	30
Seldom/Never	1	2	2
Positive attitudes toward learning (23)			
Always	96	89	84
Often	4	10	15
Seldom/Never	0	1	1

Table 1 (cont.)

*Percent of Teachers Responding Always, Often, Seldom, or Never to Statements
Concerning Knowledge and Student Learning*

Survey Item (Item Number)	School Level		
	Elementary %	Middle %	Secondary %

Expectations (cont.)

How important is it for this school to
help students acquire each of the
following:

Friendliness and respect toward
people of different races and religions
(24)

Always	89	83	79
Often	10	16	19
Seldom/Never	1	1	2

A sense of self-worth (25)

Always	94	88	83
Often	6	11	15
Seldom/Never	0	1	2

Critical thinking and reasoning skills
(26)

Always	84	78	78
Often	15	20	20
Seldom/Never	1	2	2

Independence and self-reliance (27)

Always	86	78	74
Often	14	21	24
Seldom/Never	0	1	2

Skills in evaluating information and
arguments (28)

Always	70	65	66
Often	27	31	32
Seldom/Never	3	4	2

Effective expression of opinions (29)

Always	73	64	64
Often	25	32	33
Seldom/Never	2	4	3

Table 1 (cont.)

Percent of Teachers Responding Always, Often, Seldom, or Never to Statements Concerning Knowledge and Student Learning

Survey Item (Item Number)	School Level		
	Elementary %	Middle %	Secondary %

Expectations (cont.)

How important is it for this school to help students acquire each of the following:

Vocational skills (30)

Always	35	42	50
Often	40	45	39
Seldom/Never	25	13	11

Teachers feel responsible for the social development of students. (83)

Always	37	28	13
Often	56	60	58
Seldom/Never	7	12	29

Academic learning is a top priority at this school. (67)

Always	61	46	33
Often	37	49	53
Seldom/Never	2	5	14

There is pressure on teachers for students to get high scores on achievement tests. (138)

Always	17	10	10
Often	39	35	44
Seldom/Never	44	55	46

In this school, there is a lot of pressure on students to get good grades. (77)

Always	10	11	11
Often	51	53	59
Seldom/Never	39	36	30

Teachers pressure students to get good grades. (35)

Always	7	9	9
Often	45	53	58
Seldom/Never	48	38	33

Table 1 (cont.)

Percent of Teachers Responding Always, Often, Seldom, or Never to Statements Concerning Knowledge and Student Learning

Survey Item (Item Number)	School Level		
	Elementary %	Middle %	Secondary %
Expectations (cont.)			
Achievement is more important than effort for getting good grades in this school. (127)			
Always	13	9	10
Often	46	52	62
Seldom/Never	41	39	28

Table 2

Percent of Students Responding Always, Often, Seldom, or Never to Statements Concerning Expectations for Learning

Survey Item (Item Number)	School Level		
	Elementary %	Middle %	Secondary %
Self-Expectations			
Do you expect to graduate from high school? (1)			
A. Definitely yes	73	85	93
B. Probably	20	11	5
C./D. I'm not sure/No	7	4	2
After high school, do you expect to go to college? (2)			
A. Definitely yes	52	51	49
B. Probably	27	27	23
C./D. I'm not sure/No	21	22	28
How much do you expect to learn in school this year? (6)			
A. A lot	85	72	62
B. Some	13	25	34
C./D. Not much/Very little	2	3	4
What is your favorite subject in school? (7)			
A. Language Arts/Reading/English	21	21	26
B./C. Mathematics/Science	66	59	56
D. Social Studies/History/ Geography	13	20	18
If you could choose *one* important goal for yourself, which of the following would be the most important one *for you?* (8)			
A./C. To get along well with other people/To become a better person	38	43	55
B. To learn a lot about the subjects in school	29	21	10
D. To get a good job	33	36	35

Table 2 (cont.)

Percent of Students Responding Always, Often, Seldom, or Never to Statements Concerning Expectations for Learning

Survey Item (Item Number)	School Level		
	Elementary %	Middle %	Secondary %
Expectations for Me, Personally			
Teachers believe I can learn. (23)			
Always	88	83	71
Often	9	13	24
Seldom/Never	3	4	5
Teachers expect me to learn. (75)			
Always	78	75	66
Often	18	20	29
Seldom/Never	4	5	5
Achievement Pressure			
Teachers count how hard we try as part of our grade. (11)			
Always	44	34	19
Often	39	45	47
Seldom/Never	17	21	34
Students who try hard in this school succeed. (37)			
Always	53	53	48
Often	41	42	47
Seldom/Never	6	5	5
Teachers put a lot of pressure on us to learn. (71)			
Always	26	24	19
Often	31	41	48
Seldom/Never	43	35	33
Nobody cares how hard you try in this school. (94)			
Always	12	9	6
Often	9	13	15
Seldom/Never	79	78	79

Table 3

Percent of Young Children Responding Yes or No to Statements Concerning Expectations for Learning

Survey Item (Item Number)	Percent of Young Children
My teacher thinks that I can learn. (26)	
Yes	98
No	2
My teacher thinks it's important for us to try hard. (19)	
Yes	98
No	2
My teacher cares if I learn. (17)	
Yes	96
No	4
The work we do at school is important to me. (27)	
Yes	93
No	7

Appendix C

Decision Making

Table 1

Percent of Teachers Responding Always, Often, Seldom, or Never to Statements Concerning Decision Making

Survey Item (Item Number)	School Level		
	Elementary %	Middle %	Secondary %
Response to Problems			
Schoolwide problems are identified and acted upon cooperatively by administrators, teachers, and other staff members. (115)			
Always	52	40	31
Often	40	47	55
Seldom/Never	8	13	14
People in this school do a good job of examining alternative solutions to problems before deciding what to do. (136)			
Always	46	30	22
Often	51	63	67
Seldom/Never	3	7	11
When a problem arises in this school, there are established procedures for working on it. (88)			
Always	49	38	44
Often	43	47	48
Seldom/Never	8	15	8
Our efforts to solve schoolwide problems are successful. (49)			
Always/Often	94	88	88
Seldom	5	11	11
Never	1	1	1

Table 1 (cont.)

Percent of Teachers Responding Always, Often, Seldom, or Never to Statements Concerning Decision Making

Survey Item (Item Number)	School Level		
	Elementary %	Middle %	Secondary %
Administrators' Decision Making			
Once decisions are made, the principal sees that they are carried out. (50)			
Always	63	51	41
Often	32	41	52
Seldom/Never	5	8	7
Administrators seek out teachers' suggestions for improving the school. (56)			
Always	30	28	20
Often	50	45	51
Seldom/Never	20	27	29
The principal makes the important decisions in this school. (76)			
Always	35	41	31
Often	54	49	57
Seldom/Never	11	10	12
The principal accepts staff decisions even if he or she does not agree with them. (81)			
Always	17	16	13
Often	57	52	48
Seldom/Never	26	32	39
The principal trusts teachers to use their professional judgment on instructional matters. (114)			
Always	68	61	54
Often	30	33	42
Seldom/Never	2	6	4
The principal encourages teachers with leadership abilities to move into leadership roles. (120)			
Always	43	35	27
Often	43	44	51
Seldom/Never	14	21	22

Table 1 (cont.)

Percent of Teachers Responding Always, Often, Seldom, or Never to Statements Concerning Decision Making

Survey Item (Item Number)	School Level		
	Elementary %	Middle %	Secondary %
Parents and Community			
In this school, parents and community organizations work with school personnel to identify and resolve schoolwide problems. (86)			
Always	29	13	12
Often	51	49	48
Seldom/Never	20	38	40
Parents are important members of school committees and advisory groups. (140)			
Always	49	30	23
Often	40	42	45
Seldom/Never	11	28	32
General			
The staff evaluates its programs and activities and attempts to change them for the better. (117)			
Always	51	37	29
Often	43	51	61
Seldom/Never	6	12	10
Overall, I have control over how I carry out my own job. (128)			
Always	58	51	50
Often	40	46	48
Seldom/Never	2	3	2
It is difficult for teachers to influence administrative decisions regarding school policy. (154)			
Always	9	11	9
Often	37	35	39
Seldom/Never	54	54	52
Teachers' unions or associations should bargain about curriculum and teaching materials. (100)			
Always/Often	43	37	39
Seldom	33	38	32
Never	24	25	29

Table 1 (cont.)

Percent of Teachers Responding Always, Often, Seldom, or Never to Statements Concerning Decision Making

Survey Item (Item Number)	School Level		
	Elementary %	Middle %	Secondary %
Actual and Desired Involvement in Selected Areas			
Do participate in hiring new teachers in this school. (181)			
Always/Often	7	9	12
Seldom	13	11	14
Never	80	80	74
Should participate in hiring new teachers in this school. (191)			
Always/Often	22	24	27
Seldom	31	31	36
Never	47	45	37
Do participate in selecting textbooks. (182)			
Always	40	38	45
Often	35	34	31
Seldom/Never	25	28	24
Should participate in selecting textbooks. (192)			
Always	58	50	59
Often	33	37	29
Seldom/Never	9	13	12
Do participate in resolving learning problems of individual students. (183)			
Always	54	34	30
Often	38	51	49
Seldom/Never	8	15	21
Should participate in resolving learning problems of individual students. (193)			
Always	64	45	42
Often	32	46	48
Seldom/Never	4	9	10

Table 1 (cont.)

Percent of Teachers Responding Always, Often, Seldom, or Never to Statements Concerning Decision Making

Survey Item (Item Number)	School Level		
	Elementary %	Middle %	Secondary %
Actual and Desired Involvement in Selected Areas (cont.)			
Do participate in determining appropriate instructional methods and techniques. (184)			
Always	55	47	46
Often	36	39	41
Seldom/Never	9	14	13
Should participate in determining appropriate instructional methods and techniques. (194)			
Always	67	56	56
Often	28	37	36
Seldom/Never	5	7	8
Do participate in establishing classroom disciplinary policies. (185)			
Always	67	55	50
Often	24	32	34
Seldom/Never	9	13	16
Should participate in establishing classroom disciplinary policies. (195)			
Always	75	65	61
Often	19	28	30
Seldom/Never	6	7	9
Do participate in establishing general instructional policies. (186)			
Always	33	27	24
Often	45	43	44
Seldom/Never	22	30	32
Should participate in establishing general instructional policies. (196)			
Always	47	40	36
Often	43	48	49
Seldom/Never	10	12	15

Table 1 (cont.)

Percent of Teachers Responding Always, Often, Seldom, or Never to Statements Concerning Decision Making

Survey Item (Item Number)	School Level		
	Elementary %	Middle %	Secondary %
Actual and Desired Involvement in Selected Areas (cont.)			
Do participate in determining faculty assignments in the school. (187)			
Always/Often	15	15	17
Seldom	24	21	28
Never	61	64	55
Should participate in determining faculty assignments in the school. (197)			
Always/Often	35	32	41
Seldom	32	33	33
Never	33	35	26
Do participate in evaluating the performance of teachers. (188)			
Always/Often	8	5	11
Seldom	15	17	14
Never	77	78	75
Should participate in evaluating the performance of teachers. (198)			
Always/Often	19	20	25
Seldom	30	33	31
Never	51	47	44
Do participate in selecting administrative personnel to be assigned to the school. (189)			
Always/Often	6	4	7
Seldom	10	7	10
Never	84	89	83
Should participate in selecting administrative personnel to be assigned to the school. (199)			
Always/Often	33	29	31
Seldom	27	29	30
Never	40	42	39

Table 1 (cont.)

Percent of Teachers Responding Always, Often, Seldom, or Never to Statements Concerning Decision Making

Survey Item (Item Number)	School Level		
	Elementary %	Middle %	Secondary %
Actual and Desired Involvement in Selected Areas (cont.)			
Do participate in evaluating your own job performance. (190)			
Always	39	39	34
Often	29	34	31
Seldom/Never	32	27	35
Should participate in evaluating your own job performance. (200)			
Always	57	56	47
Often	32	35	39
Seldom/Never	11	9	14
Students			
In this school, students have a chance to change things they don't like. (116)			
Always/Often	41	34	52
Seldom	50	58	45
Never	9	8	3
Students participate in the development of school policies, procedures, and programs. (143)			
Always/Often	41	35	55
Seldom	49	53	42
Never	10	12	3

Table 2

Percent of Students Responding Always, Often, Seldom, or Never to Statements Concerning Decision Making

Survey Item (Item Number)	School Level		
	Elementary %	Middle %	Secondary %
We have a chance to change things we don't like. (17)			
Always	13	8	7
Often	31	26	26
Seldom/Never	56	66	67
Students in this school participate in developing school policies and programs. (21)			
Always	23	20	15
Often	44	48	48
Seldom/Never	33	32	37
Teachers listen to our suggestions for program changes. (97)			
Always	27	18	12
Often	41	40	42
Seldom/Never	32	42	46

Appendix D

Discipline and Safety

Table 1

Percent of Teachers Responding Always, Often, Seldom, or Never to Statements Concerning Discipline and Safety

Survey Item (Item Number)	School Level		
	Elementary %	Middle %	Secondary %
Rule Enforcement			
On the average, how often do you report a student to the office for disciplinary action:			
A./B. Once a day/Once a week	5	15	5
C. Once a month	14	19	17
D. Rarely or never	81	66	78
Rules for students are fairly enforced. (42)			
Always	60	43	37
Often	37	45	54
Seldom/Never	3	12	9
Student misbehavior is dealt with firmly and swiftly. (87)			
Always	44	36	29
Often	47	46	59
Seldom/Never	9	18	12
Compliance			
Students attend class regularly and are punctual. (47)			
Always	53	32	19
Often	45	63	73
Seldom/Never	2	5	8
Students obey school rules and regulations. (149)			
Always	15	9	5
Often	82	85	88
Seldom/Never	3	6	7

Table 1 (cont.)

Percent of Teachers Responding Always, Often, Seldom, or Never to Statements Concerning Discipline and Safety

Survey Item (Item Number)	School Level		
	Elementary %	Middle %	Secondary %
Safety/Security			
The building and the school grounds are safe. (36)			
Always	65	62	52
Often	32	34	38
Seldom/Never	3	4	10
Students damage or steal other students' property. (60)			
Always/Often	12	17	31
Seldom	78	76	66
Never	10	7	3
Students damage or steal school property. (73)			
Always/Often	7	14	25
Seldom	74	74	70
Never	19	12	5
Students fight with each other. (94)			
Always/Often	14	16	12
Seldom	80	79	79
Never	6	5	9
Students physically assault teachers. (155)			
Always/Often	2	3	2
Seldom	18	24	34
Never	80	73	64
Student Behavior			
Students are taught how to behave properly so they can benefit from academic activities. (107)			
Always	56	43	25
Often	41	49	62
Seldom/Never	3	8	13

Table 1 (cont.)

Percent of Teachers Responding Always, Often, Seldom, or Never to Statements Concerning Discipline and Safety

Survey Item (Item Number)	School Level		
	Elementary %	Middle %	Secondary %
Drugs/Alcohol/Smoking			
Students violate school rules on smoking. (39)			
Always/Often	3	9	39
Seldom	9	53	53
Never	88	38	8
Students in this school drink alcohol. (62)			
Always/Often	2	7	50
Seldom	13	52	45
Never	85	41	5
Students in this school use drugs. (113)			
Always/Often	1	6	29
Seldom	18	61	67
Never	81	33	4
School Rules			
School rules for students are reasonable. (131)			
Always	78	72	55
Often	21	26	44
Seldom/Never	1	2	1

Table 2

Percent of Students Responding Always, Often, Seldom, or Never to Statements Concerning Discipline and Safety

Survey Item (Item Number)	School Level		
	Elementary %	Middle %	Secondary %
School Rules			
Rules for students are reasonable. (18)			
Always	57	42	24
Often	28	37	48
Seldom/Never	15	21	28
We have a say in making classroom rules. (64)			
Always	25	10	4
Often	28	22	15
Seldom/Never	47	68	81
Rule Enforcement			
Students know the consequences for breaking school rules. (46)			
Always	70	68	61
Often	22	24	31
Seldom/Never	8	8	8
Student misbehavior is dealt with firmly and swiftly. (54)			
Always	41	43	40
Often	37	38	43
Seldom/Never	22	19	17
Student Behavior			
In this school, we are taught how to behave properly. (53)			
Always	65	45	25
Often	26	37	43
Seldom/Never	9	18	32
Teachers are more concerned that we keep quiet than that we learn. (70)			
Always	13	12	9
Often	12	15	18
Seldom/Never	75	73	73

Table 2 (cont.)

Percent of Students Responding Always, Often, Seldom, or Never to Statements Concerning Discipline and Safety

Survey Item (Item Number)	School Level		
	Elementary %	Middle %	Secondary %
Compliance			
Students are expected to attend class regularly and to be on time. (12)			
Always	79	91	92
Often	16	7	7
Seldom/Never	5	2	1
Students obey school rules and regulations. (30)			
Always	22	10	6
Often	58	61	61
Seldom/Never	20	29	33
Students obey the school rules. (88)			
Always	23	11	7
Often	58	60	62
Seldom/Never	19	29	31
Safety/Security			
I feel safe at this school. (38)			
Always	59	41	45
Often	28	37	38
Seldom/Never	13	22	17
Students physically assault teachers. (58)			
Always/Often	12	12	7
Seldom	17	27	26
Never	71	61	67
Students fight with each other. (69)			
Always	11	15	12
Often	24	33	25
Seldom/Never	65	52	63
Students damage or steal school property. (98)			
Always	5	7	7
Often	10	17	19
Seldom/Never	85	76	74

Table 2 (cont.)

*Percent of Students Responding Always, Often, Seldom, or Never to Statements
Concerning Discipline and Safety*

Survey Item (Item Number)	School Level		
	Elementary %	Middle %	Secondary %
Drugs/Alcohol/Smoking			
Students violate school rules on smoking. (35)			
Always	8	11	22
Often	4	14	27
Seldom/Never	88	75	51
Students at this school use drugs. (85)			
Always	2	6	11
Often	3	11	30
Seldom/Never	95	83	59
Students at this school drink alcohol. (95)			
Always	3	7	20
Often	4	16	40
Seldom/Never	93	77	40

Table 3

Percent of Young Children Responding Yes or No to Statements Concerning Discipline and Safety

Survey Item (Item Number)	Percent of Young Children
School Rules	
We have too many rules at this school. (10)	
Yes	31
No	69
Rule Enforcement	
My teacher is too strict. (28)	
Yes	21
No	79
Safety/Security	
This school is a dangerous place to be. (15)	
Yes	11
No	89

Appendix E

Support Services and Facilities

Table 1

Percent of Teachers Responding Always, Often, Seldom, or Never to Statements Concerning Support Services and Facilities

Survey Item (Item Number)	School Level		
	Elementary %	Middle %	Secondary %
Library Services			
Library services meet the needs and interests of students. (37)			
Always	63	50	38
Often	31	40	46
Seldom/Never	6	10	16
Library services meet the needs of teachers. (41)			
Always	54	37	32
Often	39	48	51
Seldom/Never	7	15	17
Pleasantness/Cleanliness			
This school building is pleasant to be in. (134)			
Always	72	48	39
Often	26	43	52
Seldom/Never	2	9	9
The school building and grounds are kept clean. (159)			
Always	59	52	38
Often	36	41	54
Seldom/Never	5	7	8
Secretarial			
Adequate secretarial service is available. (64)			
Always	66	63	35
Often	26	29	41
Seldom/Never	8	8	24

Table 1 (cont.)

*Percent of Teachers Responding Always, Often, Seldom, or Never to Statements
Concerning Support Services and Facilities*

Survey Item (Item Number)	School Level		
	Elementary %	Middle %	Secondary %
Inservice Worthwhile			
Inservice programs at this school are worthwhile. (103)			
Always	28	16	13
Often	55	53	52
Seldom/Never	17	31	35
Use of Building			
Teachers and students are allowed to put things on the walls in this building. (110)			
Always	70	47	37
Often	23	39	45
Seldom/Never	7	14	18
Furniture and equipment can be rearranged as desired. (118)			
Always	85	77	65
Often	14	20	31
Seldom/Never	1	3	4

Table 2

*Percent of Young Children Responding Yes or No to Statements Concerning
Support Services and Facilities*

Survey Item (Item Number)	Percent of Young Children
Pleasantness/Cleanliness	
This school is nice to be in. (13)	
Yes	94
No	6

Appendix F

Commitment

Table 1

Percent of Teachers Responding Always, Often, Seldom, or Never to Statements Concerning Staff, Student, and Parent Commitment

Survey Item (Item Number)	School Level		
	Elementary %	Middle %	Secondary %
Indices of Student Commitment			
Students have a lot of school spirit. (130)			
Always	53	58	60
Often	40	24	15
Seldom/Never	7	18	25
There is a lot of student participation in academic clubs, sports, and music and drama activities. (33)			
Always	27	51	43
Often	46	38	38
Seldom/Never	27	11	19
Indices of Staff Commitment: Teacher Pride and Morale			
Teachers are proud to work at this school. (31)			
Always	76	57	47
Often	23	39	48
Seldom/Never	1	4	5
The morale of teachers is high. (43)			
Always	48	33	23
Often	44	53	57
Seldom/Never	8	14	20
Teachers maintain high standards for themselves. (63)			
Always	68	47	32
Often	30	51	63
Seldom/Never	2	2	5

Table 1 (cont.)

*Percent of Teachers Responding Always, Often, Seldom, or Never to Statements
Concerning Staff, Student, and Parent Commitment*

Survey Item (Item Number)	School Level		
	Elementary %	Middle %	Secondary %
Indices of Staff Commitment: Teacher and Principal Openness			
Teachers are receptive to suggestions for program improvement. (40)			
Always	56	41	31
Often	41	53	61
Seldom/Never	3	6	8
Teachers try new ideas to improve their teaching. (91)			
Always	48	32	21
Often	50	62	72
Seldom/Never	2	6	7
Staff members are flexible; they are able to reconsider their positions on issues and change their minds. (145)			
Always	30	16	15
Often	61	70	71
Seldom/Never	9	14	14
The principal encourages teachers to try out new ideas. (147)			
Always	52	35	24
Often	41	51	62
Seldom/Never	7	14	14
I participate in professional development activities outside of the school. (122)			
Always	26	23	24
Often	54	53	52
Seldom/Never	20	24	24
The principal shares new ideas with teachers. (78)			
Always	63	45	33
Often	32	41	53
Seldom/Never	5	13	14

Table 1 (cont.)

*Percent of Teachers Responding Always, Often, Seldom, or Never to Statements
Concerning Staff, Student, and Parent Commitment*

Survey Item (Item Number)	School Level		
	Elementary %	Middle %	Secondary %
Indices of Staff Commitment: Staff Acceptance of Responsibility			
Administrators, teachers, and other staff members are working hard to improve this school. (59)			
Always	71	57	45
Often	26	37	50
Seldom/Never	3	6	5
Rules and red tape in this school make it difficult to get things done. (69)			
Always/Often	14	23	28
Seldom	58	53	57
Never	28	24	15
Teachers are not responsible for what happens at this school; too many factors are beyond their control. (105)			
Always/Often	19	24	28
Seldom	46	45	50
Never	35	31	22
People in this school complain about things, but are reluctant to do anything about them. (158)			
Always/Often	26	38	47
Seldom	58	54	49
Never	16	8	4
Teachers feel responsible for student learning. (92)			
Always	73	50	38
Often	26	47	58
Seldom/Never	1	3	4
The staff is task oriented; jobs get completed and there is little wasted time. (119)			
Always	49	30	20
Often	48	64	71
Seldom/Never	3	6	9

Table 1 (cont.)

Percent of Teachers Responding Always, Often, Seldom, or Never to Statements Concerning Staff, Student, and Parent Commitment

Survey Item (Item Number)	School Level		
	Elementary %	Middle %	Secondary %
Indices of Parental Commitment			
Parents support school activities. (48)			
Always	47	25	18
Often	44	58	60
Seldom/Never	9	17	22
Parents serve as teacher aides in this school. (55)			
Always/Often	56	37	9
Seldom	24	30	30
Never	20	33	61
Parents support school rules. (68)			
Always	36	23	15
Often	60	69	75
Seldom/Never	4	8	10
Parents work in the school library. (72)			
Always/Often	49	26	5
Seldom	22	21	15
Never	29	53	80
Parents come to school to discuss their children's problems. (85)			
Always	33	13	9
Often	59	70	54
Seldom/Never	8	17	37
Parents tutor students at this school. (95)			
Always/Often	44	20	5
Seldom	35	39	35
Never	21	41	60
Parents encourage and support teachers' efforts. (129)			
Always	28	11	13
Often	65	73	66
Seldom/Never	7	16	21

Table 1 (cont.)

*Percent of Teachers Responding Always, Often, Seldom, or Never to Statements
Concerning Staff, Student, and Parent Commitment*

Survey Item (Item Number)	School Level		
	Elementary %	Middle %	Secondary %
Indices of Parental Commitment (cont.)			
Parents made sure their children do their homework. (146)			
Always	5	2	1
Often	76	51	37
Seldom/Never	19	47	62
Other Indices of Teacher Commitment			
On the average, the amount of time you spend per day on extra- or co-curricular duties such as music or athletics is: (3)			
A. Less than 1 hour	82	71	56
B. Between 1 and 2 hours	14	16	23
C./D. Between 2 and 3 hours/More than 3 hours	4	13	21
On the average, the amount of time you spend per day after regular school hours checking and grading papers and preparing for class is: (4)			
A./B. Less than a half-hour/Between a half-hour and one hour	41	51	45
B. Between one and two hours	43	38	38
C. More than two hours	16	11	16
On the average, the amount of time you spend per day after regular school hours with students is: (5)			
A. Less than a half-hour	80	64	46
B. Between a half-hour and one hour	17	25	36
C./D. Between one and two hours/More than two hours	3	11	19
On the average, the total amount of time you work per day on school-related activities is: (6)			
A./B. Less than six hours/Between six and eight hours	51	50	41
C. Between eight and ten hours	43	42	47
D. More than ten hours	6	8	12

Table 1 (cont.)

*Percent of Teachers Responding Always, Often, Seldom, or Never to Statements
Concerning Staff, Student, and Parent Commitment*

Survey Item (Item Number)	School Level		
	Elementary %	Middle %	Secondary %
Other Indices of Teacher Commitment (cont.)			
The number of teaching days you missed last year for health or personal reasons was: (7)			
A. None	13	18	20
B. 1-5	67	60	68
C./D. 6-10/More than 10	20	22	12
The number of teaching days you missed last year for professional reasons was: (8)			
A. None	49	46	39
B. 1-3	45	47	50
C./D. 4-6/7 or more	6	7	11
Teachers put in extra time and effort to improve this school. (70)			
Always	48	59	66
Often	49	31	25
Seldom/Never	3	10	9
I plan to teach until retirement. (46)			
Always	56	51	50
Often	24	22	24
Seldom/Never	20	27	26
Teachers support school policies and procedures. (137)			
Always	61	49	33
Often	38	48	65
Seldom/Never	1	3	2
Our faculty meetings are worthwhile. (141)			
Always	37	28	22
Often	53	53	55
Seldom/Never	10	19	23

Table 1 (cont.)

*Percent of Teachers Responding Always, Often, Seldom, or Never to Statements
Concerning Staff, Student, and Parent Commitment*

Survey Item (Item Number)	School Level		
	Elementary %	Middle %	Secondary %
Other Indices of Teacher Commitment (cont.)			
Teachers spend time after school with students who have individual problems. (144)			
Always	10	11	19
Often	45	47	63
Seldom/Never	45	42	18

Table 2

Percent of Students Responding Always, Often, Seldom, or Never to Statements Concerning Staff and Student Commitment

Survey Item (Item Number)	School Level		
	Elementary %	Middle %	Secondary %
Indices of Staff Commitment			
Teachers like to work at this school. (25)			
Always	58	44	33
Often	33	44	53
Seldom/Never	9	12	14
Teachers in this school help out with student activities. (59)			
Always	39	34	32
Often	46	50	54
Seldom/Never	15	16	14
Teachers spend time after school with students who have individual problems. (63)			
Always	19	21	24
Often	33	34	49
Seldom/Never	48	45	27
Teachers put a lot of time and effort into their work here. (65)			
Always	68	52	35
Often	25	38	53
Seldom/Never	7	10	12
Teachers leave the building as soon as possible when the school day ends. (84)			
Always	10	11	9
Often	18	24	26
Seldom/Never	72	65	65
Teachers and administrators work hard to improve this school. (99)			
Always	66	49	34
Often	26	36	46
Seldom/Never	8	15	20

Table 2 (cont.)

Percent of Students Responding Always, Often, Seldom, or Never to Statements Concerning Staff, Student, and Parent Commitment

Survey Item (Item Number)	School Level		
	Elementary %	Middle %	Secondary %
Indices of Student Commitment			
I tend to watch the clock and count the minutes until school ends. (20)			
Always	18	25	27
Often	14	22	28
Seldom/Never	68	53	45
There is a lot of student participation in academic clubs, sports, and music and drama activities. (45)			
Always	37	54	57
Often	38	33	31
Seldom/Never	25	13	12
The work we do in school is important to me. (61)			
Always	60	40	36
Often	32	38	48
Seldom/Never	8	12	16
This school is a good place to be. (78)			
Always	58	40	36
Often	28	38	44
Seldom/Never	14	22	20
Good luck is more important than hard work for success in school. (100)			
Always/Often	22	21	18
Seldom	19	25	32
Never	59	54	50

Table 3

Percent of Young Children Responding Yes or No to Statements Concerning Student and Parent Commitment

Survey Item (Item Number)	Percent of Young Children
Indices of Parent Commitment	
My parents think this is a great school. (11)	
Yes	93
No	7
Indices of Student Commitment	
I like to come to school. (4)	
Yes	82
No	18
This is a good school. (6)	
Yes	96
No	4
The kids in this school really like the school. (22)	
Yes	86
No	14
I am proud of this school. (24)	
Yes	93
No	7

Appendix G

Interpersonal Relations

Table 1

Percent of Teachers Responding Always, Often, Seldom, or Never to Statements Concerning Relationships Among Persons

Survey Item (Item Number)	School Level		
	Elementary %	Middle %	Secondary %

Task Support

There is someone in this school I can count on when I need help. (45)

	Elementary	Middle	Secondary
Always	78	76	66
Often	19	20	29
Seldom/Never	3	4	5

There is a great deal of cooperative effort among staff members. (51)

Always	58	48	31
Often	36	43	57
Seldom/Never	6	9	12

Teachers' accomplishments are recognized and rewarded. (82)

Always	37	27	23
Often	45	43	49
Seldom/Never	18	30	28

Other teachers in this school seek my assistance when they have teaching problems. (99)

Always	10	6	7
Often	58	57	47
Seldom/Never	32	37	46

The principal goes out of his or her way to help teachers. (124)

Always	58	46	33
Often	34	36	47
Seldom/Never	8	18	20

Teachers help each other find ways to do a better job. (160)

Always	39	20	15
Often	53	67	67
Seldom/Never	8	13	18

Table 1 (cont.)

*Percent of Teachers Responding Always, Often, Seldom, or Never to Statements
Concerning Relationships Among Persons*

Survey Item (Item Number)	School Level		
	Elementary %	Middle %	Secondary %
Personal Support			
Teachers at this school act as if things are more important than people. (65)			
Always/Often	8	11	15
Seldom	43	55	59
Never	49	34	26
Teachers trust the principal. (71)			
Always	61	50	37
Often	33	34	53
Seldom/Never	6	16	10
The work of students and awards are prominently displayed. (75)			
Always	68	48	38
Often	30	45	50
Seldom/Never	2	7	12
There is an "every person for himself" attitude in this school. (79)			
Always/Often	11	15	21
Seldom	43	50	57
Never	46	35	22
The principal is concerned about the personal welfare of teachers. (89)			
Always	64	53	42
Often	30	34	43
Seldom/Never	6	13	15
Teachers trust each other. (152)			
Always	44	33	25
Often	52	59	67
Seldom/Never	4	8	8

Table 1 (cont.)

Percent of Teachers Responding Always, Often, Seldom, or Never to Statements Concerning Relationships Among Persons

Survey Item (Item Number)	School Level		
	Elementary %	Middle %	Secondary %

Inclusion

New teachers are made to feel welcome and part of the group. (57)

Always	65	57	41
Often	30	34	49
Seldom/Never	5	9	10

There is a positive "sense of community" among students, teachers, and administrators. (84)

Always	44	24	19
Often	48	56	58
Seldom/Never	8	20	23

Teachers from one area or grade level respect those from other areas or grade levels. (123)

Always	60	46	39
Often	37	48	53
Seldom/Never	3	6	8

When the principal acts as a spokesperson for this school, he or she accurately represents the needs and interests of the staff and students. (132)

Always	65	53	42
Often	32	39	52
Seldom/Never	3	8	6

Teachers are responsive to the concerns of parents. (135)

Always	62	42	32
Often	37	56	65
Seldom/Never	1	2	3

Table 1 (cont.)

Percent of Teachers Responding Always, Often, Seldom, or Never to Statements Concerning Relationships Among Persons

Survey Item (Item Number)	School Level		
	Elementary %	Middle %	Secondary %
Respect			
Students insult teachers. (54)			
Always/Often	8	14	15
Seldom	61	71	72
Never	31	15	13
Teachers and students in this school are considerate of one another. (108)			
Always	38	23	17
Often	60	70	76
Seldom/Never	2	7	7
Teachers care about what students think. (150)			
Always	57	31	27
Often	41	65	70
Seldom/Never	2	4	3

Table 2

Percent of Students Responding Always, Often, Seldom, or Never to Statements Concerning Relationships Among Persons

Survey Item (Item Number)	School Level		
	Elementary %	Middle %	Secondary %
Task Support			
Students in this school help one another. (19)			
Always	29	17	19
Often	50	53	55
Seldom/Never	21	30	26
Teachers ignore students who aren't very smart. (33)			
Always/Often	12	14	17
Seldom	12	22	39
Never	76	64	44
Teachers get angry when students give wrong answers. (55)			
Always/Often	16	17	16
Seldom	37	46	57
Never	47	37	27
Students' accomplishments are recognized and rewarded. (68)			
Always	30	28	28
Often	43	44	48
Seldom/Never	27	28	24

Table 2 (cont.)

Percent of Students Responding Always, Often, Seldom, or Never to Statements Concerning Relationships Among Persons

Survey Item (Item Number)	School Level		
	Elementary %	Middle %	Secondary %

Personal Support

There may be a lot of things you like about this school, but if you had to choose the *one best* thing, which of the following would it be? (10)

A. My friends	55	65	63
B. The teachers	23	13	9
C. The classes I am taking	14	13	16
D. None of the above	8	9	12

Teachers at this school act as if things are more important than people. (13)

Always	6	7	7
Often	10	15	22
Seldom/Never	84	78	71

Teachers are considerate of each other. (27)

Always	74	64	45
Often	21	29	47
Seldom/Never	5	7	8

Students are friendly toward each other. (56)

Always	22	17	17
Often	60	64	69
Seldom/Never	18	19	14

Table 2 (cont.)

Percent of Students Responding Always, Often, Seldom, or Never to Statements Concerning Relationships Among Persons

Survey Item (Item Number)	School Level		
	Elementary %	Middle %	Secondary %
Inclusion			
I know most of the other students in my grade. (14)			
Always	72	54	48
Often	22	35	39
Seldom/Never	6	11	13
Teachers act as if they are always right. (39)			
Always	23	30	27
Often	28	34	41
Seldom/Never	49	36	32
It is hard to get to know teachers here. (42)			
Always/Often	17	20	21
Seldom	29	38	47
Never	54	42	32
Teachers show favoritism. (51)			
Always	19	17	17
Often	25	30	36
Seldom/Never	56	53	47
It is hard to get to know students here. (86)			
Always/Often	24	25	21
Seldom	36	42	49
Never	40	33	30
In general, I am satisfied with the way teachers and other adults in this school treat me. (89)			
Always	46	37	31
Often	39	43	52
Seldom/Never	15	20	17

Table 2 (cont.)

Percent of Students Responding Always, Often, Seldom, or Never to Statements Concerning Relationships Among Persons

Survey Item (Item Number)	School Level		
	Elementary %	Middle %	Secondary %

Respect

Teachers treat you better if you are wealthy or your parents are "important." (22)

Always	7	8	8
Often	8	9	13
Seldom/Never	85	83	79

Students respect teachers. (26)

Always	37	18	13
Often	46	53	59
Seldom/Never	17	29	28

Students in this school respect the rights of other students. (50)

Always	29	16	12
Often	49	51	56
Seldom/Never	22	33	32

Teachers care about what students think. (62)

Always	47	36	23
Often	39	44	53
Seldom/Never	14	20	24

Students in this school are treated fairly. (73)

Always	51	37	25
Often	33	44	55
Seldom/Never	16	19	20

Students are considerate of each other. (93)

Always	24	16	11
Often	57	59	65
Seldom/Never	19	25	24

Table 3

Percent of Young Children Responding Yes or No to Statements Concerning Relationships Among Persons

Survey Item (Item Number)	Percent of Young Children
The principal likes the children in this school. (3)	
Yes	98
No	2
Students here pick on each other a lot. (8)	
Yes	45
No	55
I like my teacher. (9)	
Yes	95
No	5
The teacher makes fun of students when they are wrong. (12)	
Yes	8
No	92
My teacher really likes young children. (14)	
Yes	94
No	6
I feel good about myself. (16)	
Yes	93
No	7
The principal trusts students. (18)	
Yes	90
No	10
The other kids in this school like me. (20)	
Yes	82
No	18
My teacher trusts students. (23)	
Yes	90
No	10
Students here are nice to each other. (30)	
Yes	75
No	25

Appendix H

History: Change Over Time

Table 1

Percent of Teachers Responding Always, Often, Seldom, or Never to Statements Concerning Potential School Problems Five Years Ago and Today

Survey Item (Item Number)	School Level					
	Elementary		Middle		Secondary	
	Five Years Ago	Today	Five Years Ago	Today	Five Years Ago	Today
Discipline (161/171)						
Always/Often	31	26	49	32	53	22
Seldom	48	52	40	49	37	64
Never	21	22	11	19	10	14
Student use of alcohol and drugs (162/172)						
Always/Often	3	3	18	9	59	36
Seldom	14	16	46	53	36	57
Never	83	81	36	38	5	7
Financial support (163/173)						
Always/Often	30	43	38	48	44	53
Seldom	41	34	43	36	41	34
Never	29	23	19	16	15	13
Time students spend riding the school bus (164/174)						
Always/Often	17	20	29	22	27	26
Seldom	37	37	45	49	53	53
Never	46	43	26	29	20	21
Curriculum (165/175)						
Always/Often	19	13	24	15	30	21
Seldom	47	49	54	58	54	59
Never	34	38	22	27	16	20
Academic standards (166/176)						
Always/Often	19	14	27	19	32	30
Seldom	42	43	48	50	52	52
Never	39	43	25	31	16	18

Table 1 (cont.)

Percent of Teachers Responding Always, Often, Seldom, or Never to Statements Concerning Potential School Problems Five Years Ago and Today

| Survey Item (Item Number) | School Level | | | | | |
| | Elementary | | Middle | | Secondary | |
	Five Years Ago	Today	Five Years Ago	Today	Five Years Ago	Today
Getting and keeping good teachers (167/177)						
Always/Often	17	17	32	29	39	35
Seldom	38	36	43	45	43	44
Never	45	47	25	26	18	21
Class size (168/178)						
Always/Often	39	33	46	34	43	39
Seldom	36	42	41	49	42	45
Never	25	25	13	17	13	16
Administrative leadership (169/179)						
Always/Often	21	13	32	22	40	24
Seldom	37	39	45	44	44	49
Never	42	48	23	34	16	27
Parental support (170/180)						
Always/Often	22	22	35	33	41	38
Seldom	45	47	51	53	48	51
Never	33	31	14	14	11	11

Appendix I

Goal Attainment

Table 1

Percent of Teachers Responding Always, Often, Seldom, or Never to Statements Concerning Goal Attainment

Survey Item (Item Number)	School Level		
	Elementary %	Middle %	Secondary %
How effective this school is in helping students acquire each of the following:			
Intellectual			
Reading skills (11)			
Always	71	53	32
Often	28	43	57
Seldom/Never	1	4	11
Factual knowledge and concepts in the subject area (12)			
Always	55	42	42
Often	44	56	54
Seldom/Never	1	2	4
Critical thinking and reasoning skills (16)			
Always	39	24	20
Often	55	60	60
Seldom/Never	6	16	20
Skills in evaluating information and arguments (18)			
Always	30	20	17
Often	57	55	62
Seldom/Never	13	25	21
Effective expression of opinions (19)			
Always	40	24	23
Often	52	58	60
Seldom/Never	8	18	17
Vocational			
Vocational skills (20)			
Always	13	21	32
Often	40	37	48
Seldom/Never	47	42	20

Table 1 (cont.)

Percent of Teachers Responding Always, Often, Seldom, or Never to Statements Concerning Goal Attainment

Survey Item (Item Number)	School Level		
	Elementary %	Middle %	Secondary %
How effective this school is in helping students acquire each of the following:			
Personal			
Positive attitudes toward learning (13)			
Always	66	47	41
Often	32	46	50
Seldom/Never	2	7	9
A sense of self-worth (15)			
Always	66	44	36
Often	33	50	55
Seldom/Never	1	6	9
Independence and self-reliance (17)			
Always	48	30	22
Often	47	54	59
Seldom/Never	5	16	19
Social			
Friendliness and respect toward people of different races and religions (14)			
Always	63	52	42
Often	32	40	46
Seldom/Never	5	8	12
General			
All students have a chance to do well in this school. (111)			
Always	80	75	60
Often	19	24	38
Seldom/Never	1	1	2

Table 2

Percent of Students Responding Always, Often, Seldom, or Never to Statements Concerning Goal Attainment

Survey Item (Item Number)	School Level		
	Elementary %	Middle %	Secondary %
Intellectual			
In this school, we are taught reading skills. (29)			
Always	79	63	34
Often	17	27	35
Seldom/Never	4	10	31
In this school, we are taught to read for understanding. (43)			
Always	63	49	35
Often	30	39	46
Seldom/Never	7	12	19
In this school, we are taught to read for enjoyment. (83)			
Always	34	26	14
Often	40	43	41
Seldom/Never	26	31	45
In this school, we are taught how to write effectively. (60)			
Always	54	33	26
Often	34	42	46
Seldom/Never	12	25	28
In this school, we are taught thinking and reasoning skills. (40)			
Always	49	36	26
Often	38	43	48
Seldom/Never	13	21	26

Table 2 (cont.)

Percent of Students Responding Always, Often, Seldom, or Never to Statements Concerning Goal Attainment

Survey Item (Item Number)	School Level		
	Elementary %	Middle %	Secondary %
Personal			
In this school, we are taught how to study. (15)			
Always	52	39	18
Often	30	35	36
Seldom/Never	18	26	46
In this school, we are taught to be independent and self-reliant. (92)			
Always	48	36	28
Often	39	47	53
Seldom/Never	13	17	19
Social			
In this school, we are taught to respect the rights of other individuals and groups. (36)			
Always	69	59	38
Often	24	28	39
Seldom/Never	7	13	23
In this school, we are taught to be friendly toward people of different races, religions, and cultures. (87)			
Always	65	52	38
Often	23	29	35
Seldom/Never	12	19	27

Appendix J

Instructions to Counselors

The Good Schools Project is a three-phase collaborative effort of Kappa Delta Pi members and chapters working together to learn about good schools in America. The Executive Council appointed a seven member committee in 1981 to coordinate the project, and that committee is assisted by the Laureate Counselor of Kappa Delta Pi.

The basic purpose of these materials is to provide you as a counselor with specific instructions and assistance to accomplish Phase One of the project: identifying good schools. What follows is a description of specific tasks to be accomplished, in what order, by whom, and when.

Taken together, the tasks to be accomplished in Phase One are crucial if we are to have confidence in the data that are collected. Each task is based upon certain assumptions, and these assumptions constitute the rationale underlying the processes that are involved. In describing the tasks to be accomplished, therefore, we will outline both the *what* and *why* of the project. To avoid misunderstanding, we have tried to describe everything in detail. Our hope is that these detailed descriptions will enable you to work with Kappa Delta Pi members in your area to accomplish the project and to understand what is involved and why.

Phase	Objectives	Time
One	Identify good schools	Autumn 1982
Two	Survey schools identified	Winter 1983
Three	Follow-up investigations of some good schools	Winter/Spring 1983

The instructions here relate only to Phase One of the project. Identifying schools that are good is fundamental to everything else that follows. We will begin by charting an overview of the six steps required to accomplish Phase One. After that, a detailed description of each section will be set forth.

Overview of Phase One

Step	Tasks to be Accomplished	Deadline
Step 1	Form a committee to identify good schools	September 1
Step 2	Solicit recommendations for good schools from KDP members	
Step 3	Receive recommendations for good schools	October 15
Step 4	Identify good schools in your area	
Step 5	Notify schools/verify information	
Step 6	Send information to Good Schools Project Committee	

Each of these steps is described in more detail below.

Step 1: The immediate task to be accomplished in Step 1 is for you to form a committee (probably of not less than three nor more than seven persons) to identify the good schools in your area. Our assumption is that you will probably be a member of that committee and that you will chair it. Criteria for membership on the committee include the following:

First, every person who serves on the committee to identify good schools must be a member of Kappa Delta Pi.

Second, every person who serves on the committee must be an experienced person in the field of education.

Third, every person who serves on the committee to identify good schools in your geographic area must be someone who knows the area and who knows the schools well.

A committee of three to seven persons who are members of Kappa Delta Pi, experienced professionals, and who know the schools in your area will be able to make intelligent decisions about which schools are really good and which are not. The assumptions underlying these requirements for membership are described below.

To be elected to membership in Kappa Delta Pi requires that a person demonstrate excellence and scholarship in education. Furthermore, every member of Kappa Delta Pi has made a pledge to humanity, science, service, and toil. They are intelligent, competent people who are committed to education and to solving human problems through teaching and learning. Every person who serves on the committee to identify good schools in your area should be a member of Kappa Delta Pi.

Kappa Delta Pi is a large organization—more than 50,000 members—and by far the largest portion of these members are experienced, practicing professionals. They are teachers, administrators, and professors who are "on the job" in schools and colleges, day after day. However, most of those who are "visible" as active members at the local chapter level are students—graduate and undergraduate—many of whom are *not* experienced professionals.

The Good Schools Project committee feels that only *experienced professionals* who are *members of Kappa Delta Pi* should participate in *identifying* good schools in your area. Novices, by definition, do not know enough about schooling and do not know enough about the local schools to make these judgments. "Old pros" are required, and they must be "old pros" *who know the community well.* Even seasoned professionals who are members of Kappa Delta Pi but new to your community will not be in a position to make intelligent decisions regarding which schools are good.

In this package you also have received a mailing list that includes names and addresses of members of Kappa Delta Pi who live in your general area. This list was compiled by society headquarters, and includes every paid-up member of Kappa Delta Pi who is on *The Educational Forum* and *Record* mailing list. Your list probably has from 100 to 500 names on it. Taken together, all of the lists that were mailed to all of the chapters include the names of every member of Kappa Delta Pi, wherever they may reside.

The Good Schools Project committee broke the mailing list apart by ZIP code numbers, and we tried to include on your list all of those persons who presently live in your general area. Obviously, the list will not be perfect. We undoubtedly made errors by including some persons who do not really live in your immediate geographical area, and we probably failed to include some persons who do reside in your area, also. We did the best we could, however, and the list should be reasonably accurate and up-to-date and useful.

Review the list of names carefully. Add names of others who you know are *members of Kappa Delta Pi* (or even those who used to be members—now would be a good time, in fact, to get them back). Select your committee to identify good schools in your area from that combined list of names. Make your own determination of who is *experienced* and who *knows your community* well, being sensitive to the concerns that have been articulated here. Professional leaders in your area who are not Kappa Delta Pi members and whose counsel is needed may, of course, be consulted.

We feel confident that you will understand and appreciate the rationale that has been set forth here, so form your local committee by September 1, 1982, if possible. You will have to take into consideration such other factors as availability, skills in working with other people, and the like, but form the very best committee that you can to identify the good schools in your area as quickly as you can.

At the first meeting of your committee, provide every member with a copy of these instructions.

Step 2: After you have formed your local Kappa Delta Pi committee to identify good schools, convene that group and take steps to solicit recommendations of good schools from members of Kappa Delta Pi in your local area. Note that you will need to have these recommendations returned to you before October 15, 1982.

The Good Schools Project committee has provided you with two things to help you identify good schools in your area: The Kappa Delta Pi mailing list, and a packet of materials that can be reproduced on your own letterhead and sent to every member of Kappa Delta Pi in your general area (see Appendix J-1).

We urge you to send one letter and form to every member of Kappa Delta Pi in your area. Use the modified list (to which you added names) that was described in Step 1. Invite all KDP members to recommend schools in your general area that they think are especially good, and to include with each recommendation detailed reasons stating why they think that particular school should be identified as a school to be included in the Good Schools Project.

Several things should develop as a result of this effort to solicit recommendations for good schools. First, every member of Kappa Delta Pi will have an opportunity to participate in this project. Also, by inviting every member of Kappa Delta Pi to assist in the identification of good schools in America today, we are broadening the base of involvement dramatically. If thousands of Kappa Delta Pi members (who are competent, intelligent people committed to excellence and scholarship in education) recommend schools in their own community, we are using the intelligence and professional expertise of many able people as a basis for making informed decisions about which schools are good.

Second, these same persons will be thinking about and talking about "good schools" as well as the problems and difficulties that we always seem to talk about. Shifting emphasis from the negative aspects of schooling to the positive should be worthwhile in its own right.

Finally, by asking each KDP member who recommends a school (or schools) to fill out the form and write a letter of recommendation explaining why they are recommending that school, your local committee to identify good schools will have generated an extensive list of reasons that these people think the schools are good. Those reasons can serve as a broad-based set of considerations when you establish criteria by which to make your final decisions in Step 3 (described below). The Good Schools Project committee is also deeply interested in the reasons cited by Kappa Delta Pi members in recommending schools that they consider good, and we want you to make these recommendation forms (or copies of them) available to us later for research purposes. But more about that later.

Now, please turn to the letter and form included in Appendix J-1, and study those materials carefully. Note that there are two items involved. One is a sample letter that you can send to every member of Kappa Delta Pi on your mailing list, and the second is a one-sheet form to be included with that letter on which those who recommend schools would provide factual information about each school (e.g., name of school, name of principal, address, telephone number, etc.) as well as detailed reasons as to why they feel the school is especially good. The recommendors may not know all of the factual information, but they can probably give you enough to help you "trace it out" yourself later if you decide to identify that school as one to be included in the Good Schools Project. Specifically, there are three things you need to do.

First, *prepare a copy of this letter on your stationery* (and add anything else you feel would be appropriate), with *your name and address* as a return, for each person on the mailing list of Kappa Delta Pi members that we have provided you.

Second, *prepare copies of the information sheet* (both sides) with your name and address in the upper right hand corner so respondents will send all materials back to you.

Third, *mail a copy of the letter and form* to every person on your mailing list, including those that you have added. Do this on or before *September 15, 1982.* That will give respondents several weeks to prepare their recommendations of schools in your general area that they think are especially good.

When these materials are returned to you by October 15, 1982, you and your committee will be ready to begin Step 3.

Step 3: The instructions to members of Kappa Delta Pi to whom you mailed materials directed them to return recommendations for good schools and related material to you no later than October 15, 1982. Establish a procedure for checking the recommendations for completeness and for collating the recommendations into one list to be reviewed by the committee.

Step 4: Analyze these recommendations in any way that seems appropriate and useful to you. These reasons constitute a source of ideas that can be converted to criteria for making your final determination of good schools. From the reasons cited on the forms, therefore, and from the general experience and wisdom of the members of your committee, *determine criteria* that you will use to make the final identification of schools to be included in the Good Schools Project. There are no "hard and fast" rules here. Our assumption is that by combining your committee members' experience and "know how" about schools with the reasons cited by KDP members for their recommendations, you should be able to develop a set of criteria that you can use to make intelligent decisions about which schools are especially good. When these criteria have been agreed upon by your committee, *write the criteria down.*

Now, before you proceed, we ask you and your committee to do two things through discussion. First, *develop a process* for employing the criteria to identify good schools, and *describe that process briefly.* Write it down. In our opinion, the process must be *deliberate, thoughtful, judicious,* and *unhurried.* The Good Schools Project wants to know *how you went about the business of identifying good schools.* We are not interested in "checking on you"; we are interested in *knowing* what various committees actually do. Eventually, we must be able to describe, accurately and completely, what different committees did in their efforts to identify good schools.

Second, we feel that it is imperative for your committee to "think through" some of the problems you will face in identifying good schools *before* you actually make those determinations. For example, the Good Schools Project committee has specified the following "negative criteria" for your consideration. All we ask is that you *talk about* each of these "negative criteria" in your own committee before you actually start to identify good schools.

(a) Identifying good schools should *not* be a popularity contest.

You may want to note the frequency of recommendations which different schools receive, but it would be completely inappropriate, in our judgment, to make final determinations solely or even primarily on the basis of the number of times that any particular school was recommended. Do not allow your committee to be "pushed" into identifying a particular school as good, for example, because several KDP members teach in that same building and decide to get together and give their school some publicity. The motives of such teachers may be very honorable, and the school, in fact, may be worthy of inclusion in our sample, but we implore you to be *deliberate, thoughtful, judicious,* and *unhurried* as you *apply the criteria that you have articulated* to make the final decision about which schools should be identified as good.

(b) Do not ignore different kinds of schools.

Or to say it more positively, identify the good schools, wherever those schools may be or however those schools manifest their good qualities. We hope that each Kappa Delta Pi chapter will identify *several* good schools in its area. The number of schools ultimately identified as good will be a function of the total number of schools in your general area, of course, but it is our hope that schools of different kinds and levels and serving different populations will be included.

A good school in the heart of the ghetto may be very different from a good school in a small, isolated, rural village. The Good Schools Project committee wants you to *identify good schools, wherever they may be.* Our basic assumption is that schools may differ, even dramatically, but still be good. Different schools may serve different kinds of students, different kinds of communities, and they may even exist for different kinds of purposes. Many kinds of schools can be good.

(c) Identifying good schools should *not* be a political process and should not be based on political considerations.

Do *not* get into this kind of discussion in your deliberations: "Well, we identified one school from the north part of town; maybe we should find a school on the south side." Or: "We have named four public schools; maybe we ought to name a private school, just to keep everybody happy."

We encourage you *not* to think that way. *Identify the good schools, wherever they may be.*

Our general concern in asking you to address these three negative criteria is to encourage you to make a deliberate effort to *identify the good schools in your area, wherever they may be.* Be prepared to employ the criteria that you have devised in deliberate, thoughtful, judicious, unhurried ways. You may need several meetings to *review the recommendations, develop criteria, establish processes,* and *consider the negative criteria* that we have specified. By late October, however, you should be ready to proceed.

After you have received and reviewed the recommendations, established criteria, developed a process, and considered the negative criteria, your committee to identify good schools should meet and *identify the schools* in your area that you feel meet your criteria for inclusion in the Good Schools Project. This should probably be accomplished by about November 1, 1982.

Step 5: After you have made your decisions, contact *all of the schools identi-fied* as good, and *verify the descriptive information* presented on the form that you received from the KDP member who nominated the school (i.e., name of school, address, telephone, number of students served, etc.). Wherever possible, this contact should be in person (rather than by telephone) and by you or a member of your committee. *Be sure that all information has been provided on the form.*

During the visit, *describe the general purpose and nature of the Good Schools Project* to the principal and *encourage that person to participate* in the survey that will be accomplished in early January, 1983. Any clearances required by the school or district should be arranged for at this time.

Tell the principal that the school will receive an official invitation to partici-pate in the project from the Good Schools Project committee, but *all survey materials will be brought by you to the school during the first two weeks in January, 1983.*

The principal needs to understand that participation in the project will mean that he or she will be asked to distribute questionnaires to all staff members in the school and to selected groups of students within the school, and that certain persons will be interviewed. (The Good Schools Project staff will have copies of the survey instruments and interview schedule in your hands by October 15 so clearances can be secured.) Responses by all participants will be completely anonymous, of course. Except for certain demographic data (e.g., age, sex, etc.), the only identifying information will be a different number for each school. We intend to provide printouts for you to make available to each school, if we can, so that you and the people in that school can make your own study of the data and any comparisons to the national data you want to make. The Good Schools Project will not make any comparisons between individual schools at all. Each school will receive a certificate that it was identified as a good school and that the students and the staff participated in the Good Schools Project, but no school will be publicly named without the principal's agreement in writing.

Step 6: After you have visited all of the schools and notified the principal that the school has been identified as a good school for the Kappa Delta Pi Good Schools Project, and after you have verified all of the factual information requested and secured permission from the principal to collect the data, *mail the following* to the Director of the Good Schools Project before November 15, 1982:

(a) factual information sheet/recommendation form for each school identified by your committee as good (NOTE: If a school refuses to participate, *write the word "REFUSED" in red* on the top of the infor-mation sheet, but send the form in with all of the other materials. We will *not* include that school in the project, but we do need to have the factual information and recommendation sheet, which is the last page of Appendix J-1).

(b) *a list of one or two schools* that you have identified as good that you would especially like to study in depth during the next six month period.

(c) *the criteria* you developed and used to identify good schools in your area.

(d) *a description of the process* you developed and used to identify good schools in your area.

(e) a list of the *names, addresses, and present positions* of all of the members of your local committee to identify good schools in your area.

(f) *number of letters mailed* to Kappa Delta Pi members in your area soliciting recommendations.

(g) *number of Kappa Delta Pi members who submitted recommendations.*

(h) *number of schools recommended* for inclusion in the project by various members of Kappa Delta Pi.

(i) *total number of schools* your committee finally identified for inclusion in the project (should be same as number of sheets in "a" above).

(j) *number of schools that refused to participate in the project* after you contacted them to verify factual information and explain the purposes of the Good Schools Project.

(k) *your name, address, and phone number* for contact if the Good Schools Project needs additional information from you.

Step 7: Oh! You did not think there was a Step 7, did you? Well, our hope is that you will move now to *begin work with your own students and colleagues* so that you will be able to participate in the intensive study of a few good schools to learn "how these schools came to be."

Special materials to help you do this study will be available soon from Kappa Delta Pi. In addition, each of the Kappa Delta Pi regional meetings (between February and April, 1983) will have special training sessions for those who are conducting these in-depth case studies of a few good schools. In general, though, we hope that you will form a team of people in your own area who can help conceptualize and accomplish an in-depth case study of one school, at least. Persons who have sociological or anthropological research skills would be especially helpful, as would be people who are interested in ethnographic or qualitative research. Intensive investigations of teacher–student relationships, teaching style, leadership style, policy statements, traditions, precedents, discipline practices, curriculum materials, testing procedures, communications with parents, relationships among staff, hiring procedures, supervisory activities, staff development activities, and relationships with the central office, for example, could be explored. What makes this school tick? What is the school really like, and how did it get to be that way? Our hope is that you will prepare yourself and a group of on-site investigators to study at least one school in depth between January and May, 1983.

For now, we thank you very much for all that you have done. If you have worked your way from Step 1 through Step 6, you and your chapter will have done everything that you could have possibly done to assure the success of this project.

You will receive survey materials for Phase Two for each school you have identified as good by January 1, 1983, to be distributed to the schools before January 15th, but we will be in close communication with you before that time. We will also have copies of the survey questionnaire and interview schedule to you by October 15th for you to use in securing clearance with the principal of each school that will participate in Phase Two.

Appendix J-1

(Note to counselors: Put this letter on *your* stationery and have respondents send their nominations to *you* at *your address*.)

September 1, 1982

Dear Kappa Delta Pi Member:

Our schools have been severely criticized in recent years. Confidence in the schools has dropped. Many people, in fact, are concerned about the status and future of education in America today. In an effort to increase understandings about good schools, and in an attempt to highlight outstanding practices in education, Kappa Delta Pi has initiated the Good Schools Project.

You may have read Jack Frymier's editorial in the May 1982 issue of *The Educational Forum* entitled "Good Schools Project: A Call to Action." That editorial outlined the general purposes of the project and asked all members of Kappa Delta Pi to become involved. This letter is an invitation from those of us here in our local chapter to ask you to help us identify the good schools in our general area. Regardless of what chapter you belong to, I hope you will help our local committee to identify good schools by telling us of one or more good schools that you know about, and why you think those schools are especially good. We need your recommendations on or before October 15, 1982.

Let me elaborate. I know that as a member of Kappa Delta Pi, you are committed to excellence and scholarship in education. I know that you are knowledgeable about the schools and schooling. I presume that you are deeply concerned about the status of education everywhere.

We in Kappa Delta Pi feel confident that there are hundreds of good schools all over America today: public, parochial, and private schools; elementary, middle level, and senior level schools; and urban, suburban, and rural schools.

The task of the Good Schools Project is four-fold: (1) to identify the good schools, wherever they are; (2) to study these good schools carefully to find out what they are like; (3) to study a few of these good schools intensively and over time to see how they got to be that way; and (4) to make inferences from what we learn that would be helpful to other people who want to make their own schools better.

Now, what can you do? It is very simple. Share with us your knowledge about specific schools you know. *Help us identify schools that you think are especially good.*

Think about the schools you know about, and do *three things:* One, *recommend those schools* that you think are excellent; the schools that are exceptionally good. Two, *make a recommendation* for each school that you think is good. Outline in detail just why you think each school is especially good, and send me a separate form for each school you recommend. Three, *fill out the information sheet* with as much specific information as you can provide about the school that you are recommending. You may not know all of the details, of course, but be certain that you include the *name of the school, address, phone number,* and the *name of the principal,* at least, so we can follow up later.

Our hope is that we will be able to identify the very best schools in our community from those that you and other members of Kappa Delta Pi recommend as good schools. We want very much to keep this from being a "popularity contest" or "public relations pitch," and for that reason we are dependent on *your recommendations,* explaining just why you think the school is good.

We must have your *recommendations and complete information* about the school *on or before October 15, 1982.* Let us hear from you, please.

Thank you very much.

Sincerely,

(Your Name)
Counselor

Please send all materials to:
Your name
Your institution
Your street address
Your city, state, zip code
Your phone number

(Counselor—provide all this information about *yourself* here)

INFORMATION ABOUT SCHOOL RECOMMENDED AS A GOOD SCHOOL

(Counselor—NOTE—*Your* name and address *here*)

Counselor's Name _____

FILL OUT BOTH SIDES,   Institution _____
THEN RETURN TO:

Street Address _____

City, State, ZIP _____

Phone number _____

Name of School _____

Street Address _____

City, State, ZIP _____

Name of Principal _____

Telephone _____

Name of District_____

Circle all grade levels in the school: K   1   2   3   4   5   6   7   8   9   10   11   12

Total number of Professional Staff at the school: _____

Total number of Students at the school: _____

	Large City	Suburban	Small City	Rural
How would you describe the size of the community in which the school is located?	_____	_____	_____	_____

	White	Black	Spanish	Oriental	Other (Specify)
Estimate the proportion of students in this school in terms of their ethnic background (should total 100%)	_____%	_____%	_____%	_____%	_____%

Estimate the socioeconomic background of the students in this school (should total 100%)

_____%	_____%	_____%	_____%
(Professionals)	(Technicians or Managers)	(Skilled Laborers)	(Unskilled Laborers)

Circle if the school is: Public   Parochial   Private

Please describe your reasons for recommending this school on the following form.

RECOMMENDATION FOR A GOOD SCHOOL

DIRECTIONS:

In the space below, *describe in detail* why you feel that the school you are recommending is an especially good school. Be specific. Cite all of the reasons that you can. Your description will be the primary source of information used to identify good schools. Provide illustrations, factual information, particular incidents, but *do not be brief.* Present a strong argument for why this school is especially good.

_____

_____

_____

_____

_____

_____

_____

_____

_____

_____

_____

_____

_____

(attach additional sheets if necessary)

To Kappa Delta Pi Member:

Please put *your* name and address here so we can get in touch with you in case more information is needed:

Name _____

Street _____

City, State, Zip _____

Phone _____

Please provide information requested on the other side.

Appendix K

General Instructions

Your chapter of Kappa Delta Pi identified _____ good schools to be included in the Good Schools Project. The materials you have just received include everything that you will need to collect the data for the Good Schools Project. Basically, there are four things for you to do: (1) interview the principal in every school; (2) survey all of the teachers in every school; (3) have the regular teachers survey about half of the students in every school; and (4) interview a number of teachers, students, parents, and others in one specific school. This will be a lot of work, we know, but you can do it. And you have until May 1st to get these four tasks done.

The purpose of these *General Instructions* is to "walk you through" the materials and instructions necessary to accomplish the four tasks described above. Let's start by checking the boxes that you have just received.

Check first to see if you received all of the boxes that we sent to you. On the outside of each box you will note something like this: "1 of 4" or some such notation. That means one box of four that we shipped to you. Check now to see if you received all of the boxes that we sent.

Next there should be one box for each school that you identified, and the "ID Number" that we have assigned to that school has been written on the outside of that box. (NOTE: If any of the schools that you identified were large, we may have put two boxes together for that one school and labeled both boxes with the same "ID Number.") All of the materials required for collecting data in each school are inside that box. You will need to check these materials for each school later, but keep the materials for each school together in that box.

Now, before you open any of the boxes, check to see if you have one box for each of the schools that you identified as good that has been labeled with an "ID Number" as follows:

Name of School   *ID Number Assigned*

If you *do not* have one box for each school that has been assigned the appropriate "ID Number," *call the Good Schools Project office* at 614-422-1749 immediately and explain *what you do have or what is missing.* Do that right away! We may have made an error in packaging the materials for your chapter, but we will try to straighten it out quickly.

If you *do* have one box for each school, and if each box has been labeled with the appropriate "ID Number," proceed all the way through these *General Instructions.* Read everything very carefully.

First, some general comments. We have tried to organize these materials in ways that will help you keep things straight. You already know that the materials for each school are in a separate box. A second thing that you should be aware of is the color-coding scheme that we have utilized. All of the *materials that pertain to teachers are red.* All of the materials that pertain to *students are green.* Materials for *parents are blue.* Materials that pertain to the *principal are printed on white paper.* Materials for professionals *other* than the principal or classroom teachers are *yellow.* We hope the color coding will help you keep the materials straight.

Now, what is in each box? Using the information that you gave us about each school, we put the following data collection materials in each box:

(A) *Principal's Interview Form*   (one)
(B) *Instructions for Conducting Principal's Interview*   (one)
(C) *Teacher Survey* booklets   (one for each teacher in the school)
(D) *Teacher Survey* answer blanks   (one for each teacher in the school)
(E) *Instructions for Administering Teacher Survey*   (one)
(F) *Young Children's Survey*   (one each for about half of the students)
(G) *Instructions for Administering Young Children's Survey*   (one)
(GG) *Instructions to Teachers Who Conduct the Young Children's Survey*   (ten)
(H) *Student Survey* booklets   (one each for about half of the students)
(I) *Student Survey* answer blanks   (one each for about half of the students)
(J) *Instructions for Administering Student Survey*   (one)
(JJ) *Instructions to Teachers Who Conduct the Student Survey*   (ten)

Note that the student surveys have been developed with two age levels in mind. The *Young Children's Survey* should be used with children in grades 2 and 3. The printed green *Student Survey* booklets should be used with students grades 4-12. When you study the various sets of *Instructions* that tell you how to accomplish these various surveys, you will note some duplication. To avoid any misunderstanding we have tried to be explicit every time. The repetition may be a bit bothersome, but we felt it was appropriate to be as exact as we could be. We hope that you will understand.

In every school that you identified as good you will interview the principal, survey all of the teachers, and survey about half of the students according to the instructions and with the materials that are listed above.

For one school (which has a circle around the "ID Number" on the outside of the box) we have also included a set of materials for you to use to interview several teachers, students, parents, and other persons who are associated with that school. Check to see if the following materials have been included in the box for that one school.

(K) *Set of Interview Questions* (about 300 pages)   (one)
(L) *General Summary Booklet*   (one)
(M) *Instructions for Conducting Interviews*   (one)

Check each box that you received now to see if you have the materials necessary for collecting the data for the good schools that you identified. Call the Good Schools Project office if there are any serious discrepancies that you cannot correct yourself (e.g., you may be able to xerox extra copies of some materials, but you will not be able to replace any of the survey booklets or answer blanks).

The *Instructions for Conducting Interviews,* which is packaged with the materials for the one school in which you will do intensive interviews, should also be used in conjunction with the *Principal's Interview* materials that apply to every school. For obvious reasons, we have included the instructions only at one place in the total set of materials you have received.

In making the decision about which one school these in-depth interviews with several persons should be conducted in, we considered two things: your statement of preference for a particular school, and our concern for representativeness of the national sample. That is, we have tried to honor your request to do in-depth work in a school of your choice, but we have also tried to honor such theoretical considerations as grade levels served, nature of the community, size of the school, and the like. Our hope is that you will be able to do the intensive interviews in the school we finally specified, but if—for any reason—that does not make sense to you, we will accept your decision to conduct the intensive interviews in a school of your choice. We want to get a sample of schools that is theoretically and empirically defensible, but we realize that it is important for you to work in a school that "makes sense" to you, too. We feel confident that a reasonable accommodation of these two considerations can be worked out.

If you decide to do these interviews in a school different from the one we specify, *please state that* when you send your materials back to us, and *tell us why* you made the change (i.e., what were your criteria for making the change?). Be sure to *put the correct "ID Number"* on the interview materials that you return to us.

Now, a word about the remaining portion of these *General Instructions.* Appended to these *Instructions* is one copy of each of the items (except items "K" and "L") described above. We have labeled these appended materials exactly as they have been listed here (i.e., *Principal's Interview Form* is item "A," *Instructions for Conducting Principal's Interview* is item "B," and so on). By having "one of everything" here in these *General Instructions,* you will not need to tear this document apart or make copies of anything to get the data collected from all of the schools. We have provided you in these *General Instructions* copies of everything (except for *Set of Interview Questions* and *General Summary Booklet*), so you will not have to reproduce any materials at all. Read this paper, then *read through each appended item carefully.* Also, read through the two items that are not included here so you will know exactly what those who conduct the intensive interviews in one school are expected to do. Be sure you understand *who* is to be interviewed or surveyed, *how many persons* are involved, and *how* the data are to be collected. The specific instructions on all of these matters are spelled out in the *Instructions* for each of the interviews or survey materials.

A final note: There is a check list for you to use when you are boxing up materials to send back to us. Please *tear that page off,* go through the check list carefully as you box up materials to be returned to us, then *return it* with your materials *before May 1, 1983.* You do not have to send the survey booklets back or any unused answer blanks. Return to us only those materials that have information or data that we can use in learning about good schools.

Good luck on the project. As always, we are deeply appreciative of everything that you and the members of your chapter are doing. The collaborative nature of this research project is unprecedented in the history of professional organizations in education. Kappa Delta Pi is breaking new ground, thanks to you and your chapter. Get all of the materials to us by May 1 (or earlier, if you are finished), and we will report to you at the Kappa Delta Pi convocation in Montreal in Spring, 1984. And we will see you at the regionals next Spring.

If you have any questions or problems of any kind, write or call me:

Jack Frymier
Good Schools Project
29 W. Woodruff Avenue
Columbus, Ohio 43210

Appendix L

Principal's Interview Form and Instructions

Interview the principal of every school that your chapter identified as good. If you identified more than one good school, you will conduct a series of interviews with teachers, students, parents, and others in the *one* school that we have specified, but *interview the principal in every good school.*

There are two sets of materials that you should read before you interview the principal of each good school: *Instructions for Conducting Principal's Interview* (the paper you are now reading), and *Instructions for Conducting Interviews.*

When you meet with the principal, explain the purpose of the Good Schools Project, tell that person something about Kappa Delta Pi, and give him or her a copy of "Good Schools Project: A Call to Action" that has been included with the materials you have received. Assure the principal that absolutely nothing will be done with the information that he or she provides (or with any of the other information that is collected) that will reflect unfavorably on that school. Absolutely nothing. After the data collection has been completed, Kappa Delta Pi will provide each school with a certificate of participation in the Good Schools Project, but we will not even name the school without explicit permission from the principal in any publication or presentation. Our whole purpose is to identify good schools, study those schools to see what they are like, then try to learn things from those schools that others might use to make their own schools better.

The first part of the *Principal's Interview Form* is identical to the questions asked of teachers, students, and others in the intensive interviews to be accomplished in the one good school that has been specified. The last part of the *Principal's Interview Form,* however, is different and more detailed. The principal will be able to provide the information requested.

In all probability, it will take at least two hours to interview the principal and procure the information that is requested. Be sure that you and the principal both have enough time. Try to make arrangements so you will not be interrupted, if possible, but meet in the principal's office, if you can, because most of the factual information needed will be located there.

The interview with the principal should be conducted by two people, if at all possible: one person to ask questions, and the other person to take notes. These next ten pages should be used by the question-asker, but the responses should be recorded on the *Principal's Interview Form.* The questions on the *Principal's Interview Form* are identical to those that follow here, so one person can ask questions and the other person can record. If it is necessary for one person to conduct the interview alone, read through this entire *Instructions for Conducting Principal's Interview* carefully, then use the separate form *when you do the interview* and record the principal's responses on that document. There is plenty of space for recording answers there. In some instances there may appear to be duplication of questions, but try to get answers and information about all the areas involved.

I. PRE-INTERVIEW PROCEDURES

Before you begin asking questions be sure the note taker has completed the pre-interview procedures listed in Section I of the *Principal's Interview Form.*

II. BACKGROUND QUESTIONS

The questioner should ask the following questions and the note taker should record the answers in Section II of the *Principal's Interview Form.*

1. How many grade levels are in this school?

2. How many students are in the school?

3. Briefly describe the students who attend this school and the families from which they come. For example, tell about the ethnic composition, the income level of the families, the educational background of parents, and the expectations parents have of their children.

4. How is the student population for this school determined? For example, is this a neighborhood school, a special public school where parents have to sign up to have their children attend, a private school with high tuition and/or high academic standards for admission, a parochial school where no tuition is charged, or a school for the physically handicapped?

5. How long have you been principal of this school?

6. How long have you been a principal?

7. How long have you been in education?

8. What other positions (within education and outside it) have you held?

9. What role other than principal do you perform in this school?

III. OPEN ENDED QUESTIONS

The questioner should ask the following questions and the note taker should record the answers in Section III of the *Principal's Interview Form.* The questions in Section III are purposely open ended, and the interviewer should be particularly cautious while administering Section III questions not to influence the responses of the person being interviewed.

1. (a) If you were to sum up this school in a phrase, what would that phrase be?

   (b) Could you describe some things that happen or have happened in the school which illustrates this phrase?

2. Do you think this is a good school? Why or why not?

3. A group of people who are very knowledgeable about schools think this is a good school. What are some of the things about this school that would make people say it's good?

4. Do you think this school is significantly different from most other schools? Why or why not?

5. How has this school developed into what it is today? What were the important events in its history? Who were the significant people that made a difference in what it is today?

IV. QUESTIONS ABOUT SPECIFIC ASPECTS OF SCHOOL LIFE

6. How would you describe the way teachers in this school teach?

If answer is brief or lacking specific examples, you might say:
- What would be an example of that?
- What other things do teachers do?

If the person seems to be having difficulty responding to the question, you might say:
- Do teachers in this school teach differently from teachers in other schools?
- Do teachers lecture most of the time?
- Do teachers use a lot of dittos?

7. Do students who go to this school learn different things than students who go to other schools? If so, what are those things?

If answer is brief or lacking specific examples, you might say:
- What would be an example of that?
- Are there other unique things that students learn here?

If the person seems to be having difficulty responding to the question, you might say:
- Does this school have more of an academic (or vocational or arts) orientation than most schools?
- Is responsibility stressed more here than in other schools? If so, tell me how this is stressed.

8. What persons or groups of persons make the decisions in this school? Please tell what kinds of decisions each person or group makes and provide an example of each type of decision.

If answer is brief or lacking specific examples, you might say:
- Can you give me a brief example of that type of decision?
- What other decisions does this group make?

If the person seems to be having difficulty responding to the question, you might say:
- What sorts of things does the principal decide?
- What decisions do students make at this school?

9. Please describe how students in this school behave, and also describe how teachers handle discipline. Give specific examples.

If the answer is brief or lacking specific examples, you might say:
- Please describe this discipline strategy.
- What would be a specific incident when this occurred?
- What are different ways students are punished?
- What are different ways students are rewarded?

If the person seems to be having difficulty responding to the question, you might ask:
- Is reward or punishment emphasized more?
- Do all teachers and administrators discipline in the same way? If not, how does it vary from teacher to teacher?

10. What is the relationship between the school and the community? Describe incidents that illustrate this relationship.

If the answer is brief or lacking specific examples, you might say:
- Can you think of other incidents which demonstrate this relationship?
- Can you tell me other things about the relationships between the school and the community?

If the person seems to be having difficulty responding to the question, you might ask:
- How does the community influence the school?
- Are parts of the community critical of the school?
- Does the community support the school?
- Do teachers and administrators feel threatened by segments of the community?

11. What do you believe is most important in teaching young people?

If the answer is brief or lacking specific examples, you might say:
- Can you give me an example of how these beliefs translate to actions?
- What other things do you believe are important?

If the person seems to be having difficulty responding to the question, you might ask:
- What is the philosophy in this school?
- What do you believe is important for children to learn?

12. How involved with their jobs are people who work in this school?

If the answer is brief or lacking specific examples, you might say:
- Can you give me an example?
- Can you think of anything else?

If the person seems to be having difficulty responding to the question, you might ask:
- How much time do teachers spend planning?
- Do teachers readily volunteer to do extra things? For example . . . .

13. How do people in this school get along with one another? For example, how would you characterize the relationship between teachers and administrators? How do teachers get along with one another? How do students get along with one another?

If the answer is brief or lacking specific examples, you might say:
- Can you give me an example which illustrates this?
- What about other relationships in the school?

If the person seems to be having difficulty responding to the question, you might ask:
- Do teachers socialize outside of school?
- How do teachers feel about the principal?
- How do students feel about teachers and the principal?

14. Is there anything else you can tell me which is important in understanding this school?

V. QUESTIONS ABOUT THE SCHOOL AND ITS COMMUNITY

15. Name of school district _____

16. Type of school district (i.e., city, county, etc.) _____

17. Number of students in the school district _____

18. Is this school A. Public _____
                   B. Private_____
                   C. Parochial _____

19. Is this a special purpose school (e.g., Vo-tech, alternative, special educa-
    tion)   YES _____   NO _____

    If yes, describe: _____

    _____

20./21. Would you characterize the school's community as:

(20)	(21)
_____ Rural	_____ Above average in education
_____ Urban	_____ Average in education
_____ Suburban	_____ Below average in education
_____ Small City	

22./23. Approximately what percentage of the students in this school come from
        home environments that can be characterized as:

(22)	(23)
_____ Affluent	_____ Executive
_____ Middle class	_____ Professional
_____ Working class	_____ Skilled labor
_____ Poor	_____ Unskilled or employed
100%	100%

24. What percentage of the students in this school are:

    A. Afro-American   _____

    B. American Indian _____

    C. Caucasian   _____

    D. Hispanic   _____

    E. Oriental   _____

    F. Other   _____

25. What ethnic and religious groups, if any, are predominant in the com-
    munity(s) served by this school?

    Ethnic groups:_____

    Religious groups: _____

26. In terms of people moving in and out of the community and students
    entering and leaving school during the year, how would you describe the
    stability of the community(s) that this school serves?

    _____ Very stable   _____ Moderately stable   _____ Unstable

27. Number of full-time classroom teachers in the school _____

28. Number of part-time classroom teachers in the school_____

29. Number of full-time support personnel (art, music, guidance counselor, exceptional education, etc.)_____

30. Number of part-time support personnel _____

31. Number of principals (i.e., principal, assistant principal, etc.? in the school _____

32. Number of parents who volunteer regularly (i.e., weekly, at least) in this school _____

33. How old is the school building? _____

34. How long ago was the last major addition or remodeling? _____

35. What is the average class size in this school? _____

36. What percentage of the students receive free lunch or breakfast because they cannot afford it?_____

37. What percentage of the students are relieved of textbook fees, if any, because they cannot afford them? _____

38. What is the average daily attendance this year? _____

39. What is the average daily membership (number of students enrolled in) of the school this year? _____

40. On the average, what percentage of the students drop out of school each year? _____

41. On the average, what percentage of the students transfer to another school each year? _____

42. On the average, what percentage of the students transfer into the school each year? _____

43. How many suspensions were there last year (1981-82)? _____

44. How many students were expelled last year (1981-82)? _____

45. How many incidents of vandalism were there at the school last year (1981-82)? _____

46. What was the cost of vandalism last year (1981-82)? _____

47. What was the worst incident of vandalism last year (1981-82)? _____

_____

_____

_____

48. How many incidents of personal theft were there last year (1981-82)?
    Against A. Teachers _____
             B. Students _____

49. How many incidents of physical attack were there last year (1981-82)?
    Against A. Teachers _____
             B. Other staff members _____
             C. Students _____

50. On the average, what percentage of the students failed one or more courses last year (1981-82)?_____

51. On the average, what percentage of the students were retained at grade level last year (1981-82)? _____

52. On the average, what percentage of the students in this school are college bound? _____

53. Are students in this school tracked or grouped by ability?

    Yes _____ No_____

54. For each of the following, indicate whether there is a program and, if so, the number and percentage of the student body in each program.

Program	No. of Stud.	% of Students
A. Gifted and talented	_____	_____
B. Emotionally disturbed	_____	_____
C. Learning disabled	_____	_____
D. EMR	_____	_____
E. TMR	_____	_____
F. Other	_____	_____

55. Which of the following cocurricular or extracurricular activities are available in the school? What percentage of the students participate in each?

Activity		Percentage of students
A. Music	_____	_____
B. Drama	_____	_____
C. Sports	_____	_____
D. Scholastic	_____	_____
E. Other (specify)	_____	_____
_____	_____	_____

56. Are students bused to the school? Yes _____ No _____

57. If yes, is this for purposes of

A. Racial or ethnic integration	Yes _____	No _____
B. Geographic location	Yes _____	No _____

58. What is the average distance that students are bused? _____

59. If this school is a senior high school,

    A. What percentage of entering students graduate?_____

    B. What percentage of the graduates continue their education by attending college? _____

    C. What percentage of the graduates continue their education with vocational training?_____

60. What percentage of teachers took sick leave last year? _____

61. What was the average number of sick leave days used per teacher last year? _____

62. What percentage of teachers took professional leave last year?_____

63. What was the average number of professional leave days used (e.g., for conferences) per teacher last year? _____

64. What percentage of teachers took personal leave last year? _____

65. What was the average number of personal leave days used per teacher last year? _____

66. On the average, what percentage of teachers voluntarily leave the school each year for another position? _____

67. What criteria are used for hiring teachers? _____

_____

_____

68. Who participates in making decisions to hire new teachers? _____

_____

_____

69. What is the educational background (i.e., degrees, majors, etc.) of the principal? _____

_____

70. How long has the principal been at this school? _____

71. Did the principal come from within the school? Yes _____ No _____

72. Did the principal come from within the district? Yes _____ No _____

73. Principal's age _____

74. Principal's sex Male _____ Female _____

75. Principal's race

    A. Afro-American _____

    B. American Indian _____

    C. Caucasian _____

    D. Hispanic _____

    E. Oriental _____

    F. Other _____

76. Is the school required to submit an annual report to the school district each year? Yes _____ No _____

    If yes, *please attach a copy* to this completed instrument.

77. When did the school last receive regional accreditation? _____

    If within the last five years, *please attach a copy* of the report to this completed instrument.

78. In the space below, add any other descriptive characteristics of this school that you think are important.

79. Please provide the following achievement/ability test data for the past three years for each grade level in the school. Enter the grade level at the top and then provide the achievement/ability information for that grade level in the column below. (If you can, simply get a xerox copy of the summary sheets that report the achievement data for the school instead of filling in the information below)

(1981-82)

Grade Level _____ _____ _____ _____ _____ _____ _____

Name of Ach. Test _____ _____ _____ _____ _____ _____ _____

Average Ach. Score _____ _____ _____ _____ _____ _____ _____
  (specify subject area)

Standard Deviation _____ _____ _____ _____ _____ _____ _____

% in Top Quartile _____ _____ _____ _____ _____ _____ _____

Name of Ability Test _____ _____ _____ _____ _____ _____ _____

Average Ability Score _____ _____ _____ _____ _____ _____ _____

Standard Deviation _____ _____ _____ _____ _____ _____ _____

% in Top Quartile _____ _____ _____ _____ _____ _____ _____

(1980-81)

Grade Level _____ _____ _____ _____ _____ _____ _____

Name of Ach. Test _____ _____ _____ _____ _____ _____ _____

Average Ach. Score _____ _____ _____ _____ _____ _____ _____
  (specify subject area)

Standard Deviation _____ _____ _____ _____ _____ _____ _____

% in Top Quartile _____ _____ _____ _____ _____ _____ _____

Name of Ability Test _____ _____ _____ _____ _____ _____ _____

Average Ability Score _____ _____ _____ _____ _____ _____ _____

Standard Deviation _____ _____ _____ _____ _____ _____ _____

% in Top Quartile _____ _____ _____ _____ _____ _____ _____

(1979-80)

Grade Level _____ _____ _____ _____ _____ _____ _____

Name of Ach. Test _____ _____ _____ _____ _____ _____ _____

Average Ach. Score _____ _____ _____ _____ _____ _____ _____
  (specify subject area)

Standard Deviation _____ _____ _____ _____ _____ _____ _____

% in Top Quartile _____ _____ _____ _____ _____ _____ _____

Name of Ability Test _____ _____ _____ _____ _____ _____ _____

Average Ability Score _____ _____ _____ _____ _____ _____ _____

Standard Deviation _____ _____ _____ _____ _____ _____ _____

% in Top Quartile _____ _____ _____ _____ _____ _____ _____

Appendix M

Instructions for Conducting Interviews

This manual describes procedures for conducting the Good Schools Project interviews. The principal in every school that you identified as good should be interviewed using the *Principal's Interview Form* (item "A") and the special *Instructions for Conducting Principal's Interview* (item "B"). In one school that has been specified, interview five teachers, five students, five parents, and five other school personnel with the *Set of Interview Questions* (item "K"). When you have finished all of these interviews in that one school, summarize your information about that one school in the *General Summary Booklet* (item "L").

Kappa Delta Pi's Good Schools Project depends upon the information gathered through these interviews and through surveys administered in schools around the country by chapter members. The quality of the information gathered depends upon your understanding of the questions to be asked and the process of getting and reporting answers from teachers, students, and others who are part of the good schools your chapter has identified. These instructions will provide you with information you will need in preparing for, conducting, and reporting the interviews—with the principal in every school, and with several persons in one school.

Now, take a minute to look through the *Set of Interview Questions* (item "K"). At first glance, the *Set of Interview Questions* may appear to be intimidating—it is so big. Do not be apprehensive. Actually, the *Set* is simply a series of the same questions to be asked of several different persons. Once you understand the format, it will all seem to be very straightforward and not complicated at all.

Study the *Set of Interview Questions* carefully, and you will note that there are five separate sets of questions for five teachers to be interviewed that are printed on red paper, five sets for students that are printed on green paper, five sets for parents printed on blue paper, and five sets for professionals other than the principal or teachers that are printed on yellow paper. (You will remember that the *Principal's Interview Form* is a separate document printed on white paper. It includes these same questions, plus many more, and every principal in every school identified as good should be interviewed with the *Principal's Interview Form.*)

Take another minute now and look through the *General Summary Booklet* (item "L"). This booklet is to be used *after* you have completed all of your interviews in the one school, and it is a place to summarize and generalize from what you have learned about that one school.

When you send materials back to the Good Schools Project Research Committee, you are asked to send back both the *Set of Interview Questions* (filled out) and the *General Summary Booklet* (filled out). What we will try to spell out in these *Instructions for Conducting Interviews* is how to work with the *Set of Interview Questions* and the *General Summary Booklet,* and then where to send your materials so they can be analyzed by the Good Schools Project Research Committee.

Organizing for the Interviews

To collect the interview data needed, your chapter's group of interviewers should organize themselves into pairs. Whenever possible, interviews should be accomplished by two chapter members who can share the task of asking questions and recording answers. If you operate in pairs, you will have another person both to share the work and help interpret the answers.

Several teams of two people will be needed to gather the information in the one school in which you will do intensive interviewing, since talking with several groups of people in each school will entail considerable time. Having a number of pairs working in any one school also has an advantage: each pair of interviewers will develop a perspective through their experience in the school. This variety can then contribute to the wealth and accuracy of information finally sent back to the Good Schools Project Research Committee.

Each pair of interviewers should plan to conduct interviews with a combination of people—students, teachers, parents, and others—in order to obtain a broad overview of the school. In this way, interviewers will be able to cross-check their perceptions of what parents, students, or teachers are really saying about their own experience in the school.

Team captains. One person should be appointed to coordinate all of the interviews within the one school. This "team captain" should arrange and check on all scheduling, coordinate who on the interview team does what, and check the distribution of parents, teachers, and students to assure sufficient numbers and diversity of each group. Good coordinating can also minimize disruption to the schools. Attending to all of the details necessary will make the interviews go smoothly in that school.

The first thing the team captain should do is to arrange clearance for the interviews. This should be done in conjunction with the chapter counselor, who can help team captains work within the policies and procedures of the school district. Through the counselor, too, the interview phase of the project must be coordinated with the survey phase.

Once clearance has been arranged, the team captain should maintain communication with the principal and make arrangements for interviews within the school. Team captains should work with the principal to make certain that everyone in the school will be anticipating the arrival of the interviewing teams and to work out a process of setting up interviews with the various groups of people involved. Throughout this process, team captains must be sensitive to the political and social expectations involved in selecting people to be interviewed, and be willing to go through whatever channels are necessary to make the interviews go smoothly and professionally.

Problems. If your chapter encounters any problems with making arrangements or collecting or reporting information, do not hesitate to consult with the Good Schools Project Research Committee. Call Jack Frymier at 614-422-1749 and he or one of the other members of the research committee will be in touch with you immediately. Because we are concerned that you gather the best information possible, we will discuss problems and think about options with you. If you have questions or need assistance, call the number cited above.

Materials and records. Before any interviews are conducted, interviewers should all become familiar with the materials they will be using, and should talk about plans with others conducting interviews in the same school.

The materials are constructed so that each interview can be recorded in a separate packet. The packets should be distributed to and reviewed by those who plan to do the interviews. One of the two team members should be responsible for asking the questions, the other for recording the answers. The interviews should be taped to provide a back-up record and a resource for compiling information at the end of the interviewing process. Plans will have to be made for obtaining and operating the necessary taping equipment.

All interviews should be taped and recorded in writing, unless an interviewee refuses you permission to tape or the taping is seriously inhibiting an interviewee from responding freely. Plan to use a separate tape for each interview, labeling each one carefully with all the necessary identifying information—name of inter-viewee, role (parent, teacher, student, or principal), school name, date, and name of interviewers. If you cannot provide a tape for each interview, please use a recorder with a counter, start at zero, and note exactly where on the tape each interview begins so the information on the tapes can be retrieved later.

You will probably want to refer to your tapes when you fill out the summary booklet, and the research team may need to listen to them as well. These unedited responses are potentially valuable to the research, so keep your tapes on file.

The notes you take during the interviews and the tape recordings of your conversations are both important. Both can help you remember what happened when your group meets to prepare the summary responses for the *General Summary Booklet.*

Practice. Even if you are experienced at interviewing, practicing ahead of time is a good idea. In this way, the two interviewers can become comfortable with the questioning and answer process, can practice working as a team, and can uncover potential problems (no batteries in the tape recorder, questions and answers too fast for the note taker, etc.).

For those who are not experienced at conducting interviews, practicing the skills of interviewing described below will make the process more effective. Team-mates can also offer advice to each other on such techniques as probing for answers or explaining questions when they are not understood.

Planning. Before the interviews are conducted, plans should be made for the meeting later of all those who will be collecting information. Each interviewer is asked not only to be one of a pair collecting and recording interview information, but to be a part of a larger group interpreting and reflecting on the collective experience of the people in the school, and to furnish the research team with summary information. The *General Summary Booklet,* contained with these materials, asks for summary information from those of you who conducted the interviews when you have completed the interviews. Filling out this booklet will demand some assessment from you about what is happening in the school. The *General Summary Booklet* should be filled out by team captains after one or more discussion meetings following the completion of the interviews. Scheduling and planning for these meetings should be done in this initial stage of organization.

Details. Setting up the interviews themselves might be done in a variety of ways. The team captain might personally select or approve the room for interviews when he or she is making other arrangements. In that way, interviewers would be assured of a good environment for conducting the interviews. It is not necessary that interviews be held at the school. School may be more convenient for interviewees, but a room at the central office, a nearby university, or any other convenient place is equally acceptable—as long as it is conducive to holding an interview of high professional quality.

After the people have been contacted and have agreed to hold the interview, other details or arrangements will still have to be made. These will include setting the date and time, and finding a suitable room if the team captain has not already found one. A mutually convenient date should be set in the immediate future. Do not let so much time elapse that one or both of you forget it. And the time should be one in which neither you nor the interviewee will feel rushed or pressured to get finished. Allow approximately one hour for each interview so that you will have enough time to collect the needed data and yet not waste time. Avoid scheduling interviews just before classes start in the morning, during breaks, or at other times when interviewees might feel resentful, pressured, or distracted. Try to arrange for a space where both you and the interviewee will be comfortable and thoughtful and have a minimum of interruptions. The questions to be asked in the interview are sometimes complicated, so a chance for him or her to think in peace is essential.

Conducting the Interviews

If you are the person conducting the interviews, you should begin each interview with an explanation of the Good Schools Project, your role in it, and why your interviewee has been asked to participate. This sets the stage for a professional interview in which it is made clear that the interviewee's time and thoughts are valued and will be used by competent people. Then you might explain why interviews are being conducted in addition to the questionnaires. We want to find out how significant people perceive that school. Emphasize that the interviews are important in helping us round out the picture of the school which we have obtained from the questionnaires.

It is important that you ask the questions in the order listed in the materials. Questions have been arranged so that the answers of the interviewees will not be influenced by preceding questions. The more open-ended questions have been placed first and the pointed ones toward the end. This will help ensure that the responses we get are the real thoughts and feelings of the people being questioned.

During the interview, do everything you can to put the interviewee at ease. Answer questions as completely as you can. Take time to assure the person that their participation is valued. Make certain they are as comfortable as possible. Evidence of preparation by you will assure the interviewee that it is a professional situation in which they can expect to be treated accordingly.

Focusing. One of the difficulties often encountered in conducting an interview is keeping it on target. Stories told may be fascinating to both you and the interviewee, and yet not at all related to the intended purposes of the interview. Because it is essential for the project that you obtain answers to the questions listed, please do all you can to keep the interview on specific topics. This must be done politely and gently, of course, without offending the interviewees. Sometimes such comments as, "That's fascinating, but can we return to that toward the end of the interview?," or "That's so interesting—could we schedule another time to talk about it more?" would be good ways to bring your interviewee back to the topic in our research study. Remember—time will be limited.

Not judging. In the course of the interview you might be asked for your own opinions, views, or perceptions about policies or people within the school or school district. This can put you in a delicate position. You should be careful to react in a professional manner and not offend the interviewee. To agree that a given policy is stupid or that the principal at that school is the best in the district would open the possibility of being quoted later. When asked for your opinions or reactions to such topics, respond in ways that are non-evaluative. Avoid commenting about people, especially within the same school. In response to a query as to whether you agree that some school is the best in the district, you might respond in a friendly, joking fashion. In this way, you avoid slighting other schools or influencing answers with your opinions. What you say might be quoted to other parents, faculty members, or students, so be cautious and judicious in your comments.

Listening. One of the most important things you can do to assure a successful interview is to be an appreciative listener. It is essential for you to speak to set the stage for the interview, to ask the questions listed, to probe when the answers are not clear or need further clarification, and to conclude the interview. The rest of the time you should listen intently, cooperate as needed with your partner, and restrain yourself from conversing with the interviewees.

Probing. There will be times, of course, when you must probe for greater clarification, further expansion, additional data, or for other such reasons. Do not hesitate to do this. It is essential that you are clear about the meaning of the responses you are getting and that answers are as complete as possible. Suggestions for probes are included with some of the questions listed. Questions or comments such as, "Can you give me an example of what you mean?" or "I'm not sure what you mean by that," are usually enough to help the person continue a train of thought. When you probe, be careful not to influence their answers any more than necessary. Avoid saying what you think, and then asking them if that is what they mean; their responses might end up reflecting more accurately what *you* think than what *they* think.

Waiting. A difficult task for most interviewers is to tolerate some silence. Most people are tempted to fill in with small talk or repetitious thoughts. Silences, however, are often necessary for the interviewee to collect his or her thoughts and organize the response. Some people are slower than others in their answers. Be careful not to rush the process. Allow time for thought. Do not feel compelled to keep up the conversation. Silence can be golden if it is conducive to thoughtful, complete, organized responses to your questions.

Concluding. When the interview is finished, express appreciation for the person's time and effort. Without their help, as well as yours, the Good Schools Project could not be accomplished.

Reporting the interviews

After all the interviews in the one school have been conducted, all the pairs of interviewers working in that school should gather to talk out the responses requested in the *General Summary Booklet.* Before going to that meeting (or series of meetings), interviewers should not only review their notes and tapes, but should also work in pairs to prepare summaries of each response to a question they have asked. From these individual summaries, collective responses can be thought out when the various interviewers gather. Detailed instructions for this phase are given in the *General Summary Booklet.*

Summarizing: Your summary of responses *from each group within the school* is the basic material that the Good Schools Project research team will work from to understand what is happening within this school. For this reason, interviewers should take care in reaching agreement on statements that they believe accurately represent the reality of life within that school.

You should remind one another to be careful to distinguish between what people actually said and your own thoughts about the school. Both kinds of information are needed, but it is important for the research team to know from you which is which. What the *interviewees said* and what *interviewers perceived* are both useful to the project, but these must be separated clearly for us to understand what they mean.

Returning the materials. The *General Summary Booklet,* as well as the complete *Set of Interview Questions,* should be returned to the Good Schools Project office, along with all of the answer blanks from the surveys, the *Principal's Interview Form,* and other materials. The research team will read all interview materials carefully. *Do not send tapes* unless they are requested by the research team. Hold onto tapes until you hear whether they will be needed.

We want to express our appreciation to you for all of your work and cooperation. Without your efforts, the Good Schools Project could not happen. We on the research team believe in the importance of this project. Because of your efforts, we can deliver a message that needs to be heard: There *are* good schools and this is how they operate. You are to be commended for your willingness to devote so much time and effort to the project. We thank you sincerely for your participation.

Do not hesitate to call any member of the research staff if you need any further advice or assistance. We will be glad to help you in any way possible throughout your efforts on the project.

On or before May 1, 1983, send the complete *Set of Interview Questions* and the *General Summary Booklet,* along with all of the other materials (i.e., *Student Surveys, Teacher Surveys,* and *Principal's Interview Form*) to:

> Jack Frymier
> Good Schools Project
> 29 W. Woodruff Avenue
> Columbus, Ohio 43210

Appendix N

Instructions for Administering Student Survey

The *Student Survey* is to be given to *about half of the students* (who are in grades 4 through 12) in *each of the schools* identified as good. The printed green booklets titled *Student Survey* are to be used with students in grades 4 through 12. The *Young Children's Survey* forms are to be used with students in grades 2 and 3.

If a school is a typical K-6 elementary school, for example, use the *Young Children's Survey* forms with students in grades 2 and 3, and use the printed green *Student Survey* booklets and answer blanks with students in grades 4 through 6. If the school identified as good is a middle level or junior or senior high school, use the green *Student Survey* booklets and answer sheets with the students in that school. These *Instructions for Administering Student Survey* that you are currently reading pertain only to the survey data that you will collect from students in grades 4 through 12 who respond to the *Student Survey* on the printed answer blanks.

Get one copy of the *Student Survey* booklet (printed in green) and one copy of the *Student Survey* answer blank (printed in green), and study those materials carefully. Note that "Side 1" has space for responses to a hundred questions, and "Side 2" has space for responses to another hundred questions. For the purposes of this student survey, students will use only "Side 1" of the answer blank. If you look at the *Student Survey* booklet, you will note that there are only 100 questions.

Open the *Student Survey* booklet and read the first page, titled "Directions—Please Read Carefully." In the sixth paragraph on that first page you will note that the students who complete the survey are asked to look at the left-hand corner of the answer blank, side one. That paragraph states:

> Now, in the upper left-hand corner of your answer blank you will see a series of columns labeled "A" through "Q." The first three columns of circles labeled "A" have already been marked to indicate the identification number that has been assigned to your school. Do not make any other marks on that section of your answer blank. Move directly to item number "1."

Your local Kappa Delta Pi chapter members must *put the appropriate "ID Number" for that school on the answer blank for each student* before you take the survey materials to the school. If your chapter identified more than one school to be included in the Good Schools Project, each *school will have a different "ID Number."* That number has been written on the outside of the box that contains all data collection materials for that school, and it has also been written at the bottom of page "1" of the *General Instructions.*

Check to be certain that you have the correct "ID Number" for the school, then *put that "ID Number" on every answer blank* before you go to the school. We are asking you to do this to guarantee that there will be no errors.

Your first reaction to this request will probably be: "That will be a big job!" We know that, and we hate to ask you to put those "ID Numbers" on every answer blank, but we are scared that there will be too many mistakes if we ask students to fill that out.

The students at each school will not know their school's "ID Number," since we have arbitrarily assigned that number to their school for research purposes. Furthermore, many young students, especially, might find it confusing to blacken the spaces correctly. However, once that data gets into the computer, a mistaken "ID Number" will cause us to lose those data. That means that we would not have complete information to make available to you when we provide you with printouts later, and it also means that any inferences we make from the data would be in error. To avoid that kind of mix-up, we are asking you to *put the appropriate "ID Number" on each green answer blank* before you go to the school. And if you identified more than one good school, please note that *each school will have a different "ID Number."*

On each *Student Survey* green answer blank, therefore, *fill in the appropriate circles in the three columns labeled "School ID - A." For example,* if the "ID Number" that we assigned to a particular school was "148," use a No. 2 lead pencil and fill in the circles under "A" on each green answer blank for that one school as follows:

Now, since only a portion (about half) of the students in each school are to be surveyed, the problem you will have to address is how to get a representative sample of students in that school. Ideally, a sample would be selected using a procedure that would give each student in the school an equal probability of being included in the survey. Such a procedure is known as "random sampling." While it does not ensure representativeness, random sampling does increase the likelihood of drawing a representative sample.

However, practical considerations make it very difficult to select a truly random sample of students in a school, so other procedures will have to be used. Our concern is that you do everything you can to select students by using procedures that will approximate randomness and try to guarantee representativeness.

Students must be selected in ways that will avoid systematic biases. Students who are selected should be representative of all of the students in the school as far as *grade level, ability, achievement, sex, race,* and *ethnic background* are concerned.

We suggest that you make arrangements through the principal of the school so that the *Student Survey* will be administered to *about half* of the students *at each grade level* (4 through 12) in *intact classes* that are representative of all of the students in the school. At the junior and senior high school levels, that may mean that students should be selected only in classes in required subject areas, such as English, rather than from elective courses, such as foreign language or physics or band. If classes have been organized according to ability grouping, try to get equal numbers of classes from the various ability groups. Do everything you can to identify intact classroom groups of students that will be representative of the school in terms of grade level, ability, achievement, sex, race, and ethnic background. And we hope that you will be able to use all of the answer blanks that we have provided—a larger sample is likely to be more representative than a smaller sample.

During the process of making this determination of classroom groups to be surveyed, establish procedures to make sure that you do *not* get the same student responding to the survey more than once. In a secondary school, at least, that may mean conducting the surveys simultaneously, for example. However you do it, avoid repetition among students responding.

Once you and the principal have identified intact groups that will include about half of the students in the school, make arrangements with the principal to get copies of *Student Survey* booklets and answer blanks to each teacher in those classrooms. The regular classroom teacher should administer the surveys, according to the *Instructions to Teachers Who Conduct the Student Survey.* Enough copies of those instructions for each teacher who will administer the surveys have been included with the box of materials for each school.

After the teachers have administered the surveys to their students, *the teachers should return all completed answer blanks* to the principal, who will return them back to you and the local chapter of Kappa Delta Pi. The completed *Student Survey* answer blanks should be returned by May 1, 1983, along with the other survey and interview materials, to:

> Jack Frymier
> Good Schools Project
> 29 W. Woodruff Avenue
> Columbus, Ohio 43210

Appendix O

Teacher Survey

Directions—Please read carefully

Kappa Delta Pi, an honor society in education, is conducting a study of good schools in America. Your school has been identified as one of the schools to be included in this project. We would like to ask you to respond to this questionnaire as a way of helping us understand what good schools are like. Will you help us, please? The questionnaire is fairly long, but it is easy to respond to.

Note that you have been provided a separate answer blank. Check first to *be certain that this test booklet and the answer blank are both the same color.* If they are not the same, return the materials and get a matched set.

Use a No. 2 lead pencil only. Do *not* use a pen.

Now, turn your answer blank to "SIDE 1," and turn the page horizontally, with the places for response for items 1 through 100 on the right side of the page.

In the left-hand corner of the answer blank, you will see a series of vertical columns labeled "A" through "Q." Mark the appropriate circles for those questions. Column "A," which actually consists of three separate columns of numbers, has already been marked to indicate the "ID" number for your school.

Begin now with question "B," and answer each question, "B" through "Q."

Mark only on the answer blank. Fill in each circle which represents the correct answer completely, but *do not write any place else* on the answer blank, and *do not write on this test booklet.*

A. School ID
   In order to avoid error, the three circles in column "A" on your answer blank have already been filled in to indicate your school's "ID" number. Go now to question "B."
B. Is this school
   A. Public
   B. Parochial
   C. Independent—Private
C. Is the school community primarily
   A. Small City
   B. Large City
   C. Suburban
   D. Rural

D. Number of students in school district

A.	1,000 or less	F.	20,001 to 25,000
B.	1,001 to 5,000	G.	25,001 to 30,000
C.	5,001 to 10,000	H.	30,001 to 35,000
D.	10,001 to 15,000	I.	35,001 to 50,000
E.	15,001 to 20,000	J.	50,001 or higher

E. Number of students in this school

A.	100 or less	F.	901 to 1,100
B.	101 to 300	G.	1,101 to 1,300
C.	301 to 500	H.	1,301 to 1,500
D.	501 to 700	I.	1,501 to 2,000
E.	701 to 900	J.	2,001 or higher

F. Number of *full time* classroom teachers in your school

A.	10 or less	F.	51 to 60
B.	11 to 20	G.	61 to 70
C.	21 to 30	H.	71 to 80
D.	31 to 40	I.	81 to 90
E.	41 to 50	J.	91 or higher

G. Grade levels in this school

     Please fill in *all* appropriate circles.

H. Your years of teaching experience, including this year

A.	1	E.	11 to 13
B.	2 to 4	F.	14 to 16
C.	5 to 7	G.	17 to 19
D.	8 to 10	H.	20 or more

I. Years you have taught at *this* school, including this year

A.	1	E.	11 to 13
B.	2 to 4	F.	14 to 16
C.	5 to 7	G.	17 to 19
D.	8 to 10	H.	20 or more

J. Your age

     Please fill in the appropriate circles. The left-hand column represents the first digit of your age. The right-hand column represents the second digit.

K. Marital Status

     A. Married
     B. Single
     C. Divorced
     D. Spouse Deceased

L. Race/Ethnic Background

     A. Afro-American
     B. American Indian
     C. Caucasian/White
     D. Hispanic
     E. Oriental
     F. Other

M. Grade levels you teach

     Please fill in *all* appropriate circles.

N. What is the average number of students in your class
    A. less than 10
    B. 11 to 15
    C. 16 to 20
    D. 21 to 25
    E. 26 to 30
    F. 31 to 35
    G. More than 35

O. Do you currently work in this school
    A. Full time
    B. Part time

P. How would you describe your primary responsibility in this school
    A. Classroom teacher
    B. Support staff (principal, counselor, etc.)

Q. Hypothetically, which one of the following reasons would *most likely* cause you to leave your present position
    A. More money
    B. Severe staff conflict
    C. Higher status job
    D. Inadequate instructional materials
    E. Personal conflict with the administration
    F. Personal frustration or lack of satisfaction with my own job performance
    G. Difficult student population

NOTE: Where it says "Sex," mark the M or F circle to indicate whether you are male or female. Where it says "Grade," indicate the grade levels that you *prefer* to teach by marking all of the circles that are appropriate.

1. Indicate which one of the following best describes your usual teaching situation.
    A. Teach alone
    B. Teach alone with regular assistance from one or more specialists (e.g., art, music, special education)
    C. Teach with one or more aides
    D. Teach as a member of a teaching team

2. Indicate your highest degree
    A. Less than Baccalaureate
    B. Bachelor's
    C. Master's
    D. Doctor's

3. On the average, the amount of time you spend per day on extra- or co-curricular duties such as music or athletics is:
    A. Less than 1 hour
    B. Between 1 and 2 hours
    C. Between 2 and 3 hours
    D. More than 3 hours

4. On the average, the amount of time you spend per day after regular school hours checking and grading papers and preparing for class is:
   A. Less than a half-hour
   B. Between a half-hour and one hour
   C. Between one and two hours
   D. More than two hours

5. On the average, the amount of time you spend per day after regular school hours with students is:
   A. Less than a half-hour
   B. Between a half-hour and one hour
   C. Between one and two hours
   D. More than two hours

6. On the average, the total amount of time you work per day on school-related activities is:
   A. Less than six hours
   B. Between six and eight hours
   C. Between eight and ten hours
   D. More than ten hours

7. The number of teaching days you missed last year for health or personal reasons was:
   A. None
   B. 1-5
   C. 6-10
   D. More than 10

8. The number of teaching days you missed last year for professional reasons was:
   A. None
   B. 1-3
   C. 4-6
   D. 7 or more

9. On the average, how often do you report a student to the office for disciplinary action:
   A. Once a day
   B. Once a week
   C. Once a month
   D. Rarely or never

10. How much time do you expect students to spend on homework each day:
    A. None
    B. Less than 30 minutes
    C. Between 30 and 60 minutes
    D. More than 60 minutes

More Directions—Please Read Carefully

Now look at your answer blank again. Items "11" through "200" look like this:

A   N
0 0 0 0

"A" means "Always"
"N" means "Never"
When you look at your answer blank, think of it this way.

Always Often Seldom Never
0   0   0   0

For example, if you think your school is "always" like the statement says, mark your answer blank this way:

A   N
● 0 0 0

If you think your school is "never" like the statement says, mark your answer blank this way:

A   N
0 0 0 ●

If you think your school is somewhere in between—"often" like that, or "seldom" like that—fill in the appropriate circle.

All right. Go now to item "11." Respond to every statement, please.

You may begin.

Schools have many kinds of objectives. Listed below are several things that are often suggested as appropriate objectives for a school. Please respond to each of these items two ways. First, indicate *how effective* this school is in helping students acquire each of the following. Second, indicate *how important you feel it is* for the school to help students acquire each of these things. Indicate *how effective this school is* by marking numbers 11 through 20 on your answer blank. Indicate *how important each objective is to you* by marking numbers 21 through 30 on your answer blank.

How Effective   **How Important**

11	Reading Skills	21
12	Factual knowledge and concepts in the subject area	22
13	Positive attitudes toward learning	23
14	Friendliness and respect toward people of different races and religions	24
15	A sense of self-worth	25
16	Critical thinking and reasoning skills	26
17	Independence and self-reliance	27
18	Skills in evaluating information and arguments	28
19	Effective expression of opinions	29
20	Vocational skills	30

31. Teachers are proud to work at this school.
32. I encourage students to disagree with me.
33. There is a lot of student participation in academic clubs, sports, and music and drama activities.
34. It is more important that students learn what is right than to think for themselves.
35. Teachers pressure students to get good grades.
36. The building and the school grounds are safe.
37. Library services meet the needs and interests of students.
38. In this school, most classes are well-organized, and little time is wasted.
39. Students violate school rules on smoking.
40. Teachers are receptive to suggestions for program improvement.
41. Library services meet the needs of teachers.
42. Rules for students are fairly enforced.
43. The morale of teachers is high.
44. It is important for students to learn what is in the textbook.
45. There is someone in this school I can count on when I need help.
46. I plan to teach until retirement.
47. Students attend class regularly and are punctual.
48. Parents support school activities.
49. Our efforts to solve schoolwide problems are successful.
50. Once decisions are made, the principal sees that they are carried out.
51. There is a great deal of cooperative effort among staff members.
52. All students are capable of higher-level learning.
53. I use standardized test results for making instructional decisions.
54. Students insult teachers.
55. Parents serve as teacher aides in this school.
56. Administrators seek out teachers' suggestions for improving the school.
57. New teachers are made to feel welcome and part of the group.
58. Students are encouraged to examine different points of view rather than to expect that there are right answers.
59. Administrators, teachers, and other staff members are working hard to improve this school.
60. Students damage or steal other students' property.

61. I encourage students to work together on topics they are studying.
62. Students in this school drink alcohol.
63. Teachers maintain high standards for themselves.
64. Adequate secretarial service is available.
65. Teachers at this school act as if things are more important than people.
66. Students learn best when new content and skills are related to their previous experiences.
67. Academic learning is a top priority at this school.
68. Parents support school rules.
69. Rules and red tape in this school make it difficult to get things done.
70. Teachers put in extra time and effort to improve this school.
71. Teachers trust the principal.
72. Parents work in the school library.
73. Students damage or steal school property.
74. I encourage students to raise questions about what they are studying.
75. The work of students and awards are prominently displayed.
76. The principal makes the important decisions in this school.
77. In this school, there is a lot of pressure on students to get good grades.
78. The principal shares new ideas with teachers.
79. There is an "every person for himself" attitude in this school.
80. If teachers expect students to learn, students will learn.
81. The principal accepts staff decisions even if he or she does not agree with them.
82. Teachers' accomplishments are recognized and rewarded.
83. Teachers feel responsible for the social development of students.
84. There is a positive "sense of community" among students, teachers, and administrators.
85. Parents come to school to discuss their children's problems.
86. In this school, parents and community organizations work with school personnel to identify and resolve schoolwide problems.
87. Student misbehavior is dealt with firmly and swiftly.
88. When a problem arises in this school, there are established procedures for working on it.
89. The principal is concerned about the personal welfare of teachers.
90. Students learn best when they begin with discrete skills and information rather than broad ideas.
91. Teachers try new ideas to improve their teaching.
92. Teachers feel responsible for student learning.
93. I let students select the curriculum materials they use.
94. Students fight with each other.
95. Parents tutor students at this school.
96. Teachers individualize instruction.
97. The curriculum materials available are appropriate for the students in my classes.
98. The tests and examinations I give my students accurately represent the goals and objectives of this school.
99. Other teachers in this school seek my assistance when they have teaching problems.
100. Teachers' unions or associations should bargain about curriculum and teaching materials.

101. Students learn best when they have some choice in the selection of materials and activities.
102. Teachers in this school expect students to learn.
103. Inservice programs at this school are worthwhile.
104. I let students select learning activities.
105. Teachers are not responsible for what happens at this school; too many factors are beyond their control.
106. I use the textbook as the primary source of information.
107. Students are taught how to behave properly so they can benefit from academic activities.
108. Teachers and students in this school are considerate of one another.
109. I use my own teacher-made tests for making instructional decisions.
110. Teachers and students are allowed to put things on the walls in this building.
111. All students have a chance to do well in this school.
112. Open-ended questions are confusing to students.
113. Students in this school use drugs.
114. The principal trusts teachers to use their professional judgment on instructional matters.
115. Schoolwide problems are identified and acted upon cooperatively by administrators, teachers, and other staff members.
116. In this school, students have a chance to change things they don't like.
117. The staff evaluates its programs and activities and attempts to change them for the better.
118. Furniture and equipment can be rearranged as desired.
119. The staff is task oriented; jobs get completed and there is little wasted time.
120. The principal encourages teachers with leadership abilities to move into leadership roles.
121. I give my students the option to do projects such as pictures or models rather than written assignments.
122. I participate in professional development activities outside of the school.
123. Teachers from one area or grade level respect those from other areas or grade levels.
124. The principal goes out of his or her way to help teachers.
125. Students learn best when a wide variety of activities are provided.
126. Teachers in this school were well-prepared in their undergraduate programs.
127. Achievement is more important than effort for getting good grades in this school.
128. Overall, I have control over how I carry out my own job.
129. Parents encourage and support teachers' efforts.
130. Students have a lot of school spirit.
131. School rules for students are reasonable.
132. When the principal acts as a spokesperson for this school, he or she accurately represents the needs and interests of the staff and students.
133. Audio-visual materials and equipment are available when needed.
134. This school building is pleasant to be in.
135. Teachers are responsive to the concerns of parents.

136. People in this school do a good job of examining alternative solutions to problems before deciding what to do.
137. Teachers support school policies and procedures.
138. There is pressure on teachers for students to get high scores on achievement tests.
139. Given the opportunity, students will choose activities that are educationally worthwhile.
140. Parents are important members of school committees and advisory groups.
141. Our faculty meetings are worthwhile.
142. What is considered to be true or important changes as conditions change.
143. Students participate in the development of school policies, procedures, and programs.
144. Teachers spend time after school with students who have individual problems.
145. Staff members are flexible; they are able to reconsider their positions on issues and change their minds.
146. Parents make sure their children do their homework.
147. The principal encourages teachers to try out new ideas.
148. Students tutor or assist other students in my classes.
149. Students obey school rules and regulations.
150. Teachers care about what students think.
151. School supplies are readily available for classroom use.
152. Teachers trust each other.
153. Information is learned primarily so it can be applied to real-life situations.
154. It is difficult for teachers to influence administrative decisions regarding school policy.
155. Students physically assault teachers.
156. Content is integrated across subject boundaries to promote learning.
157. Most of the time in class is spent on academic activities.
158. People in this school complain about things, but are reluctant to do anything about them.
159. The school building and grounds are kept clean.
160. Teachers help each other find ways to do a better job.

For the next several items, you are asked to respond in two ways. First, indicate the extent to which you feel that each of the following areas *was a problem at this school five years ago*. Second, indicate the extent to which you feel that each *is a problem today*. On your answer blank, mark the extent to which each *was a problem by using numbers 161 through 170. Indicate the extent to which you feel each is a problem today* by using numbers 171 through 180.

Was a Problem		Is a Problem
161	Discipline	171
162	Student use of alcohol and drugs	172
163	Financial support	173
164	Time students spend riding the school bus	174
165	Curriculum	175
166	Academic standards	176
167	Getting and keeping good teachers	177
168	Class size	178
169	Administrative leadership	179
170	Parental support	180

For each of the following items you are asked to respond two ways. First, indicate *how often you do participate* in making decisions in each of these areas. Second, indicate *how often you think you should participate* in making decisions in each of these areas. On your answer blank, indicate the extent to which you *do participate* by marking numbers 181 through 190. Indicate the extent to which you think you *should participate* by marking numbers 191 through 200.

Do Participate		Should Participate
181	Hiring new teachers in this school	191
182	Selecting textbooks	192
183	Resolving learning problems of Individual students	193
184	Determining appropriate instructional methods and techniques	194
185	Establishing classroom disciplinary policies	195
186	Establishing general instructional policies	196
187	Determining faculty assignments in the school	197
188	Evaluating the performance of teachers	198
189	Selecting administrative personnel to be assigned to the school	199
190	Evaluating your own job performance	200

Appendix P

Student Survey

Directions—Please read carefully

We are doing a study of good schools in America. Your school has been identified as one of the schools to be included in this project. We want to know *how you feel about your school.*

You have been given a separate answer blank. It should be green, like this test booklet. If the answer blank is not green, return it and get a green one.

Use a No. 2 lead pencil, only. Do *not* use a pen, and *do not write your name* on this answer blank.

First, turn your answer blank to "Side 1," and turn the page so that the places for your responses to questions "1" through "100" are on the right side of the page.

Go first to the middle of the page, and fill in the "M" or "F" circle which indicates your sex as male or female. Underneath that, where it says "GRADE," fill in the circle which indicates your grade in school.

Now, in the upper left-hand corner of your answer blank you will see a series of columns labeled "A" through "Q." The first three columns of circles labeled "A" have already been marked to indicate the identification number that has been assigned to your school. Do not make any other marks on that section of your answer blank. Move directly to item number "1."

Items "1" through "10" look like this on your answer blank:

A B C D
0 0 0 0

Read each question, then fill in the circle which represents your best answer. For example, if you think option "B" is best, mark your answer blank like this:

A B C D
0 ● 0 0

Fill in the circle completely. Mark only on the answer blank. Do not write on this booklet.

You may begin.

1. Do you expect to graduate from high school?
    A. Definitely yes
    B. Probably
    C. I'm not sure
    D. No

2. After high school, do you expect to go to college?
    A. Definitely yes
    B. Probably
    C. I'm not sure
    D. No

3. What is your racial or ethnic background?
    A. Afro-American/Black
    B. Hispanic
    C. Caucasian/White
    D. Other

4. What grades do you usually get in school?
    A. A
    B. B
    C. C
    D. D or F

5. How much time do you spend on homework each day?
    A. None
    B. Less than 30 minutes
    C. Between 30 and 60 minutes
    D. More than 60 minutes

6. How much do you expect to learn in school this year?
    A. A lot
    B. Some
    C. Not much
    D. Very little

7. What is your favorite subject in school?
    A. Language Arts/Reading/English
    B. Mathematics
    C. Science
    D. Social Studies/History/Geography

8. If you could choose *one* important goal for yourself, which of the following
   would be the most important one *for you?*
    A. To get along well with other people
    B. To learn a lot about the subjects in school
    C. To become a better person
    D. To get a good job

9. How do you spend *most* of your time during the school day?
    A. Listening to the teacher talk with the whole group
    B. Working by myself on workbooks or reading
    C. Working with other students on special projects
    D. Taking tests to see how much I have learned

10. There may be a lot of things you like about this school, but if you had to choose the *one best* thing, which of the following would it be?
    A. My friends
    B. The teachers
    C. The classes I am taking
    D. None of the above

Please Read Carefully

Now look at your answer blank again. Items "11" through "100" look like this:

A   N
0   0   0   0

"A" means "Always"
"N" means "Never"
When you look at your answer blank, think of it this way.

Always Often Seldom Never
0   0   0   0

For example, if you think your school is "always" like the statement says, mark your answer blank this way:

A   N
●   0   0   0

If you think your school is "never" like the statement says, mark your answer blank this way:

A   N
0   0   0   ●

If you think your school is somewhere in between— "often" like that, or "seldom" like that—fill in the appropriate circle.
All right. Go now to item "11." Respond to every statement, please.
You may begin.

Mark your answer blank according to this scale:

Always Often Seldom Never
0   0   0   0

11. Teachers count how hard we try as part of our grade.
12. Students are expected to attend class regularly and to be on time.
13. Teachers at this school act as if things are more important than people.
14. I know most of the other students in my grade.
15. In this school, we are taught how to study.
16. Teachers ask us to explain how we got an answer.
17. We have a chance to change things we don't like.
18. Rules for students are reasonable.
19. Students in this school help one another.

20. I tend to watch the clock and count the minutes until school ends.
21. Students in this school participate in developing school policies and programs.
22. Teachers treat you better if you are wealthy or your parents are "important."
23. Teachers believe I can learn.
24. Everybody works on the same things in class.
25. Teachers like to work at this school.
26. Students respect teachers.
27. Teachers are considerate of each other.
28. Teachers encourage us to question what's in the book.
29. In this school, we are taught reading skills.
30. Students obey school rules and regulations.
31. What we do in class is well organized and little time is wasted.
32. We have a choice about the amount of time we spend working on assignments.
33. Teachers ignore students who aren't very smart.
34. Most of our class assignments are interesting.
35. Students violate school rules on smoking.
36. In this school, we are taught to respect the rights of other individuals and groups.
37. Students who try hard in this school succeed.
38. I feel safe at this school.
39. Teachers act as if they are always right.
40. In this school, we are taught thinking and reasoning skills.
41. Teachers encourage us to raise questions about what we are studying.
42. It is hard to get to know teachers here.
43. In this school, we are taught to read for understanding.
44. Teachers encourage us to work together on what we're studying.
45. There is a lot of student participation in academic clubs, sports, and music and drama activities.
46. Students know the consequences for breaking school rules.
47. Most of the work in my classes comes from the textbook.
48. Teachers try to explain things in terms of other things we already know.
49. Teachers let us select the materials we use in class.
50. Students in this school respect the rights of other students.
51. Teachers show favoritism.
52. We have a chance to decide what to study.
53. In this school, we are taught how to behave properly.
54. Student misbehavior is dealt with firmly and swiftly.
55. Teachers get angry when students give wrong answers.
56. Students are friendly toward each other.
57. Class assignments are too hard for me.
58. Students physically assault teachers.
59. Teachers in this school help out with student activities.
60. In this school, we are taught how to write effectively.
61. The work we do in school is important to me.
62. Teachers care about what students think.
63. Teachers spend time after school with students who have individual problems.

64. We have a say in making classroom rules.
65. Teachers put a lot of time and effort into their work here.
66. What teachers expect us to learn is clear to me.
67. We use different kinds of materials in class, such as newspapers and photographs.
68. Students' accomplishments are recognized and rewarded.
69. Students fight with each other.
70. Teachers are more concerned that we keep quiet than that we learn.
71. Teachers put a lot of pressure on us to learn.
72. We are encouraged to study topics that interest us.
73. Students in this school are treated fairly.
74. Teachers encourage us to examine different points of view rather than just find the right answers.
75. Teachers expect me to learn.
76. Teachers let us do projects such as pictures or models rather than written assignments.
77. Students fool around a lot in class.
78. This school is a good place to be.
79. There is a lot of cooperative effort among students.
80. We are free to question or disagree with our teachers.
81. I have enough time in class to finish my assignments.
82. We get the grades we deserve, whether or not the teacher likes us.
83. In this school, we are taught to read for enjoyment.
84. Teachers leave the building as soon as possible when the school day ends.
85. Students at this school use drugs.
86. It is hard to get to know students here.
87. In this school, we are taught to be friendly toward people of different races, religions, and cultures.
88. Students obey the school rules.
89. In general I am satisfied with the way teachers and other adults in this school treat me.
90. We are encouraged to express our opinions in class.
91. Most of our classwork is busy work—a waste of time.
92. In this school, we are taught to be independent and self-reliant.
93. Students are considerate of each other.
94. Nobody cares how hard you try in this school.
95. Students at this school drink alcohol.
96. We spend a lot of time memorizing things.
97. Teachers listen to our suggestions for program changes.
98. Students damage or steal school property.
99. Teachers and administrators work hard to improve this school.
100. Good luck is more important than hard work for success in school.

Appendix Q

Young Children's Survey

A. School "ID Number" _____

DIRECTIONS: Read each question, then *draw a circle* around the right answer.

B. What is your sex?   BOY   GIRL

C. What is your age?   6   7   8   9   10   11

D. What is your race?   Black
                          Hispanic
                          Oriental
                          White
                          Other

E. What grade levels are in this school? (Circle *all* that apply)

    K   1   2   3   4   5   6   7   8   9   10   11   12

DIRECTIONS: Read each sentence, then draw a circle around the YES or NO, which shows *how you feel about this school.*

1. This school is kept clean.	YES	NO	1.
2. Students fool around a lot in class.	YES	NO	2.
3. The principal likes the children in this school.	YES	NO	3.
4. I like to come to school.	YES	NO	4.
5. I usually know what my teacher wants me to do.	YES	NO	5.
6. This is a good school.	YES	NO	6.
7. My class assignments are hard.	YES	NO	7.
8. Students here pick on each other a lot.	YES	NO	8.
9. I like my teacher.	YES	NO	9.
10. We have too many rules at this school.	YES	NO	10.
11. My parents think this is a great school.	YES	NO	11.
12. The teacher makes fun of students when they are wrong.	YES	NO	12.
13. This school is nice to be in.	YES	NO	13.
14. My teacher really likes young children.	YES	NO	14.
15. This school is a dangerous place to be.	YES	NO	15.
16. I feel good about myself.	YES	NO	16.
17. My teacher cares if I learn.	YES	NO	17.
18. The principal trusts students	YES	NO	18.
19. My teacher thinks it's important for us to try hard.	YES	NO	19.
20. The other kids in this school like me.	YES	NO	20.
21. I do a lot of homework every night.	YES	NO	21.
22. The kids in this school really like the school.	YES	NO	22.
23. My teacher trusts students.	YES	NO	23.
24. I am proud of this school.	YES	NO	24.
25. We spend a lot of time memorizing things.	YES	NO	25.
26. My teacher thinks that I can learn.	YES	NO	26.
27. The work we do at school is important to me.	YES	NO	27.
28. My teacher is too strict.	YES	NO	28.
29. Students in this school work very hard.	YES	NO	29.
30. Students here are nice to each other.	YES	NO	30.

Appendix R

Information About Participating Schools

School ID	Level	Full Time	Part Time	Support Staff	Teachers Surveyed	Students Enrolled	Students Surveyed	Principal Surveyed	Young Surveyed	Complete Interview	Achievement Data
151	5	7	0	4	11	181	89	yes	0	yes	yes
152	K-5	13	0	5	17	317	72	yes	52	no	yes
153	K-4	22	3	5	26	455	45	yes	91	no	yes
154	K-5	30	0	14	35	820	187	yes	174	no	yes
155	7-9	50	1	5	41	1030	492	yes	0	yes	yes
156	K-5	39	0	10	44	760	150	yes	156	no	yes
157	K-5	17	1	13	22	335	92	yes	97	yes	yes
158	6-8	32	2	21	44	550	456	yes	0	yes	yes
159	6-8	25	5		43	630	567	yes	0	yes	yes
162	4-7	23	0	8	32	605	304	yes	0	yes	yes
163	K-6	46	1	13	33	648	285	yes	197	no	yes
164	K-5	6	0	4	9	135	29	yes	36	no	yes
165	7-12	17	4	8	24	400	168	yes	0	yes	yes
166	K-6	21	1	5	23	535	106	yes	137	no	yes
167	K-6	19	0	6	27	540	136	yes	124	no	no
168	K-6	14	0	14	16	310	84	yes	80	yes	yes
169	9	25	3	3	36	500	244	yes	0	no	no
171	K-5	23	2	9	31	700	133	yes	127	no	yes
172	K-5	35	0	10	32	654	97	yes	90	no	yes
173	K-6	20	1	4	22	553	139	yes	72	yes	yes
174	K-6	13	0	15	17	325	63	yes	40	no	yes
175	K-6	13	7	7	17	455	101	yes	51	no	yes
176	10-12	32	2	4	31	456	185	yes	0	yes	yes
178	K-5	27	0	22	36	776	139	yes	141	no	yes
181	9-12	25	4	1	33	520	274	yes	0	yes	yes
182	K-3	27	0	11	33	700	0	yes	122	no	yes
183	10-12	69	2	10	48	1160	532	yes	0	no	no
184	6	26	2	3	23	475	199	yes	0	no	yes
185	K-6	22	0	14	15	612	154	yes	127	no	yes
186	K-6	25	0	8	25	468	65	yes	38	no	yes
187	K-5	14	2	4	22	360	92	yes	0	yes	yes
188	K-7	15	0	7	20	397	200	yes	111	yes	yes
189	K-7	19	5	7	18	355	138	yes	187	yes	yes
190	9-12	79			75	1261	315	no	0	no	no
191	K-5	26	0	11		485		yes	0	yes	yes
193	K-6	28	1	2	27	523	147	yes	95	no	yes
194	10-12	46	8	7	26	759	263	yes	0	yes	yes
195	10-12	49	2	12	47	1023	377	yes	0	no	yes

School ID	Level	Full Time	Part Time	Support Staff	Teachers Surveyed	Students Enrolled	Students Surveyed	Principal Surveyed	Young Surveyed	Complete Interview	Achievement Data
196	K-6	13	3	4	16	288	82	yes	48	no	yes
197	K-6	22	0	4	20	554	158	yes	100	no	no
198	K-6	44	0	17	53	1333	234	yes	186	yes	yes
199	K-5	19	0	7	24	535	103	yes	104	no	no
200	K-6	19	0	10	29	409	117	yes	55	yes	no
201	K-6	31	0	9	21	470	36	yes	37	no	yes
202	K-6	30			37	330	83	yes	50	no	yes
203	9-12	57	0	3	60	1100	477	yes	0	yes	no
204	K-4	30	0	6	33	691	143	yes	214	no	yes
205	K-5	20	0	8	28	374	71	yes	60	no	yes
206	K-5	26	1	6	27	624	101	yes	82	no	yes
211	K-3	20	0	5	18	427	0	yes	89	yes	no
212	K-3	20	4	4	20	380	0	yes	109	no	no
213	9-12	7	6	2	9	106	40	yes	0	no	yes
214	K-6	27	0	10	26	665	182	yes	67	no	yes
219	7-9	42	0	13	40	789	363	yes	0	yes	yes
220	K-8	16	0	7	22	365	98	yes	83	no	yes
221	K-6	19	0	7	20	514	129	yes	100	yes	yes
222	K-5	27			23	355	48	no	51	yes	no
223	9-12	225	5	30	159	3750	1545	yes	0	no	yes
224	K-8	13	0	8	17	335	95	yes	38	yes	yes
225	K-6	16	0	4	17	286	165	yes	124	no	yes
226	K-2	22	5	0	18	640	0	yes	393	no	yes
227	11-12	121	2	57	57	1038	365	yes	0	no	no
228	10-12				105	2238	1064	no	0	yes	no
229	K-6	25	2	10	33	614	199	yes	97	no	yes
230	K-8	8	7	5	16	221	81	yes	45	no	yes
231	K-6	34	0	14	44	820	219	yes	153	no	yes
232	K-3	19	4	0	16	350	0	yes	56	no	yes
233	6-8	35	0	20	35	976	408	yes	0	yes	yes
234	6-8	14	2	6	16	268	137	yes	0	no	yes
235	K-5	10	0	6	9	250	60	yes	40	yes	yes
236	9-12	44	7	17	48	962	462	yes	0	no	yes
237	7-9	30	3	13	34	663	317	yes	0	no	yes
241	K-4	23	3	8	26	550	46	yes	76	no	yes
242	9-12	117	8	8	95	2240	750	yes	0	no	yes
243	K-5	12	1	12	19	285	52	yes	53	no	yes
244	6-8	28			24	354	167	no	0	no	no
245	K-7	13	6	9	19	325	56	yes	34	no	yes
247	K-7	24	0	13	27	490	106	yes	76	no	no
248	7-8	33	3	17	40	825	407	yes	0	no	no
249	K-6	20	0	8	19	392	72	yes	65	no	yes
251	K-3	25	1	8	30	600	3	yes	269	yes	yes

School ID	Level	Full Time	Part Time	Support Staff	Teachers Surveyed	Students Enrolled	Students Surveyed	Principal Surveyed	Young Surveyed	Complete Interview	Achievement Data
254	K-6	11	0	15	16	260	63	yes	56	no	yes
255	7-8	44			40	530	284	no	0	no	no
256	K-3	22			24	340	0	no	71	yes	no
257	9-12	42	2	8	29	584	245	yes	0	no	yes
258	K-6	26	2	26	31	678	132	yes	121	no	no
259	K-5	25	5	7	18	354	51	yes	59	no	yes
261	K-5	17	0	5	19	438	82	yes	74	yes	no
263	8-12	80	4	19	61	1540	634	yes	0	no	yes
264	K-5	10	4	6	9	269	57	yes	26	no	yes
266	K-7	11	5	6	10	243	67	yes	67	no	yes
267	K-5	14	5	8	23	355	51	yes	64	no	no
268	6-8	34	0	23	41	1021	567	yes	0	no	yes
269	K-5	17	3	7	19	344	102	yes	51	no	yes
270	10-12	92	2	19	39	1950	875	yes	0	yes	yes
271	5-6	29	0	19	30	775	400	yes	0	no	yes
274	9-12	70	0	14	69	1375	697	yes	0	no	yes
275	6-12	22	1	8	26	450	202	yes	0	no	yes
276	K-5	13	1	3	16	339	56	yes	52	no	yes
278	K-3	16	0	25	17	259	1	yes	97	no	yes
279	9-12	96	4	20	89	1753	650	yes	0	no	yes
280	K-8	25	0	7	34	664	216	yes	70	yes	yes
282	K-5	49			32	536	40	no	22	no	no
283	K-7	19	5	0	19	308	87	yes	33	no	yes
284	K-7	17	6	17	27	420	86	yes	40	no	yes
285	K-7	16	6	17	26	356	83	yes	32	no	yes

Appendix S

Criteria

Table 1

Number and Percentages of Criteria by Category and Subcategories within Categories Used to Identify Good Schools

Category and Subcategories	N	%
I. *Curriculum or Programs of the School*	86	100
Providing for Student Needs	14	16
Orientation to Achievement or Academic Excellence	13	15
Clear Expectations	13	15
Flexible or Balanced Curriculum	10	12
Innovative, Unique, or Creative Curricula	8	9
Opportunities for Learning Beyond the Classroom	6	7
Varied Emphases other than Academic in the Curriculum	6	7
Specific Desirable Practices	5	6
Personal Development Emphasis	4	5
Provision for Change	3	4
Focus upon Evaluation	2	2
Nonspecific Mention of Curriculum	2	2
II. *Climate or Atmosphere of the School*	52	100
Interrelationships Among People	11	21
General Characteristics	9	17
Orderliness and Discipline	8	15
Learning Climate	6	12
Emotional Climate	6	12
Morale and Pride	4	7
Decision Making and Involvement	3	6
Focus on Students	3	6
School is Desirable to Attend	1	2
Extra Effort From Faculty	1	2

Table 1 (cont.)

Number and Percentages of Criteria by Category and Subcategories within
Categories Used to Identify Good Schools

Category and Subcategories	N	%
III. *School and Community Relations*	41	100
Parent and School Relationships	12	29
Community to School Relationships	8	20
Community Involvement and Cooperation	8	20
Community Recognition	7	17
Community and Family Involvement and Support	3	7
General Support From Parents	3	7
IV. *Facilities and Resources*	30	100
Adequacy, Size, and Design of Building	8	27
General Adequacy of Facilities and Resources	5	17
Adequacy of Learning Resources	5	17
Pride, Aesthetics, and Safety of Facilities	4	14
Facilities or Resources Promoted Learning	3	10
Financial Resources	1	3
Intellectual Support for Array of Activities	1	3
Technical Support	1	3
Unspecified Resources	1	3
Television Station	1	3

Table 1 (cont.)

Number and Percentages of Criteria by Category and Subcategories within Categories Used to Identify Good Schools

Category and Subcategories	N	%
V. *Qualities of Administrative Leadership*	27	100
General Nonspecific Qualities	12	44
Instructional Leadership	3	11
Recognizes Accomplishments	1	4
Concern for Students	1	4
High Expectations	1	4
Participation in Total School Process	1	4
Supports Faculty, Staff, and Community	1	4
Shares Decision Making	1	4
Wise Use of Authority	1	4
Use of Technical, Human, and Conceputal Skills	1	4
Stability	1	4
Open Communication	1	4
Provides Adequate Support Systems	1	4
Process for Policy Development, Interpretation, and Implementation	1	4
VI. *Characteristics of the Faculty or Teachers*	25	100
Competencies and Qualifications	5	20
Professional Pride, Dedication, or Enthusiasm	3	12
Specific Foci for Encouraging Learning	3	12
Emotional Response to Students	3	12
Teacher Attitudes	2	8
Interpersonal Relationships	2	8
Availability of Specialists and other Teachers	2	8
Responsive to Curriculum	1	4
Openness to New Ideas	1	4
Stability	1	4
Leadership Roles	1	4
Content	1	4

Table 1 (cont.)

*Number and Percentages of Criteria by Category and Subcategories within
Categories Used to Identify Good Schools*

Category and Subcategories	N	%
VII. *Staff Characteristics*	24	100
Staff Development and Growth	7	29
Quality of Staff Relations	6	25
Qualifications of Staff	4	18
Collaborative Leadership	2	8
Support Personnel	2	8
Staff Commitment	1	4
Planning and Decision Making Procedures	1	4
Staff Morale	1	4
VIII. *Student Characteristics*	13	100
Active and Disciplined	4	31
Attitudes Toward Learning	3	23
Performance After Leaving School	2	15
Happy	2	15
Pride	1	8
Responsible Citizenship	1	8

Table 1 (cont.)

Number and Percentages of Criteria by Category and Subcategories within Categories Used to Identify Good Schools

Category and Subcategories	N	%
IX. *Miscellaneous*	<u>22</u>	<u>100*</u>
Accreditation	5	23
Demographics	4	18
Student-Teacher Ratio	2	9
School Improvement	2	9
School Accountable for Performance	1	5
Openness to Challenges in Census Areas	1	5
Classroom Management	1	5
Cooperation with Local and State Educational Institutions	1	5
Uniqueness	1	5
Low Truancy	1	5
Minimum Vandalism	1	5
Production Recordkeeping	1	5
Documentation	1	5

*Each single criterion accounted for slightly under 1%. Thus, the total is over 100%.

OTHER PUBLICATIONS AVAILABLE FROM KAPPA DELTA PI

Order the above from: Kappa Delta Pi, P.O. Box A, West Lafayette, Indiana 47906

Kappa Delta Pi an honor society in education
is proud to announce the publication of

ONE HUNDRED GOOD SCHOOLS

BY JACK FRYMIER AND OTHERS

YES SEND ME _____ COPIES OF **ONE HUNDRED GOOD SCHOOLS**

By Jack Frymier and Others

1-9 copies	$12.50 each
10-24 copies	$10.00 each
25-100 copies	$7.50 each
More than 100 copies	Contact Kappa Delta Pi for Special Price

Available From
Kappa Delta Pi
An Honor Society in Education
P.O. Box A
West Lafayette, IN 47906

Orders of more than $10 may be billed.

Amount Enclosed $ _____

Name _____

Address _____

City _____ State _____ Zip _____

YES SEND ME _____ COPIES OF **ONE HUNDRED GOOD SCHOOLS**

By Jack Frymier and Others

1-9 copies	$12.50 each
10-24 copies	$10.00 each
25-100 copies	$7.50 each
More than 100 copies	Contact Kappa Delta Pi for Special Price

Available From
Kappa Delta Pi
An Honor Society in Education
P.O. Box A
West Lafayette, IN 47906

Orders of more than $10 may be billed.

Amount Enclosed $ _____

Name _____

Address _____

City _____ State _____ Zip _____

ORDER NOW!

Extra copies are available at special prices.

BUSINESS REPLY MAIL

FIRST CLASS   PERMIT NO. 620   LAFAYETTE, INDIANA

POSTAGE WILL BE PAID BY ADDRESSEE

KAPPA DELTA PI

P.O. Box A
West Lafayette, Indiana 47906

NO POSTAGE
NECESSARY
IF MAILED
IN THE
UNITED STATES

BUSINESS REPLY MAIL

FIRST CLASS   PERMIT NO. 620   LAFAYETTE, INDIANA

POSTAGE WILL BE PAID BY ADDRESSEE

KAPPA DELTA PI

P.O. Box A
West Lafayette, Indiana 47906